Advances in Japanese Business and Economics

Volume 13

Advances in Japanese Business and Economics showcases the research of Japanese scholars. Published in English, the series highlights for a global readership the unique perspectives of Japan's most distinguished and emerging scholars of business and economics. It covers research of either theoretical or empirical nature, in both authored and edited volumes, regardless of the sub-discipline or geographical coverage, including, but not limited to, such topics as macroeconomics, microeconomics, industrial relations, innovation, regional development, entrepreneurship, international trade, globalization, financial markets, technology management, and business strategy. At the same time, as a series of volumes written by Japanese scholars, it includes research on the issues of the Japanese economy, industry, management practice and policy, such as the economic policies and business innovations before and after the Japanese "bubble" burst in the 1990s.

Overseen by a panel of renowned scholars led by Editor-in-Chief Professor Ryuzo Sato, the series endeavors to overcome a historical deficit in the dissemination of Japanese economic theory, research methodology, and analysis. The volumes in the series contribute not only to a deeper understanding of Japanese business and economics but to revealing underlying universal principles.

More information about this series at http://www.springer.com/series/11682

Kazuo Mino

Growth and Business Cycles with Equilibrium Indeterminacy

Springer

Kazuo Mino
Kyoto University Institute of Economic Research
Kyoto
Kyoto, Japan

ISSN 2197-8859 ISSN 2197-8867 (electronic)
Advances in Japanese Business and Economics
ISBN 978-4-431-55608-4 ISBN 978-4-431-55609-1 (eBook)
DOI 10.1007/978-4-431-55609-1

Library of Congress Control Number: 2017943342

Printed on acid-free paper

This Springer imprint is published by Springer Nature
The registered company is Springer Japan KK
The registered company address is: Chiyoda First Bldg. East, 3-8-1 Nishi-Kanda, Chiyoda-ku, Tokyo 101-0065, Japan

Preface

Why do macroeconomic variables of an economy fluctuate, even though no fundamental shock hits the economy? Why do countries with similar initial conditions sometimes display very different patterns of growth and development? To answer these questions, it is often helpful to use growth and business cycle models that give rise to multiple equilibria. In these models, the equilibrium path of an economy is indeterminate without specifying agents' expectations. Therefore, in the presence of equilibrium indeterminacy, extrinsic uncertainty that only affects expectations of agents may alter patterns of business cycles and long-run growth. Over the last two decades, the issue of equilibrium indeterminacy has been a well-explored research theme in macroeconomics. The central concern of this book is to elucidate various topics discussed in this line of research.

Chapter 1 provides the readers with basic concepts and analytical methods used in the literature on macroeconomic models with equilibrium indeterminacy. After presenting a brief historical review, we consider two simple examples: a univariable rational expectations model and a monetary dynamic model of an exchange economy. When analyzing both models, we classify the models into three cases: the steady-state equilibrium of the model economy is (i) unique, (ii) multiple, and (iii) a continuum. Those classifications apply to the growth and business cycle models examined in the subsequent chapters.

Chapters 2 and 3 explore baseline models of growth and business cycles that hold equilibrium indeterminacy. Chapter 2 focuses on the real business cycle models with external increasing returns and clarifies the conditions under which equilibrium indeterminacy emerges. This chapter also examines related studies that extend the baseline model into various directions. In Chap. 3, we study equilibrium indeterminacy in endogenous growth models. We treat the basic models of endogenous growth and reveal the similarities and differences in indeterminacy conditions between the real business cycle models and the endogenous growth models.

Chapter 4 considers growth models that involve multiple steady states. We examine a neoclassical growth model with threshold externalities and an endogenous growth model with global indeterminacy.

Chapters 5 and 6 discuss applied topics. Chapter 5 investigates how fiscal and monetary policy rules give rise to equilibrium indeterminacy in both real business cycle models and endogenous growth models. Chapter 6 considers equilibrium indeterminacy in open-economy models. We discuss indeterminacy conditions in small open-economy models as well as in two-country models. When inspecting both types of models, we consider both exogenous and endogenous growth settings. The final short chapter (Chap. 7) refers to a sample of recent studies that intended to pursue new directions.

Although this book is not a mere collection of my publications, the main content of the book is based on my foregoing research on macroeconomic models with equilibrium indeterminacy. First of all, I would like to thank my coauthors, Daisuke Amano, Been-Lon Chen, Koichi Futagami, Seiya Fujisaki, Yu-Shan Hsu, Yunfang Hu, Jun-ichi Itaya, Yasuhiro Nakamoto, Kazuo Nishimura, Akihisa Shibata, (late) Koji Shimomura, and Ping Wang, for their productive collaboration. At various stages of my research, many people provided useful comments. Among others, I particularly thank Shin-ichi Fukuda, Jang-Ting Guo, Makoto Saito, Danyang Xie, and Chon-Ki Yip for their constructive comments and suggestions on my papers on which this book partially depends.

Professor Ryuzo Sato, chief editor of the *Advances in Japanese Business and Economics* series, encouraged me to publish this book. I am grateful for his continuing support, since I learned economics under his guidance as a graduate student at Brown University in the early 1980s. I also thank Juno Kawakami of Springer Japan for her helpful editorial assistance. Finally, I thank my wife, Yoko Hayami, for her understanding and constant support.

Kyoto, Japan
March 2017

Kazuo Mino

Contents

About the Author

Kazuo Mino is a professor of economics at Doshisha University and a professor emeritus of Kyoto University. He is the former president of the Japanese Economic Association and the former editor of the *Japanese Economic Review*. Prior to joining Doshisha University, he worked at Hiroshima, Tohoku, Kobe, and Osaka Universities as well as at the Kyoto Institute of Economic Research at Kyoto University. Mino has published extensively on various topics in macroeconomic theory including growth and business cycle models, monetary and fiscal policies, and open-economy macroeconomics.

Chapter 1
Introduction

This chapter reviews the issue of equilibrium indeterminacy in macroeconomics. Instead of providing a broad literature survey, we consider two simple examples. One is a univariable rational expectations model of asset price determination. The other is a general equilibrium model of monetary economy. When discussing both examples, we classify the models into three categories: the steady state of the model economy is (i) unique, (ii) multiple, and (iii) a continuum. The majority of foregoing studies have treated models with a unique steady state. However, there are some interesting situations in which multiple steady state equilibria exist or the steady state of the economy constitutes a continuum. The main parts of the subsequent chapters in this book also treat case (i). Chapters 2, 3 and 5 focus on the models that have a unique interior steady state. Most of Chaps. 5 and 6 also discuss this case. On the other hand, Chap. 4 examines the models with multiple steady states, while Chap. 6 refers to the models that yield a continuum of steady states.

The models treated in this chapter are much simpler than the growth and business cycle models explored in the main body of this book. However, they are helpful for clarifying the key concepts and analytical methods used in the subsequent chapters.

1.1 A Brief Overview

If the equilibrium path of a dynamic macroeconomic model is not uniquely determined under rational expectations, which path is realized depends on a specification of expectations of agents. In this situation, non-fundamental shocks that only affect expectations of economic agents fluctuate economic activities. Therefore, in the presence of equilibrium indeterminacy, extrinsic uncertainty is a driving force of business cycles. Furthermore, if the equilibrium path of an economy is

K. Mino, *Growth and Business Cycles with Equilibrium Indeterminacy*,
Advances in Japanese Business and Economics 13,
DOI 10.1007/978-4-431-55609-1_1

indeterminate, the long-run growth and development process of the economy would be affected by extrinsic uncertainty.[1]

Early studies on rational expectations models in the 1970s found that the rational expectations equilibrium may be multiple without imposing ad hoc restrictions.[2] Since most of the early rational expectations models lacked microfoundations, it was expected that the indeterminacy problem can be resolved, if one constructs models in which rational agents solve their dynamic optimization problems. However, as revealed by Brock (1974) and Calvo (1979), monetary dynamic models with optimizing agents easily exhibit equilibrium indeterminacy. Hence, constructing microfounded models cannot resolve the indeterminacy problem.

While the presence of equilibrium indeterminacy poses a difficult question for policy makers, it can give an alternative source of business fluctuations. This idea led to a line of research that focuses on the role of extrinsic uncertainty in macroeconomic models. Using a two-period model of general equilibrium, Cass and Shell (1983) revealed that if some agents cannot participate insurance contracts, extrinsic uncertainty has real effects even in the presence of complete financial markets. Cass and Shell (1983) called extrinsic uncertainty "sunspots."[3] Azariadis (1981) examined a two-period-lived overlapping generations model and found that extrinsic uncertainty, which is called "self-fulfilling prophecies," may generate cyclical behavior of the aggregate economy. Since then, extrinsic uncertainty has also been called "animal spirits," "sentiments," or "market psychology".

Although the sunspot-driven business cycles theory developed in the 1980s made an important theoretical contribution, it had little impact on the empirical research on business cycles. This is because in the two-period lived overlapping generations economy, the length of one period is about 30 years, so that fluctuations in such an environment are not suitable for describing business cycles in the conventional sense. A special issue of the *Journal of Economic Theory* published in 1994 substantially changed the situation. The articles in this issue explored equilibrium indeterminacy in infinite horizon models of growth and business cycles. Among others, Benhabib and Farmer (1994) introduced external increasing returns into an otherwise standard real business cycle model and revealed that there exists a continuum of equilibrium paths that converge to the steady state if the degree

[1]Cass and Shell (1983) distinguished extrinsic uncertainty from intrinsic uncertainty. The former has no effect on the fundamentals of an economy such as preferences and technologies, whereas the latter affects the fundamentals.

[2]"Multiple equilibria" and "equilibrium indeterminacy" are sometimes used as interchangeable terms. Precisely speaking, the presence of multiple equilibria in macrodynamic models is necessary but not sufficient for equilibrium indeterminacy In the literature, if a model economy involves multiple paths under rational expectations (perfect foresight in the case of deterministic environment), then the equilibrium path of the economy is called indeterminate.

[3]As is well known, Jevons (1884) claimed that solar activities could generate business cycles, because they could affect weather condition for agriculture. Hence, as opposed to Cass and Shell (1983), Jevons consided that sunspots represent intrinsic uncertainty that directly affects the agricultural production condition.

of increasing returns is sufficiently strong. Moreover, Farmer and Guo (1994) examined a calibrated version of the Benhabib and Farmer model. They found that if indeterminacy holds, the model economy exhibits empirically plausible fluctuations even in the absence of fundamental technological shocks. The Benhabib-Farmer-Guo line of research attracted a considerable attention and spawned a large body of literature in the last 20 years. The main concern of this book is to elucidate relevant issues discussed in this class of studies.

Before examining growth and business cycle models in the subsequent chapters, the rest of this chapter considers two simple examples that do not involve capital and investment.

1.2 A Univariable Rational Expectations Model

1.2.1 Base Model

In this section we focus on a univariable dynamic system given by

$$p_t = f\left(E_t p_{t+1}\right), \tag{1.1}$$

where p_t denotes the price of some asset whose initial value is not historically specified. This equation means that the price in period t is determined by the conditional expected price in period $t+1$. If the system does not involve uncertainty, then $E_t p_{t+1} = p_{t+1}$ for all $t \geq 0$, so that perfect foresight prevails. To avoid unnecessary classification of patterns of dynamics, we assume that function $f(.)$ is monotonically increasing. Additionally, we assume that agents anticipate that p_t will converge neither to $+\infty$ nor to zero. Therefore, we exclude asset price bubbles.

1.2.1.1 The Case with a Unique Steady State

We first specify (1.1) as a linear system in such a way that

$$p_t = \alpha E_t p_{t+1} + b, \quad a > 0, \quad a \neq 1. \tag{1.2}$$

Here, we assume that a and b are deterministic parameters and that fundamental shocks do not hit this dynamic system. However, there may exist non-fundamental shocks that only affect expectations of economic agents. If there is no extrinsic uncertainty that gives rise to non-fundamental shocks, perfect foresight holds and the dynamic system becomes

$$p_t = a p_{t+1} + b. \tag{1.3}$$

An obvious solution of (1.2) is the stationary one given by

$$p_t = p^* = \frac{b}{1-a} \quad \text{for all } t \geq 0. \tag{1.4}$$

When this condition holds, we can set $E_t p_{t+1} = p^*$.

Now assume that there is extrinsic uncertainty that only affects agents' expectations. For example, suppose that agents believe that $p_t = p_H$ if the state of period t is H, while $p_t = p_L$ if the state of period t is L. We also assume that $p_L < p^* < p_H$. Furthermore, the transition of two states follows a stationary Markov chain whose transition matrix is given by

$$Q = \begin{bmatrix} q & 1-q \\ 1-s & s \end{bmatrix}. \quad 0 < s, q < 1.$$

Thus, for example,

$$\Pr\{\text{state of period } t+1 = H, \text{ state of period } t = H\} = q,$$
$$\Pr\{\text{state of period } t+1 = L, \text{ state of period } t = H\} = 1-q.$$

Given the above assumptions, it holds that

$$E_t p_{t+1} = q p_H + (1-q) p_L \text{ if the state in period } t \text{ is } H,$$
$$E_t p_{t+1} = (1-s) p_H + s p_L \text{ if the state in period } t \text{ is } L.$$

First, suppose that $0 < a < 1$ and $b > 0$. Then, $p_L < E_t p_{t+1} < p_H$, which means that

$$p_H > \alpha E_t p_{t+1} + b > p_L.$$

In this case, it is impossible to find $q, s \in (0,1)$ that support

$$\begin{aligned} p_H &= a\left[q p_H + (1-q) p_L\right] + b, \\ p_L &= a\left[(1-s) p_H + s p_L\right] + b. \end{aligned} \tag{1.5}$$

As a result, agents' predictions under which p_t may be either p_H or p_L cannot be self-fulfilled. The only equilibrium price that will not continue diverging is the stationary price, so that under $1 < a < 1$, it holds that $p_t = p^* = \frac{b}{1-a}$ for all $t \geq 0$. In this sense, the equilibrium path of p_t is determinate, and non-fundamental shocks fail to affect the equilibrium price levels.

Conversely, suppose that $a > 1$ and $b < 0$. Then we see that

$$p_H < a p_H + b,$$
$$p_L > a p_L + b.$$

Since $p_L < E_t p_{t+1} < p_H$, it is possible to find $q, s \in (0, 1)$ that establish (1.5) for any levels of p_H and p_L satisfying $p_L < p^* < p_H$. Namely, the system supports non-fundamental equilibrium prices $p_t = p_H$ and $p_t = P_L$ as well as the fundamental equilibrium, $p_t = c/(1-a)$.

Note that the assumption of a two-state, stationary Markov chain is made only for simplicity of discussion. We may find various forms of sunspots. For example, if $\hat{p}_t$ satisfies (1.2), then $p_t = \hat{p}_t + \varepsilon_t$ is also its solution, where ε_t is white noise. In this case the, stochastic disturbance, ε_t, represents a sunspot shock that hits the agents' expectations in period t.

If there is no extrinsic uncertainty, then $E_t p_{t+1} = p_{t+1}$. In this case (1.2) can be written as

$$p_{t+1} = \frac{1}{a} p_t - \frac{b}{a}. \tag{1.6}$$

Since the characteristic root of the above system is $1/a$, the dynamic system has a stable root if $a > 1$, while it has an unstable root if $0 < a < 1$. Note that this system does not involve non-jump state variables. Thus, if $0 < a < 1$, the number of stable roots equals the number of non-jump variables, which is zero in this example. In contrast, if $a > 1$, the number of stable roots, which is one in our model, exceeds the number of non-jump state variables. In other words, if $a > 1$ and there is no uncertainty, p_t may converge to p^* from any initial level of p_0, implying that p_0 is indeterminate so that the subsequent path of $\{p_t\}_{t=0}^{\infty}$ converging to p^* is indeterminate as well.

The above discussion can be applied to the original nonlinear system (1.1). If $p_t = f(p_{t+1})$ has a stationary solution satisfying $f(p^*) = p^*$, the linear approximation system at $p_t = p^*$ is expressed as

$$p_{t+1} = \frac{1}{f'(p^*)} (p_t - p^*) + p^*.$$

Hence, setting $1/f'(p^*) = a$ and $p^*(1 - 1/f'(p^*)) - p = b$, we see that system (2.1) is locally determinate (indeterminate) around the steady state if and only if $0 < f'(p^*) < 1$ $(f'(p^*) > 1)$.

To sum up, local determinacy/indeterminacy around the interior steady state can be shown by checking the following conditions. Namely, the necessary and sufficient conditions for local determinacy is:

number of non-jump variables = number of stable roots.

On the other hand, the necessary and sufficient conditions for local indeterminacy is:

number of non-jump variables < number of stable roots.

These criteria have been used frequently in the literature.

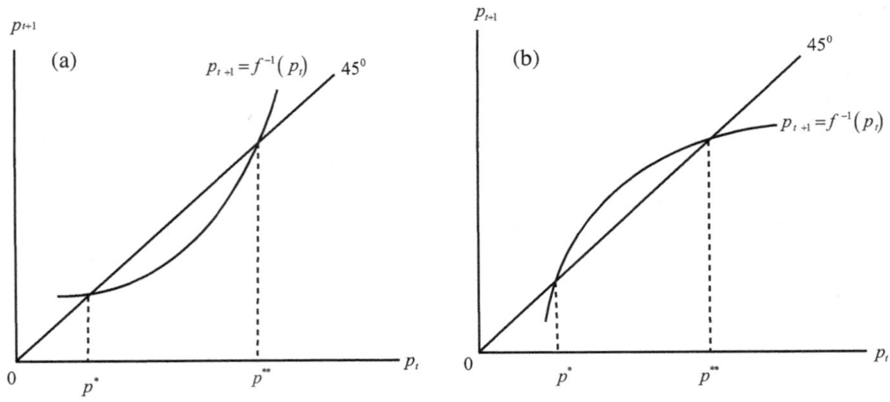

Fig. 1.1 (**a**) f(.) is strictly concave. (**b**) f(.) is strictly convex

1.2.1.2 The Case with Multiple Steady States

Next, assume that $f(.)$ in (1.1) is either a strictly convex function with $f(0) > 0$ or a strictly concave function with $f(0) < 0$. Since $f(.)$ is assumed to be invertible, the dynamic system under perfect foresight is written as

$$p_{t+1} = f^{-1}(p_t). \tag{1.7}$$

Figure 1.1a, b depict the relation between p_{t+1} and p_t given by (1.7). The figures show that the system has dual interior steady states. According to the criteria mentioned above, p^* is locally determinate and p^{**} is locally indeterminate in Fig. 1.1a, while the opposite results hold in Fig. 1.1b. The initial level of p_t can be selected from $[0, p^{**}]$ in case (a), while it can be chosen from $[p^*, +\infty)$ in case (b). In both cases, global indeterminacy is established.

1.2.1.3 The Case with a Continuum of Steady States

Again, we use the linear system (1.2) and set $a = 1$ and $b = 0$, which leads to

$$p_t = E_t p_{t+1}. \tag{1.8}$$

The corresponding deterministic system is $p_t = p_{t+1}$ and, hence, p_t stays constant:

$$p_t = p^* \text{ for all } t \geq 0.$$

However, in this case, the dynamic system fails to pin down the level of p^*. Therefore, any feasible price level can be a stationary solution, and sunspot shocks may affect the selection of p^*. Furthermore, even if we select a particular level of p^* as an equilibrium solution, $p^* + \varepsilon_{t+1}$ with $E_t\varepsilon_{t+1} = 0$ also fulfills (1.8). Namely, even after the deterministic system selects the stationary level of p_t, the asset price may fluctuate due to the presence of non-fundamental shocks.

1.2.2 Fundamental Disturbances

So far, we have assumed that there are no fundamental shocks. To check whether the baseline results shown above will not change in the presence of fundamental shocks, let us consider the following model:

$$p_t = aE_t p_{t+1} + b_t, \tag{1.9}$$

$$b_t = (1-\theta)\bar{b} + \theta b_{t-1} + \varepsilon_t, \quad 0 < \theta < 1, \ \bar{b} > 0. \tag{1.10}$$

In this model, b_t is not stationary and is disturbed by an exogenous shock, ε_t, in each period. Here, ε_t is represents an independent and identically distributed (i.i.d) stochastic variable. We seek non-divergent solutions.

First, suppose that $0 < a < 1$. In this case, iterative substitution in (1.9) up to $t = T > 0$ presents

$$p_t = E_t \sum_{j=1}^{T} a^j b_{t+j} + b_t + a^{t+T} E_t p_{t+T}.$$

Hence, in view of $0 < a < 1$, when T goes to infinity, we obtain

$$p_t = E_t \sum_{j=1}^{\infty} a^j b_{t+j} + b_t = E_t \sum_{j=0}^{\infty} a^j \theta^j b_t + (1-\theta)\bar{b}_t \sum_{j=1}^{\infty} a^j, \tag{1.11}$$

which yields

$$p_t = \frac{1}{1-a\theta} b_t + \frac{a(1-\theta)}{1-a}\bar{b}. \tag{1.12}$$

As a result, p_t is uniquely determined. Note that if there is no fundamental uncertainty ($\varepsilon_t = 0$ for all $t \geq 0$) and b_t is fixed at $\bar{b}$ (so $\theta = 0$), then the above reduces to $p_t = \bar{b}/(1-a)$. This is the steady state solution of the deterministic system.

Next, consider the case of $a > 1$. We assume that $a\theta \neq 1$. As a possible solution, we try $p_t = \phi b_t + \lambda$, where ϕ and λ are unknown constants. Then, it holds that $\phi b_t + \lambda = a\phi E b_{t+1} + a\lambda + b_t$, which leads to

$$\phi b_t + \lambda = a\phi\theta b_t + a(1-\theta)\bar{b} + a\lambda + b_t.$$

Thus, we find

$$\phi = \frac{1}{1 - a\theta}, \quad \lambda = \frac{a(1-\theta)\bar{b}}{1-a},$$

so that we again obtain (1.12).

Note that (1.12) is derived by letting $T \to \infty$ in (1.11). Therefore, if $0 < a < 1$, then (1.12) is a unique, non-diverging solution. In the case of $a > 1$, let us define a fundamental solution as

$$\hat{p}_t = \frac{1}{1 - a\theta} b_t + \frac{a(1-\theta)\bar{b}}{1-a}.$$

Then it is obvious that the following also fulfills $p_t = aE_t p_{t+1} + b_t$:

$$p_t = \hat{p}_t + \xi_{t,}$$

where ξ_t is a white noise with $E_t \varepsilon_{t+j} = 0$ for all $j \geq 0$. Consequently, the necessary condition for the presence of sunspot equilibrium is $a > 1$, which ensures the local indeterminacy condition for the corresponding system without fundamental disturbances.

1.3 General Equilibrium Models of the Monetary Economy

The simple model examined in the previous section lacks microfoundation. In this section, we reconsider indeterminacy and sunspots in general equilibrium models of monetary economies in which agents' optimization behaviors are explicitly formulated. As shown in the previous section, the key condition for the presence of sunspot-driven fluctuations in a stochastic model is that the corresponding deterministic models with perfect foresight display equilibrium indeterminacy. For expositional convenience, in this section we focus on continuous-time, deterministic models of monetary economies.

1.3.1 Base Model

Consider a money-in-the-utility function model of an exchange economy. There is an infinitely lived representative household that maximizes a discounted sum of utilities

$$U = \int_0^\infty e^{-\rho t} u\left(c, \frac{M}{p}\right) dt, \quad \rho > 0$$

subject to the flow budget constraint:

$$\dot{B} + \dot{M} = RB + p(y + \tau - c).$$

Here, c is consumption, y is the real income, M is the nominal money stock, B is the stock of private bond, p is the price level, R is the nominal interest rate, and τ denotes a real transfer from the government. The initial holdings of nominal stocks of money and bond, M_0 and B_0, are exogenously specified. For simplicity, we assume that the real income y is an exogenously given endowment that is a positive constant.

Let us define $A = B + M,\ a = A/p,\ m = M/p$ and $\pi = \dot{p}/p$. Then, we find that the flow budget constraint given above is expressed as

$$\dot{a} = (R - \pi)a + y + \tau - c - Rm.$$

The instantaneous utility function, $u(c, m)$, is assumed to be monotonically increasing and strictly concave with respect to consumption, c, and real money balances, M/p.

Denoting the implicit price of total asset, a, by q, the household's optimization conditions include the following:

$$u_c(c, m) = q, \tag{1.13}$$

$$u_m(c, m) = Rq. \tag{1.14}$$

Conditions (1.13) and (1.14) yield

$$\frac{u_m(c, m)}{u_c(c, m)} = R, \tag{1.15}$$

which means that the marginal rate of substitution between consumption and real balances equals the nominal interest rate. The implicit price of asset, q, changes according to

$$\dot{q} = q(\rho + \pi - R). \tag{1.16}$$

Additionally, the implicit value of asset, qa, should fulfill the transversality condition, $\lim_{t\to\infty} e^{-\rho t} q_t a_t = 0$.

The market equilibrium condition for final goods is

$$c = y. \tag{1.17}$$

Since there is no outstanding bond, the equilibrium condition for the financial market is

$$b = 0. \tag{1.18}$$

Finally, we assume that the seigniorage revenue of the government is distributed back the households as a lump-sum transfer. Thus, the government's budget constraint is

$$\dot{M} = p\tau. \tag{1.19}$$

1.3.2 The Case with a Unique Steady State

We now assume that the monetary authority keeps the growth rate of nominal money stock at a constant rate of μ. Hence, the government's budget (1.19) is expressed as $\tau = \mu m$. Equations (1.13) and (1.15), together with (1.17), present

$$\frac{\dot{m}}{m} = \frac{u_c(y,m)}{u_{cm}(y,m)}\left[\rho + \pi - \frac{u_m(y,m)}{u_c(y,m)}\right].$$

Eliminating π from the above by use of $\pi = \mu - \dot{m}/m$, we obtain a complete dynamic system with respect to the real money balances as follows:

$$\dot{m} = \frac{u_c(y,m)\,m}{u_{cm}(y,m) + u_c(y,m)}\left[\rho + \mu - \frac{u_m(y,m)}{u_c(y,m)}\right]. \tag{1.20}$$

Now assume that there is a stationary solution of m^* that fulfills

$$\rho + \mu = \frac{u_m(y,m^*)}{u_c(y,m^*)}.$$

Since $m_t = M_t/p_t$ is a jump variable, local determinacy holds if

$$\left.\frac{d\dot{m}_t}{dm_t}\right|_{m_t=m^*} = -\frac{u_c(y,m^*)\,m^*}{u_{cm}(y,m^*) + u_c(y,m^*)}\frac{d}{dm}\left[\frac{u_m(y,m^*)}{u_c(y,m^*)}\right] > 0.$$

Since the above shows that the linearized system has an unstable root and $m_t\,(= M_t/p_t)$ is a jump variable, the economy always stays in the steady state so that local indeterminacy cannot emerge.

Conversely, if the following condition holds, the steady state of the monetary economy exhibits local indeterminacy:

$$\left.\frac{d\dot{m}_t}{dm_t}\right|_{m_t=m^*} = -\frac{u_c(y,m^*)\,m^*}{u_{cm}(y,m^*) + u_c(y,m^*)}\frac{d}{dm}\left[\frac{u_m(y,m^*)}{u_c(y,m^*)}\right] < 0.$$

Under the above condition, the linearized system has a stable root so that any m_0 around m^* can lead the economy to the steady state equilibrium.

It is to be noted that non-separability of the utility function is a key condition for holding local intermediacy. To see this, suppose that the utility function is additively separable in such a way that

$$u(c, m) = v(v) + x(m),$$

where $v(c)$ and $x(m)$ satisfy strict concavity. Given this specification, (1.20) becomes

$$\dot{m} = m\left[\rho + \mu - \frac{x'(m)}{v'(y)}\right]. \tag{1.21}$$

It is easy to confirm that this system gives a unique steady value of m_t and that

$$\left.\frac{d\dot{m}_t}{dm_t}\right|_{m_t = m^*} = -m^* \frac{x''(m^*)}{v'(y)} > 0,$$

where m^* is the steady state level of real money balances.

1.3.3 *The Case with Multiple Steady States*

Monetary economies often involve multiple steady states. In the following, we examine two typical examples.

1.3.3.1 Hyper Inflation

Brock (1974) is the first study on the perfect-foresight competitive equilibrium of money in the utility function model (the Sidrauski model). He pointed out that the hyper-deflationary path on which real money balances go to infinity can be eliminated by the transversality condition on the household's optimization behavior. At the same time, Brock (1974) also reveals that the hyper inflationary path on which real money balances converge to zero may be supported as a perfect-foresight competitive equilibrium.

Obstfeld and Rogoff (1983) present a comprehensive discussion on the presence of hyper-inflationary equilibrium. According to their analysis, when the utility function is additively separable, the phase diagram of (1.21) has three alternative patterns as depicted by Paths A, B and C in Fig. 1.2. We see that each path satisfies

Fig. 1.2 Alternativve paths

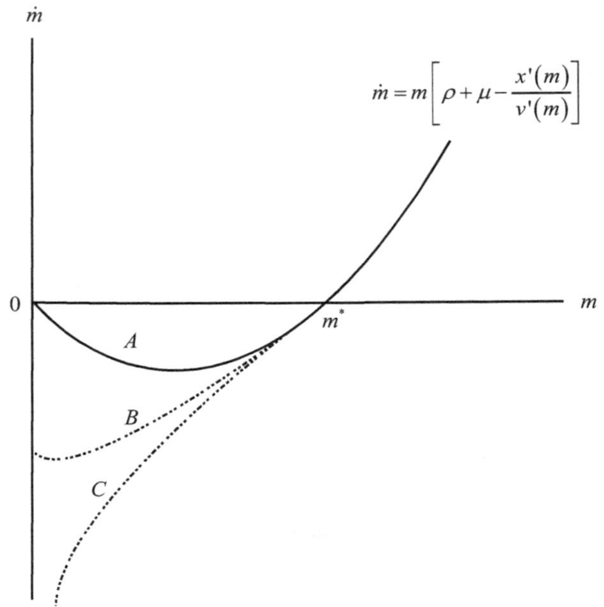

the following conditions:

$$\text{Path } A: \lim_{m_t \to 0} \left(-m_t v'(m_t)\right) = 0,$$

$$\text{Path } B: -\infty < \lim_{m_t \to 0} \left(-m_t v'(m_t)\right) < 0,$$

$$\text{Path } C: \lim_{m_t \to 0} \left(-m_t v'(m_t)\right) = -\infty.$$

Path A has two steady states, that is, an interior steady state wherein $m_t = m^*$ and a non-monetary steady state wherein $m_t = 0$. As claimed by Brock (1974), since the non-monetary steady state satisfies the transversality condition, it fulfills all the conditions for perfect-foresight competitive equilibrium. On the other hand, if the equilibrium path is either Path B or Path C, the transversailty condition is violated, so that the hyperinflationary path cannot be in competitive equilibrium. However, Obstfeld and Rogoff (1983) prove that to realize Paths B and C, the utility function should satisfy

$$\lim_{m_t \to 0} v(m_t) = -\infty,$$

implying that the household's utility becomes minus infinity when its real balance holding conveyers to zero. This is obviously an extreme assumption as to the utility of holding money. As a result, the feasible equilibrium is Path A alone. This means that the equilibrium of the economy is either the interior steady state, $m_t = m^*$, or a path that converges to $m_t = 0$. In this sense, the economy exhibits global indeterminacy.

1.3.3.2 Taylor Rule

In the previous example, one of the dual steady states is a boundary point $(m_t = 0)$. We now consider the case of dual interior steady states. Suppose that the monetary authority adjusts nominal interest rate in response to the rate of inflation in such a way that

$$R = R(\pi), \quad R'(\pi) > 1. \tag{1.22}$$

That is, the monetary authority follows the Taylor principle under which a rise in the rate of inflation increases the real interest rate, $r = R - \pi$. Notice that in this policy regime, the nominal money stock is adjusted in order to support the interest-rate control rule mentioned above.

In this example, we use a non-separable utility function in which the consumption and real money balances are Edgeworth complements to each other so that $u_{cm}(c, m) > 0$. First, condition (1.13) and the market equilibrium condition, $y = c$, give $u_c(y, m) = q$. Thus, due to the assumption of $u_{cm} > 0$, the relation between m and q is expressed as $m = m(q)$ with $m'(m) > 0$. Then, (1.14) leads to $u_m(y, m(q)) = qR$. As a result, the relation between q and R is given by

$$q = Q(R), \quad Q'(R) = \frac{u_{mm} m' q - u_m q}{q^2} < 0. \tag{1.23}$$

From (1.22) and (1.23), we obtain

$$\frac{\dot{q}}{q} = \frac{Q'(R)}{Q(R)} \dot{R} = \frac{Q'(R)}{Q(R)} R' \dot{\pi}.$$

By use of (1.16), the above equation yields a complete dynamic system of the rate of inflation in such a way that

$$\dot{\pi} = \frac{Q(R(\pi))}{R'(\pi) Q'(R(\pi))} [\rho + \pi - R(\pi)]. \tag{1.24}$$

The steady state rate of inflation denoted by π^* satisfies

$$R(\pi^*) = \rho + \pi^*,$$

which is uniquely given if $R'(\pi) > 1$ holds for all π. Then, we see that

$$\left.\frac{d\dot{\pi}}{d\pi}\right|_{\pi=\pi^*} = \frac{Q(R(\pi^*))}{R'(\pi^*)\,Q'(R(\pi^*))}\left[1 - R'(\pi^*)\right].$$

Since $Q'(R) < 0$ and $R'(\pi^*) > 1$, the above demonstrates that $d\dot{\pi}/d\pi > 0$ at $\pi_t = \pi^*$, meaning that the economy establishes local determinacy under the Taylor principle. It is to be noted that if the interest-rate control rule is passive so that $R'(\pi) < 1$, then $d\dot{\pi}/d\pi < 0$, and thus the steady state exhibits local indeterminacy. As result, the Taylor principle plays the role of stabilizer in the sense that it eliminates the possibility of local indeterminacy.

So far, we have ignored the zero lower bound of the nominal interest rate. The presence of the zero lower bound means that $R'(\pi)$ is close to zero for low rates of inflation. Hence, the monetary authority cannot follow the Taylor rule for all rates of inflation. If this is the case, there generally exist dual steady state rates of inflation that satisfy

$$R'\left(\pi^*\right) > 1, \quad R'\left(\pi^{**}\right) \approx 0, \quad \pi^* > \pi^{**}.$$

Since it holds that

$$\left.\frac{d\dot{\pi}}{d\pi}\right|_{\pi=\pi^{**}} = \frac{Q(R(\pi^{**}))}{R'(\pi^{**})\,Q'(R(\pi^{**}))}\left[1 - R'(\pi^{**})\right] < 0,$$

the steady state in the liquidity trap is locally indeterminate. Figure 1.3 depicts the graph of (1.24) in the presence of a liquidity trap. This figure shows that although the Taylor rule ensures local determinacy in the high interest rate regime, the presence of zero lower bound of the nominal interest rate generates global indeterminacy.

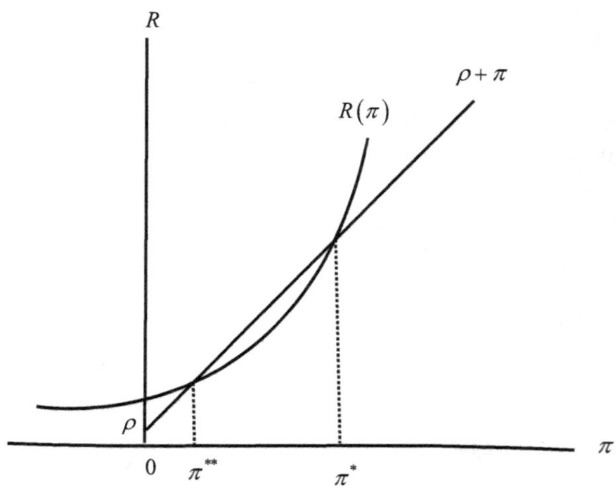

Fig. 1.3 Taylor rule with a lower bound

Benhabib et al. (2001a) present a detailed investigation of the global indeterminacy under the Taylor rule in both flexible and sticky price models.

1.3.4 A Model with a Continuum of Steady States

Finally, we examine a model with a continuum of steady state equilibria. In contrast to the classical monetary economy model with flexible prices examined above, in this subsection we consider a simple New Keynesian-type model with fixed prices. The following example depends on Kaplan et al. (2016).

Consider a production economy in which the aggregate production function is given by

$$y_t = n_t, \tag{1.25}$$

where y_t is the aggregate output and n_t is labor input at time t. For expositional convenience, in this subsection we add a time subscript to each endogenous variable. The representative household solves

$$\max \int_0^{\infty} e^{-\rho t} \log c_t dt, \quad \sigma > 0,$$

subject to the flow budget constraint

$$\dot{B}_t = R_t B_t + w_t n_t - p_t c_t,$$

as well as to the non-Ponzi-game constraint:

$$\lim \exp\left(- \int_0^t R_s ds \right) B_t \geq 0. \tag{1.26}$$

where B_t is the nominal stock of private bond, R_t is the nominal interest rate, w_t is the nominal wage, p_t is the nominal price, and c_t is consumption.

In this model, we assume that money serves as an accounting unit alone. We also assume that both nominal wage and nominal price are fixed. We normalize these variables to satisfy

$$p_t = w_t = 1. \tag{1.27}$$

Thus the real wage is unity which equals the marginal productivity of labor.

Since the real wage is fixed in our economy, we should drop the full-employment condition of labor. Here, we assume that the representative household supplies its labor in response to the aggregate employment determined by the economy as a whole. The monetary authority controls the nominal interest rate. Since the price is fixed, this assumption means that the sequence of real interest rate is set by the monetary authority. The market equilibrium conditions for the final goods and bonds are respectively given by

$$y_t = c_t, \quad B_t = 0. \tag{1.28}$$

The optimal consumption of the household satisfies the following Euler equation,

$$\frac{\dot{c}_t}{c_t} = R_t - \rho,$$

together with the transversality condition, $\lim_{t\to\infty} e^{-\rho t} c_t^{-\sigma} B_t = 0$.

The Euler equation gives

$$c_t = c_0 \exp\left(\int_0^t (\rho - R_s)\, ds\right). \tag{1.29}$$

Since the transversality condition as well as the non-Ponzi-game condition (1.26) are assumed to be fulfilled, the intertemporal budget constraint for the household is expressed as

$$B_0 + \int_0^\infty \exp\left(-\int_0^t R_s ds\right) y_t dt = \int_0^\infty \exp\left(-\int_0^t R_s ds\right) c_t dt.$$

Substituting (1.29) into the above yields

$$c_0 = \rho\left[B_0 + \int_0^\infty \exp\left(-\int_0^t R_s ds\right) y_t dt\right]. \tag{1.30}$$

First, suppose that the monetary authority keeps the real interest rate at ρ. Then, (1.30) is reduced to

$$c_0 = \rho\left(B_0 + \int_0^\infty e^{-\rho t} y_t dt\right).$$

In view of (1.29), when the monetary authority keeps $R_t = \rho$, the optimal consumption stays constant for all $t \geq 0$. Considering the equilibrium condition for the private bond, $B_t = 0$, and the final good market equilibrium, $c_t = y_t$, we find that (1.29) becomes

$$c_0 = c^* = y_t.$$

Namely, since the consumption stays constant over time, the firms always produce c^*. The level of c^* (and thus the steady state income) is determined by the expectations of households. In this situation, a sunspot shock may change c^*, and thus the aggregate income $\bar{y}$ accordingly responds to the sunspot disturbance. This conclusion demonstrates that the present model has an old Keynesian flavor in the sense that the aggregate employment is determined by the "animal spirits" of agents regarding the expectations of aggregate demand denoted by c^*.

Next, assume that the monetary authority adjusts the real interest rate according to

$$R_t = \rho + e^{-\phi t} (\rho - R_0), \quad \phi > 0. \tag{1.31}$$

Thus, the monetary authority gradually changes the real interest rate toward its steady state level of ρ. In this policy regime, the optimal consumption is adjusted according to

$$\frac{\dot{c}_t}{c_t} = e^{-\phi t} (R_0 - \rho),$$

implying that the rate of change in consumption continues declining over time.

Since $\lim_{t\to\infty} R_t = \rho$ under this policy rule, the consumption converges to a constant level as time goes infinity. Again, the steady state level of c_t is a continuum, and its selection is indeterminate without specifying the steady state level of income, y_t. Once y^* $(= c^*)$ is selected, the consumption at time t is given by

$$c_t = c^* \exp\left(\int_0^t (R_s - \rho)\, ds\right) = y^* \exp\left(\int_0^t \left(e^{-\phi t} (\rho - R_0)\right) ds\right).$$

Therefore, given the interest-rate control policy, the entire path of consumption depends on the selection of y^*. In this case, considering $B_0 = 0$, equation (1.30) is expressed as

$$c_0 = \rho \int_0^\infty \exp\left(-\int_0^t \left(\rho + e^{-\phi s} (\rho - R_0)\right) ds\right) y_t dt.$$

In this policy regime, there is a transition process toward a steady state. In the steady state, it holds that $R_t = \rho$ so that consumption stays constant at its steady state level, c^*. Again, the magnitude of c^* is indeterminate. Under a sequence of nominal interest rate, $\{R_t\}_{t+0}^{\infty}$, determined by (1.31), once the steady state level income y^* is selected, the initial level of consumption is pinned down. If a sunspot shock changes y^*, the entire paths of consumption and income will change. A pessimistic expectation shock may reduce y^* so the entire path of c_t and y_t will be dumped. On the other hand, an optimistic expectation shock gives rise to the opposite outcome. Accordingly, the main source of business fluctuations in this model is a change in the animal spirits of agents.

1.4 References and Related Studies

The solution concepts of the linear rational expectations model discussed in Sect. 1.1 are based on Blanchard and Kahn (1980) and McCallum (1983). Many authors explore equilibrium indeterminacy in monetary dynamic models under perfect foresight. In addition to Brock (1974), Calvo (1979), and Obstfeld and Rogoff (1983) cited above, we only refer to Black (1974), Matsuyama (1990), and Fukuda (1993). The Taylor rule with the zero interest lower bound in Sect. 1.2.2 is based on Benhabib et al. (2001a). See also Benhabib et al. (2001b) for further investigation of the destabilization effect of the Taylor principle. The example of the model with a continuum of equilibria in Sect. 1.2.3 follows Kaplan et al. (2016). Similar discussion is found in Roger Farmer's series of studies on models with labor market frictions: see, for example, Farmer (2010).[4]

The well-cited studies on sunspot equilibria in general equilibrium settings include Azariadis (1981), Cass and Shell (1983), and Azariadis and Guesnerie (1986). Boldrin and Woodford (1990) provide a useful survey over the early studies on dynamic macroeconomic models that display indeterminacy and cycles. It is also to be noted that Howitt and McAfee (1992) and Weil (1989) are early contributions to the animal spirits theory. Benhabib and Farmer (1999) present a comprehensive survey of the studies on equilibrium indeterminacy in real and monetary business cycle models as well as in endogenous growth models. An updated review is given by Farmer (2016). Farmer (2008b) also gives a nice overview of the development in the macroeconomic theory of animal spirits.

[4] We refer to Farmer's studies on unemployment equilibria in Chap. 7.

Chapter 2
Indeterminacy in Real Business Cycle Models

The baseline real business cycle (RBC) model is a stochastic optimal growth model with flexible labor supply. The typical driving force of business fluctuations is a technological shock hitting the total factor productivity (TFP) of the aggregate economy in each period. In RBC models with equilibrium determinacy, the economy never fluctuates in response to non-fundamental shocks that only affect expatiations of households and firms. As discussed in the previous chapter, the necessary condition for the existence of sunspot-driven business cycles is that the equilibrium path of the economy is indeterminate. Therefore, if an RBC models allows equilibrium indeterminacy, then sunspots would yield business fluctuations. This chapter focuses on the neoclassical growth models in which production externalities may give rise to equilibrium indeterminacy. We first discuss the models with fixed labor supply and then consider the prototype RBC model that allows labor-leisure choice of the representative household.

2.1 One-Sector Growth Models with Fixed Labor Supply

While the prototype RBC model assumes that the labor supply is endogenously determined by the representative household, we first examine models with fixed labor supply. Our discussion reveals that endogenous labor supply plays a critical role in generating equilibrium intermediacy in one-sector RBC models.

2.1.1 A Model with Production Externalities

Consider a representative agent economy in which a continuum of identical firms produce homogeneous goods. We normalize the mass of firms to unity. The

K. Mino, *Growth and Business Cycles with Equilibrium Indeterminacy*,
Advances in Japanese Business and Economics 13,
DOI 10.1007/978-4-431-55609-1_2

production function of an individual firm is

$$Y = F\left(K, N,\ \bar{K}\right), \tag{2.1}$$

where $Y,\ K$, and N denote output, capital, and labor, respectively. Here, $\bar{K}$ is the aggregate capital stock and it represents external effects generated by the intangible knowledge spillover associated with the capital stock in the economy at large. We assume that function $F\,(.)$ is homogeneous of degree one in private inputs, K and N, and it satisfies the standard neoclassical properties with respect to K and N. Note that since the number of firms is normalized to one, $Y,\ K$ and N express their aggregate values as well. Therefore, in the equilibrium it holds that $\bar{K} = K$.

Each firm takes external effects shown by $\bar{K}$ as given, meaning that the competitive factor prices are given by

$$r = F_1\left(K, N, \bar{K}\right),$$
$$w = F_2\left(K, N, \bar{K}\right),$$

where r and w respectively denote rent and real wage.

The representative household maximizes a discounted sum of utilities

$$U = \int_0^{\infty} e^{-\rho t} u\left(C\right) dt, \quad \rho > 0$$

subject to the flow budget constraint

$$\dot{K} = rK + w - C - \delta K, \quad 0 \leq \delta < 1,$$

where δ is the depreciation rate of capital. In the above, we assume that the representative household supplies one unit of labor in each moment so that we set $N = 1$. We assume that the instantaneous utility function $u\left(C\right)$ is monotonically increasing and strictly concave in C, and it satisfies the Inada conditions.

As is well known, the perfect foresight equilibrium path is described by the following pair of differential equations

$$\dot{K} = F\left(K, 1, \bar{K}\right) - C - \delta K, \tag{2.2}$$

$$\dot{C} = \frac{C}{\sigma\left(C\right)}\left[F_1\left(K, 1, K\right) - \rho - \delta\right], \quad \sigma\left(C\right) = -\frac{u''\left(C\right)C}{u'\left(C\right)} > 0, \tag{2.3}$$

together with the initial value of capital stock as well as with the transversality condition: $\lim_{t\to\infty} e^{-\rho t} u'\left(C_t\right) K_t = 0$.

We assume that the dynamic system constituting (2.2) and (2.3) has a unique steady state in which it holds that

$$C = F(K, 1, K) - \delta K,$$
$$F_1(K, 1, K) = \rho + \delta.$$

Linear approximation of the above system around the steady state presents the following coefficient matrix:

$$J_1 = \begin{bmatrix} \rho + F_3 & -1 \\ \frac{C}{\sigma(C)}(F_{11} + F_{13}) & 0 \end{bmatrix}.$$

Since the system involves one jump variable, C, and one non-jump variable, K, the presence of local indeterminacy around the steady state means that the steady state is a sink; that is, J_1 has two stable roots. The necessary and sufficient conditions for local indeterminacy are thus given by

$$\det J_1 = \frac{C}{\sigma(C)}(F_{11} + F_{13}) > 0,$$
$$\operatorname{trace} J_1 = \rho + F_3 < 0.$$

Notice that our assumption about the production technology means that $F_{11} < 0$. Hence, the presence of equilibrium indeterminacy requires that $F_{13} > 0$ and $F_3 < 0$. Namely, the aggregate capital has negative external effects.[1] For example, an increase in the aggregate capital enhances congestion of production activities, which lowers the productivity of private technology of each firm.

An example of a production function that satisfies $F_{11} < 0$ and $F_{13} > 0$ is

$$F\left(K, N, \bar{K}\right) = AK^{\alpha}N^{1-\alpha} + \theta K\bar{K} - \frac{\eta}{2}\bar{K}^2, \qquad A > 0.\ 0 < \alpha < 1, \ \ \theta > 0, \ \ \eta > 0,$$

which yields $F_3 = \theta K - \eta\bar{K} > 0$ for $\theta > \eta$ and $F_{13} = \theta - \eta\bar{K} > 0$ for $\bar{K} = K < \theta/\eta$. As a result, if $\theta > \eta > 0$ and if the steady state capital stock is less than θ/η, then the steady state is locally indeterminate.

Ever since Romer (1986), the endogenous growth theory has emphasized positive production externality that brings about external increasing returns. Hence, although the negative externality presents a theoretical possibility of indeterminacy in the neoclassical growth model with fixed labor supply, its theoretical relevancy is rather small.

---

[1] As to this result, see the detailed investigations by Boldrin (1992) and Boldrin and Rustichini (1994).

2.1.2 A Model with Productive Consumption

We next consider another example in which the level of aggregate consumption has a positive external effect on production. We assume that the production function of each firm is

$$Y = F\left(K, N, \bar{C}\right),$$

where $F_3 > 0$. For example, suppose that a higher consumption raises the nutrition of agents, which raises the social productivity of labor. Thus, a rise in the aggregate consumption may have a positive impact on the productivity of firms as well. However, an individual firm does not perceive such a positive effect of the consumption on production.[2]

In the equilibrium, it holds that $\bar{C} = C$ and $N = 1$, and, thus, the complete dynamic system in this setting consists of (2.2) and

$$\dot{C} = \frac{C}{\sigma(C)}\left[F_1(K, 1, C) - \rho - \delta\right]. \tag{2.4}$$

Again, we assume that there is a unique steady state that fulfills the following conditions:

$$C = F(K, 1, C) - \delta K,$$

$$F_1(K, 1, C) = \rho + \delta.$$

The coefficient matrix of the linearized system around the steady state is

$$J_2 = \begin{bmatrix} \rho & F_3 - 1 \\ \frac{C}{\sigma(C)} F_{11} & \frac{C}{\sigma(C)} F_{13} \end{bmatrix}.$$

It is easy to see that the necessary conditions for indeterminacy are $F_3 > 1$ and $F_{13} < 0$. If one of these conditions is not satisfied, the steady state is either a saddle point or a source (total instability).

A sample of production function that holds $F_3 > 1$ and $F_{13} < 0$ is

$$Y = AK^{\alpha}N^{1-\alpha} - \theta K\bar{C} + \frac{\eta}{2}\bar{C}^2, \quad A > 0, \quad 0 < \alpha < 1, \quad \theta > 0, \quad \eta > 0.$$

In this example, the necessary conditions for indeterminacy are

$$\eta C > \theta K + 1 \ \text{ and } \theta > \eta C.$$

[2]The role of productive consumption is explored by Daito (2009), Steger (2002), and others.

2.2 The Benhabib-Farmer-Guo Approach

As shown above, if there are external effects in production or consumption, the one-sector neoclassical growth model with fixed labor supply may yield equilibrium indeterminacy. However, judging from the common sense of economics, the conditions for holding indeterminacy mentioned above are rather restrictive. Such a shortcoming can be avoided if the model economy allows the labor-leisure choice of the representative household. Benhabib and Farmer (1994) introduce external increasing returns into an otherwise standard one-sector RBC model. They show that sunspot-driven fluctuations can be observed if the degree of social increasing returns is high enough. Farmer and Guo (1994) examine a calibrated version of the Benhabib-Farmer model. They find that the model displays empirically plausible patterns of business cycles, even though fluctuations of the model economy are generated by sunspot shocks alone.

2.2.1 Base Model

In Benhabib and Farmer (1994), the objective function of the representative household is a discounted sum of utilities given by

$$U = \int_0^\infty e^{-\rho t}\left(\log C - \frac{N^{1+\gamma}}{1+\gamma}\right)dt, \quad \rho > 0, \quad \gamma > 0,$$

where C is consumption and N denotes hours worked. The flow budget constraint for the household is

$$\dot{K} = rK + wN - C - \delta K, \tag{2.5}$$

where K is capital stock owned by the household, r is the rate of return to capital, and w is the real wage rate. In addition, δ denotes the deprecation rate of capital. Controlling consumption, C, and labor supply (hours worked), N, the household maximizes U subject to the flow budget constraint and a given initial holding of capital, K_0. In solving this problem, the representative household takes sequences of factor prices, $\{r_t, w_t\}_{t=0}^\infty$, as given.

We set up the current value Hamiltonian function in such a way that

$$\mathcal{H} = \log C - \frac{N^{1+\gamma}}{1+\gamma} + q(rk + wN - C - \delta K),$$

where q denotes the price of capital measured in utility. Then, the optimization conditions for the above problem are

$$\max_C \mathcal{H} \Longrightarrow 1/C = q, \tag{2.6}$$

$$\max_N \mathcal{H} \Longrightarrow N^{\gamma} = qw, \tag{2.7}$$

$$\dot{q} = q\left(\rho + \delta - r\right), \tag{2.8}$$

together with the budget constraint (2.5) and the transversality condition such that

$$\lim_{t\to\infty} e^{-\rho t} q_t k_t = 0. \tag{2.9}$$

From (2.6) and (2.7), we obtain

$$CN^{\gamma} = w. \tag{2.10}$$

This condition means that the marginal rate of substitution between labor supply and consumption equals the real wage rate. In addition, (2.6) and (2.8) present the Euler equation of the optimal consumption:

$$\frac{\dot{C}}{C} = r - \rho - \delta. \tag{2.11}$$

As for the production side, it is assumed that there is a continuum of identical firms with a unit mass. The production function of the representative firm is

$$Y = XK^{a}N^{1-a}, \quad 0 < \alpha < 1,$$

where TFP of the private technology, X_t, is given by

$$X = A\bar{K}^{\alpha-a}\bar{N}^{\beta-(1-a)}, \ A > 0, \ \alpha > a, \quad \beta > 1 - a.$$

Here, $\bar{K}$ and $\bar{N}$ respectively denote aggregate levels of capital and labor in the economy at large. Since the mass of firms is normalized to one, Y, K and N also represent their aggregate values. Hence, the consistency conditions require that

$$\bar{K} = K, \quad \bar{N} = N \quad \text{for all } t \geq 0,$$

implying that the social production function internalizing external effects is

$$Y = AK^{\alpha}N^{\alpha}, \quad \alpha + \beta > 1. \tag{2.12}$$

As a result, the social technology exhibits increasing returns to scale, and A stands for TFP of the social technology.

When maximizing its profits, an individual firm takes the external effects as given. Hence, the competitive rate of rate of return and the real wage rate are respectively expressed as

$$r = a\frac{Y}{K} = aAK^{\alpha-1}N^{\beta}, \tag{2.13}$$

$$w = (1-a)\frac{Y}{N} = (1-a)AK^{\alpha}N^{\beta-1}. \tag{2.14}$$

Finally, the equilibrium condition of the final goods is given by

$$Y = C + \dot{K} + \delta K. \tag{2.15}$$

Note that the competitive equilibrium of this model can be defined by solving the following pseudo planning problem. In this problem, the planner controls C and N to maximize U subject to

$$\dot{K} = AK^{a}N^{1-a}\bar{K}^{\alpha-a}\bar{N}^{\beta-(1-a)} - C - \delta K.$$

When solving the problem, the planner takes the sequences of $\{\bar{K}_t\}_{t=0}^{\infty}$ and $\{\bar{N}_t\}_{t=0}^{\infty}$ as given. It is easy to see that the optimization conditions of the planner's problem, together with the consistency conditions, $\bar{K} = K$ and $\bar{N} = N$, yield (2.10) and (2.11).

2.2.2 Dynamic System

Equations (2.10) and (2.14) yield

$$CN^{\gamma} = (1-a)AK^{\alpha}N^{\beta-1}. \tag{2.16}$$

The conventional analysis of the equilibrium dynamics of this model is that using (2.16), we express N as a function of K and C. Then, we substitute this relation into $Y = AK^{\alpha}N^{\beta}$, $r = aAK^{\alpha-1}$, and $w = (1-\alpha)AK^{\alpha}N^{\beta-1}$ to derive a complete dynamic system of K and C. After confirming that the steady state values of K and C are uniquely given, we linearize the dynamic system around the steady state and check the signs of characteristic roots of the coefficient matrix. In what follows, we focus on a dynamic system of Y/K and C/K, because it is more convenient for driving the indeterminacy conditions than the conventional method mentioned above. To do this, we rewrite (2.10) as

$$CN^{\gamma} = (1-a)\frac{Y}{N},$$

which gives

$$N = \left[(1-a)\frac{x}{z} \right]^{\frac{1}{1+\gamma}}.$$

Here, we denote $x = Y/K$ and $z = C/K$. As a result, the aggregate output is written as

$$Y = AK^{\alpha} \left[(1-a)\frac{x}{z} \right]^{\frac{\beta}{1+\beta}}.$$

Noting that $r = aY/K = ax$, the growth rates of capital, consumption and output are respectively given by

$$\frac{\dot{K}}{K} = x - z - \delta, \tag{2.17}$$

$$\frac{\dot{C}}{C} = ax - \rho - \delta, \tag{2.18}$$

$$\frac{\dot{Y}}{Y} = \alpha\frac{\dot{K}}{K} + \frac{\beta}{1+\gamma}\left(\frac{\dot{x}}{x} - \frac{\dot{z}}{z}\right). \tag{2.19}$$

Using (2.17), (2.18), and (2.19), together with $\dot{x}/x = \dot{Y}/Y - \dot{K}/K$ and $\dot{z}/z = \dot{C}/C - \dot{K}/K$, we obtain the following dynamic system of x and z:

$$\frac{\dot{x}}{x} = \frac{1}{1-\phi}\left\{ [\alpha - 1 + \phi(1-a)]\, x - [\alpha - 1 + \phi]\, z + (1-\alpha)\delta - \phi\rho \right\}, \tag{2.20}$$

$$\frac{\dot{z}}{z} = (a-1)\, x + z - \rho, \tag{2.21}$$

where $\phi + \beta/(1+\gamma).\phi = \frac{\beta}{1+\gamma}$.

In the steady state, K, Y and C stay constant over time. The conditions for $\dot{K} = 0$ and $\dot{z} = 0$ respectively yield

$$x - z - \delta = 0,$$

$$(1-a)\, x + z - \rho = 0.$$

Thus, the steady state levels of x and z are

$$x^* = \frac{\rho + \delta}{a}, \quad z^* = \frac{\rho + (1-a)\,\delta}{a}. \tag{2.22}$$

2.2.3 *Indeterminacy Conditions*

The coefficient matrix of (2.20) and (2.21) evaluated at the steady state is

$$J = \begin{bmatrix} x^* \frac{1}{1-\phi} \left[\alpha - 1 + \phi \left(1 - a\right)\right] & x^* (\alpha - 1 + \phi) \\ z^* \left(a - 1\right) & z^* \end{bmatrix}.$$

The determinant of this matrix is

$$\det J = x^* z^* \frac{1}{1-\phi} a \left(\alpha - 1\right).$$

Since $0 < \alpha < 1$, if $\phi < 1$ so that

$$1 + \gamma > \beta, \tag{2.23}$$

then the steady state is a saddle point. Hence, there is a linear relation between x and z on the stable saddle path, which is written as $z_t = \bar{m} x_t$, where $\bar{m}$ is a constant. Therefore, on the stable saddle path, it holds that

$$Y_t = AK_t^{\alpha} \left[\left(1 - a\right) \bar{m}\right]^{\frac{\beta}{1+\gamma}}.$$

Hence, if the initial level of K_0 is given, Y_0 is given, implying that $x_0 = Y_0/K_0$ is determine as well so that the equilibrium path of the economy is determinate.

If the equilibrium path is indeterminate, the initial level of C is indeterminate under a given level of K_0. This requires the steady state of our dynamic system to be a sink so that the coefficient matrix J has two stable roots. The necessary and sufficient conditions for the presence of two stable roots are $\det J > 0$ and trace $J < 0$. The trace of J is given by

$$\begin{aligned} \text{trace } J &= x^* \left[\frac{1}{1-\phi} \left(\alpha - 1\right) + \phi \left(1 - a\right)\right] + z^* \\ &= \frac{\rho + \delta}{a} \left[\frac{1}{1-\phi} \left(\alpha - 1\right) + \phi \left(1 - a\right)\right] + \frac{\rho + \left(1 - a\right) \delta}{a}. \end{aligned}$$

Consequently, the necessary and sufficient conditions for indeterminacy in terms of model parameters are the following:

$$1 + \gamma < \beta, \tag{2.24}$$

$$\frac{\rho + \delta}{a} \left[\frac{1+\gamma}{1+\gamma-\beta} \left(\alpha - 1\right) + \frac{\beta \left(1 - a\right)}{1+\gamma}\right] + \frac{\rho + \left(1 - a\right) \delta}{a} < 0. \tag{2.25}$$

The first condition requires that the external effect associated with aggregate labor is high enough. The second condition shows that even if $\beta > 1 + \gamma$, indeterminacy may not hold. For example, suppose that the aggregate capital does not yield external effects so that $\alpha = a$. Then if $\beta > 1 + \gamma$, the left hand side of the second inequality condition becomes

$$\frac{(\rho + \delta)(1 - a)}{a} \left[\frac{\beta}{1 + \gamma} - \frac{1 + \gamma}{1 + \gamma - \beta} \right] + \frac{\rho + (1 - a)\delta}{a} > 0,$$

which violates (2.25). Therefore, the presence of equilibrium indeterminacy requires that the aggregate capital should exhibit external effects as well.

2.2.4 Calibration

Farmer and Guo (1994, 1995) examine a stochastic, discrete time version of the Benhabib-Farmer model. Using the pseudo-planning formulation, we assume that the planner solves the following problem:

$$\max E_0 \sum_{t=0}^{\infty} \left(\frac{1}{1 + \rho} \right)^t \left[\log C_t - \frac{N_t^{1+\gamma}}{1 + \gamma} \right]$$

subject to

$$K_{t+1} = (1 - \delta) K_t + A_t K_t^a N_t^{1-a} \bar{K}_t^{\alpha - a} \bar{N}_t^{\beta - (1-a)} - C_t, \tag{2.26}$$

$$\log A_{t+1} = \theta \log A_t + (1 - \theta) \log A^* + \varepsilon_{t+1}, \quad 0 < \theta < 1. \tag{2.27}$$

Here, equation (2.27) means that the TFP follows a first-order stochastic difference equation in which ε_{t+1} is a white noise (an exogenous disturbance hitting the TFP in period $t + 1$) and A^* is the steady state level of TFP in the deterministic world. When solving the optimization problem, the planner takes the sequences of external effects, $\{\bar{K}_t, \bar{N}_t\}_{t=0}^{\infty}$, as given.

Using the consistency conditions, $\bar{K}_t = K_t$ and $\bar{N}_t = N_t$, the optimal choice conditions for C_t and N_t give

$$C_t N_t^{\gamma} = (1 - a) \frac{Y}{N_t} = A_t K_t^{\alpha} N_t^{\beta - 1},$$

which leads to

$$N_t = \left[\frac{1 - \alpha}{C_t} A_t K_t^{\alpha} \right]^{\frac{1}{1 - \gamma - \beta}}. \tag{2.28}$$

The Euler equation of the optimal consumption is

$$\frac{1}{C_t} = \frac{1}{1+\rho} E_t \frac{1}{C_{t+1}} \left(a\frac{Y_{t+1}}{K_{t+1}} + 1 - \delta \right).$$

Substituting (2.28) into (2.26) and the Euler equation, we obtain the following:

$$K_{t+1} = A_t K_t^{\alpha} \left[\frac{1-\alpha}{C_t} A_t K_t^{\alpha} \right]^{\frac{\beta}{1-\gamma-\beta}} + (1-\delta) K_t - C_t, \tag{2.29}$$

$$\frac{1}{C_t} = \frac{1}{1+\rho} E_t \frac{1}{C_{t+1}} \left(K_{t+1}^{\alpha} \left[\frac{1-\alpha}{C_t} A_{t+1} K_{t+1}^{\alpha} \right]^{\frac{\beta-1}{1-\gamma-\beta}} + 1 - \delta \right). \tag{2.30}$$

Now, let us define $x_t = \log(X_t/X^*)$ $(X_t = K_t, C_t, A_t)$. Then, log-linearizing (2.29), (2.30), and (2.27) at the steady state yields

$$\begin{bmatrix} k_{t+1} \\ E_t c_{t+1} \\ a_{t+1} \end{bmatrix} = J \begin{bmatrix} k_t \\ c_t \\ a_t \end{bmatrix} + \begin{bmatrix} 0 \\ 0 \\ \varepsilon_{t+1} \end{bmatrix}, \tag{2.31}$$

where

$$J = \begin{bmatrix} \psi_{kk} & \psi_{kc} & \psi_{ka} \\ \psi_{ck} & \psi_{cc} & \psi_{ca} \\ 0 & 0 & \theta \end{bmatrix},$$

and ψ_{ij} $(i,j = c,k)$ denotes coefficient evaluated at the deterministic steady state.

When determinacy holds, the optimal consumption is uniquely related to k_t and a_t on the stable saddle path. Thus, the policy function of c_t approximated around the steady state is expressed as

$$c_t = \lambda_k k_t + \lambda_a a_t, \tag{2.32}$$

where λ_k and λ_a are undetermined coefficients. Using (2.32), $E_t c_{t+1}$ in the left hand side of (2.31) is written as

$$\begin{aligned} E_t c_{t+1} &= \lambda_k E_t k_{t+1} + \lambda_a E_t a_{t+1} \\ &= \lambda_k (\psi_{kk} k_t + \psi_{kc} c_t + \psi_{ka} a_t) + \lambda_a \theta a_t \\ &= (\psi_{kk} \lambda_k + \psi_{kc} \lambda_k^2) k_t + (\lambda_k \psi_{ka} + \psi_{kc} \lambda_k \lambda_a + \lambda_a \theta) a_t. \end{aligned}$$

The second equation in (2.31) gives

$$E_t c_{t+1} = (\psi_{kk} + \lambda_k k_{kc}) k_t + (\lambda_a \psi_{kc} + \theta) a_t.$$

Hence, we see that the following is established for any k_t and a_t:

$$\begin{aligned}&(\psi_{kk}\lambda_k + \psi_{kc}\lambda_k^2)k_t + (\lambda_k\psi_{ka} + \psi_{kc}\lambda_k\lambda_a + \lambda_a\theta)\, a_t \\ &= (\psi_{kk} + \lambda_k k_{kc})\, k_t + (\lambda_a\psi_{kc} + \theta)\, a.\end{aligned}$$

Comparing the coefficients of k_t and a_t in the above identity, we obtain

$$\begin{aligned}\psi_{kk}\lambda_k + \psi_{kc}\lambda_k^2 &= \psi_{kk} + \lambda_k k_{kc},\\ \lambda_k\psi_{ka} + \psi_{kc}\lambda_k\lambda_a + \lambda_a\theta &= \lambda_a\psi_{kc} + \theta.\end{aligned}$$

Solving these two equations with respect to λ_k and λ_a, we can express λ_k and λ_a in terms of ψ_{ij} $(i, j = k, c, a)$.[3] Consequently, the dynamic system is summarized by the following stochastic difference equations of k_t and a_t:

$$\begin{aligned}k_{t+1} &= (\psi_{kk} + \psi_{kc}\lambda_k)k_t + (\psi_{ka} + \lambda_a\psi_{ka})\, a_t,\\ a_{t+1} &= \theta a_t + \varepsilon_{t+1}.\end{aligned}$$

Under a given sequence of stochastic disturbance $\{\varepsilon_t\}_{t=0}^{\infty}$, we can conduct numerical simulations and impulse response analysis based on the above set of stochastic difference equations.

On the other hand, if the steady state is a sink and indeterminacy holds, we cannot relate c_t to k_t and a_t in the way as (2.32). In such a case, we exploit the fact that the rational expectations hypothesis means that $c_{t+1} - E_t c_{t+1} = \zeta_{t+1}$, where ξ_t is white noise. Therefore, if equilibrium indeterminacy holds, the dynamic system is expressed as

$$\begin{bmatrix} k_{t+1} \\ c_{t+1} \\ a_{t+1} \end{bmatrix} = J \begin{bmatrix} k_t \\ c_t \\ a_t \end{bmatrix} + \begin{bmatrix} 0 \\ \xi_{t+1} \\ \varepsilon_{t+1} \end{bmatrix}. \tag{2.33}$$

Here, the expectations error, ξ_{t+1}, represents a sunspot shock. In particular, if there is no fundamental shock so that $a_t = 0$ for all $t \geq 0$, then the dynamic system becomes

$$\begin{aligned}k_{t+1} &= \psi_{kk}k_t + \psi_{kc}c_t,\\ c_{t+1} &= \psi_{ck}k_t + \psi_{cc}c_t + \xi_{t+1}.\end{aligned}$$

Without stochastic disturbances, the deterministic steady state $(k^*, c^*) = (0, 0)$ is a sink. In this system, the driving force of business fluctuations is the sunspot

[3] There are two solutions of λ_k. We select one that corresponds to the stable saddle path.

shock, ξ_t, alone. Farmer and Guo (1994) confirm that even in this simple case, the calibrated model performs reasonably well as compared with the standard RBC dynamic system summarized by (2.31).

In fact, Kamihigashi (1996) reveals that the canonical RBC model and the corresponding sunspot model may show observationally equivalent time series data of macroeconomic variables. Kamihigashi's theoretical contribution suggests that as far as performances of calibrated models are concerned, it is difficult to evaluate whether sunspot models can substitute the canonical RBC model. Consequently, the evaluation of the sunspot models focuses on whether or not the indeterminacy conditions shown by (2.24) and (2.25) are empirically plausible. We discuss this point in Sect. 2.4.1.

2.3 The Source of Indeterminacy

2.3.1 Strategic Complementarity

The Benhabib-Farmer model assumes that there are many identical, competitive firms and that the production activity of an individual firm gives rise to a positive impact on the other firms' production activities. Such a situation can be captured as a coordination game. Cooper and John (1988) explore the symmetric, Nash equilibrium in a static game in which there are identical agents. Cooper (1999) presents various examples of coordination games including macro-dynamic models.

Suppose that there are multiple identical agents. Each agent selects an activity a_i in order to maximize its objective function

$$u_i = u\left(a_i,\ a_{-i}, \theta_i\right).$$

In the above, a_{-i} is a vector whose elements are other agents' activities. It is assumed that $u\left(.\right)$ is monotonically increasing and strictly concave in a_i. Moreover, θ_i is an agent-specific parameter that affects the agent's felicity. Here, we focus on the symmetric equilibrium, and thus we assume that

$$\theta_i = \theta \ \text{ for all } i.$$

Since $u_i\left(.\right)$ is strictly concave in a_i, if a rise in $a_j \ \ (j \neq i)$ decreases the marginal benefit of agent $i \ \ (= \partial u_i / a_i)$, then a higher a_j lowers the optimal choice of a_i. In this case, agents' actions are strategic substitutes each other. Conversely, if a higher $a_j \ \ (j \neq i)$ increases $\partial u_i / a_i u_i$, then a rise in a_j increases the optimal level of a_i, so that agents' actions are strategic complements each other.

Each agent maximizes $u(.)$ by selecting a_i under given levels of other agents' strategies expressed by a_{-i}. The first-order conditions are

$$\frac{\partial u(a_i, a_{-i}, \theta)}{\partial a_i} = 0 \text{ for all } i. \tag{2.34}$$

Since each agent has an identical objective function, the optimal choice of agent i is expressed as

$$a_i = \phi(a_{-i}, \theta)$$

If we find a set of solutions satisfying all the conditions in (2.34), then the optimal solutions fulfill the symmetric conditions, namely,

$$a_i^* = \phi\left(a_{-i}^*, \theta\right) = a^* \text{ for all } i,$$

This is the symmetric Nash equilibrium.

The main findings by Cooper and John (1988) are the following:

1 If the game exhibits strategic sustitutability, there is a unique symmetric Nash equilibrium.
2 In the case of strategic complementarity, there may exist multiple symmetric Nash equilibria and these equilibria are Pareto ranked.

To confirm the above propositions, assume that there are two symmetric Nash equilibria, a^* and a^{**} $(>a^*)$, Then, we obtain

$$a_i^* = \phi\left(a_{-i}^*, \theta\right) = a^* \text{ for all } i,$$
$$a_i^{**} = \phi\left(a_{-i}^{**}, \theta\right) = a^{**} \text{ for all } i.$$

In the case of strategic substitutability, if $a_j^* < a_j^{**}$, the optimal choice of agent i $(\neq j)$ yields $a_i^* > a_i^{**}$. However, this contradicts our assumption that the symmetric Nash equilibrium satisfies

$$a^* = \phi\left(a_{-i}^*, \theta\right) > \phi\left(a_{-i}^{**}, \theta\right) = a^{**}.$$

In contrast, if strategic complementarity holds, then it is possible to hold that

$$a^* = \phi\left(a_{-i}^*, \theta\right) < \phi\left(a_{-i}^{**}, \theta\right) = a^{**}.$$

In this case, a^{**} is better for all the agents, and, hence, the Nash equilibrium with $a_i = a^{**}$ dominates the equilibrium with $a_i = a^*$ in the Pareto sense.

The presence of external increasing returns assumed by Benhabib and Farmer (1994) and Farmer and Guo (1994) is a typical situation in which the Nash equilibrium is characterized by strategic complementarity. In the presence of positive technological spillover, when an individual firm expands its production, it yields a positive impact on the other firms' production activities. If there are two symmetric equilibria and if every firm becomes optimistic, then the equilibrium with higher levels of production can be realized. By contrast, if every firm is pessimistic, the lower equilibrium will emerge.

2.3.2 Intuitive Implication of Indeterminacy Conditions

To apply the above discussion to the Benhabib-Farmer model, it is useful to note how the current consumption, C_t, is determined. First, consider the intertemporal budget constraint for the household such that

$$K_t + \int_t^{\infty} \exp\left(-\int_t^s (r_v - \delta)\, dv\right) C_s ds = \int_t^{\infty} \exp\left(-\int_t^s (r_v - \delta)\, dv\right) w_s N_s ds.$$

The Euler equation of the optimal consumption gives

$$C_s = C_t \exp\left(\int_t^s (r_v - \delta - \rho) dv\right).$$

Substituting this into the intertemporal budget constraint leads to

$$C_t = \rho\,(K_t + H_t)\,, \tag{2.35}$$

where H_t is the human wealth defined by

$$H_t = \left(\int_t^{\infty} \exp\left(-\int_t^s (r_v - \delta)\, dv\right) w_s N_s ds\right). \tag{2.36}$$

We re-express (2.10) as

$$CN^{\gamma} = w = \bar{\Omega} A K^{\alpha} N^{1-a}, \tag{2.37}$$

where $\bar{\Omega} = \bar{K}^{\alpha - a} \bar{N}^{\beta-(1-a)}$ represents the external effects associated with aggregate capital and labor. Since the marginal utility of consumption is $1/C$, if we fix C, the left hand side of (2.37) represents the Frisch labor supply curve. On the other hand, the right hand side is the labor demand curve of firms under a given level of external effect, $\bar{\Omega}_t$.

Suppose that a positive sunspot shock makes the households anticipate that their future wage income increases. This enhances the expected present value of human wealth given by (2.36). Hence, from (2.35) such an income effect will raise the current consumption. In the standard RBC model without production externalities ($\bar{\Omega}_t = 1$), a rise in C_t shifts the Frisch labor supply curve upward,

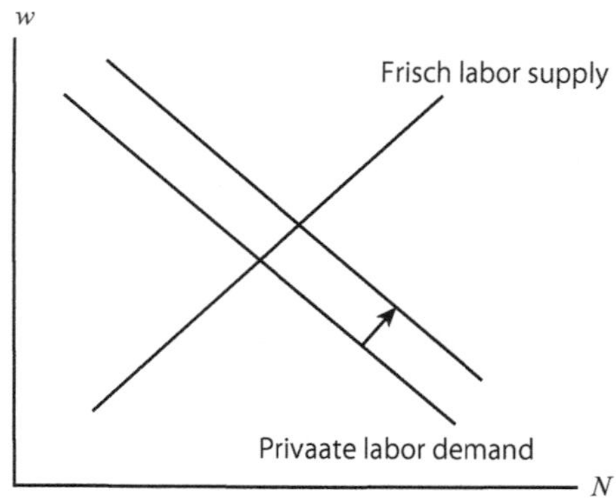

Fig. 2.1 A shift of the private labor demand curve

so that the equilibrium level of hours worked decreases. Under a given level of K_t, the decline in N_t depresses Y_t, implying that the investment in period t is lowered. This lowers capital accumulation, thereby declining future income, which contradicts the initial expectation that the future income will rise. This outcome demonstrates that a sunspot shock will not affect the equilibrium of the economy. By contrast, in the presence of production externalities, if firms increase their labor inputs, strategic complementarity among the firms' decisions raises the labor wedge, $\bar{\Omega} = \bar{K}^{\alpha-a}\bar{N}^{\beta-(1-a)}$. Note that if $\beta > 1 + \gamma$, a rise in the aggregate hours, N, increases labor wedge, and thus the individual labor demand curve shifts up. If such a shift dominates the shifts of the labor supply curve, then the equilibrium level of hours worked may increase (see Fig. 2.1).

To see the above result more clearly, note that since the number of firms is normalized to unity, the social labor demand curve that internalizes external effects is given by $w = AK^{\alpha}N$. Therefore, in the standard case of $\beta < 1 + \gamma$, the social labor demand curve is still downward sloping. On the other hand, if $\beta > 1 + \gamma$, then the social labor demand curve that internalizes externalities is upward sloping and it is stepper than the Frisch labor supply curve. Suppose that a positive, non-fundamental shock hits the economy and, thus, households anticipate that their real wage will increase. This increases the anticipated value of the human wealth, so that the households raise their current consumption C_t. As a result, the Frisch labor supply curve shifts upward. In the standard case in which $1+\gamma > \beta$, the equilibrium employment and the current output will decline. Consequently, a higher C_t with a lower Y_t discourages investment of the households. Therefore, the future capital will be lowered, which contradicts the initial anticipation of higher levels of future wages. In contrast, if $\beta > 1 + \gamma$, an upward shift of the Frisch labor supply curve raises the equilibrium levels of employment and output. If such a rise in output is large enough to enhance the current investment despite the increase in C_t, the future capital stock becomes larger and the real wage will actually rise: the initial change in expectations caused by the sunspot shock will be self-fulfilled (see Fig. 2.2).

Using a discrete-time counterpart of the model discussed so far, Wen (2001) presents a more precise argument. In our continuous-time setting, his discussion

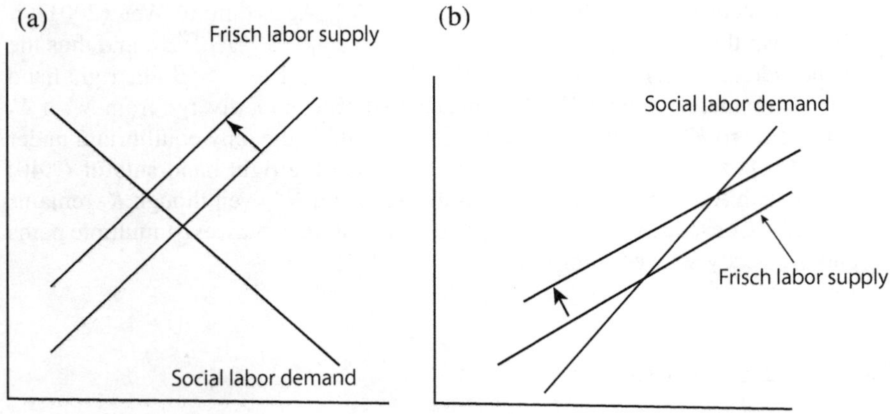

Fig. 2.2 (**a**) The case of $1+\gamma > \beta$. (**b**) The case of $\beta > 1+\gamma$

is as follows. Substituting $w_s = C_s N_s^{\gamma}$ into (2.36) gives

$$H_t = \left(\int_t^{\infty} \exp\left(-\int_t^{s} (r_v - \delta)\, dv \right) C_s N_s^{1+\gamma} ds \right).$$

Substituting (2.35) again into the above, we obtain

$$H_t = C_t \int_t^{\infty} e^{-\rho s} N_s^{1+\gamma} ds,$$

which means that the current level of optimal consumption is written as

$$C_t = \frac{\rho K_t}{1-\rho \int_t^{\infty} e^{-\rho s} N_s^{1+\gamma} ds}. \tag{2.38}$$

From $C_t = w_t N_t^{-\gamma}$, (2.38) gives

$$1-\rho \int_t^{\infty} e^{-\rho s} N_s^{1+\gamma} ds = \frac{\rho K_t}{w_t N_t^{-\gamma}}. \tag{2.39}$$

Note that the term$-\int_t^{\infty} e^{-\rho t} N_s^{\gamma+1} ds$ represents a (subjectively) discounted sum of the disutility of labor (divided by $1+\gamma$).

Suppose that at the outset ($t=0$), the economy stays at the steady state so that $K_0 = K^*$ and $N_0 = N^*$. Now, let us raise $N_0 > N^*$ and keep $K_t = K^*$. To establish (2.39), it should hold that

$$1-\rho \int_0^{\infty} e^{-\rho t} N_s^{1+\gamma} dt = \frac{\rho K^*}{w_0 N_0^{-\gamma}}. \tag{2.40}$$

Since the system is stable, N_t must converge to N^*. According to Wen (2001), it can be shown that a higher N_0 ($> N^*$) yields a larger $\int_t^{\infty} e^{-\rho t} N_s^{1+\gamma} ds$, and thus the left hand side of (2.40) decreases with N_0. Moreover, if $1 + \gamma > \beta$, the right hand side of (2.40) increases with N_0. This means that N_0 cannot diverge from N^* if K_t remains equal to K^*. In other words, the steady state is the only equilibrium under $K_t = K^*$. On the other hand, if $1 + \gamma < \beta$, then the right hand side of (2.40) decreases with N_0, implying that N_0 can diverge from N^* even though K_t remains equal to K^*. Consequently, in the case of $\beta > 1 + \gamma$, they may exist multiple paths around the steady state equilibrium.

2.4 Related Issues

2.4.1 Indeterminacy Under Mild Increasing Returns

We have seen that the necessary condition for indeterminacy in the baseline RBC model is $\beta > 1 + \gamma$. In our specification of the utility function, $1/\gamma$ represents the (Frisch) elasticity of labor supply with respect to real wage. The conventional estimated range of $1/\gamma$ is from 1.0 to 2.0, meaning that the minimum level of γ is 0.5. Thus, if β exceeds 1.5, the degree of social returns to scale, $\alpha + \beta$, is higher than 1.8 even if the external effects of capital is relatively small. (Remember that the presence of capital externality, i.e. $\alpha > a$, is necessary to generate indeterminacy). If we follow the indivisible labor supply hypothesis given by Hansen (1985) and Rogerson (1988) (so the instantaneous utility function is $u(C,N) = \log C - BN,\ B > 0$), then $\alpha + \beta$ should be at least higher than 1.4. Since the foregoing studies on returns to scale of aggregate production functions such as Basu and Fernald (1997) suggested that the aggregate production technology is close to constant or mild increasing returns, the indeterminacy conditions for the baseline RBC model with production externalities are empirically implausible. Researchers of the mainstream RBC theory criticized this point and claimed that the sunspot-driven business cycles are convincing; see, for example, Aiyagari (1995). Such a criticism turned the researchers' attention to the models that exhibit indeterminacy under empirically plausible external effects in production. In what follows, we refer to two ideas.

2.4.1.1 Endogenous Capital Utilization

Wen (1998) shows that if capital utilization is associated with convex costs, then the degree of external increasing returns to generate indeterminacy can be reduced. If capital stock is not fully used, the production function of an individual firm is given by

$$Y_t = A\,(s_t K_t)^a\, N_t^{1-\alpha}\, \left(\bar{s}\bar{K}\right)^{\alpha - a}\, \bar{N}^{\beta-(1-a)}, \tag{2.41}$$

where s denotes the capital utilization rate. According to the standard assumption on capital utilization, we assume that the depreciation rate of capital is an increasing, convex function of s. Here, we specify the depreciation function in such a way that

$$\delta = \frac{\delta_0}{1+\theta} s^{1+\theta} = \delta(s), \quad \theta > 0.$$

The optimal rate of capital utilization maximizes the net output, $Y - \delta(s) K$, which is given by

$$s = \left(\frac{a}{\delta_0} Y \right)^{\frac{1}{1+\theta}}. \tag{2.42}$$

The social production function is obtained by setting $\bar{K} = K$, $\bar{N} = N$, and $\bar{s} = s$, so that the aggregate output, Y, fulfills

$$Y = A (sK)^{\alpha} N^{\beta} = A \left(\frac{a}{\delta_0} Y \right)^{\frac{\alpha}{1+\theta}} (K)^{\alpha} N^{\beta}.$$

If we ignore endogenous capital utilization, then $A \left(\frac{a}{\delta_0} Y \right)^{\frac{\alpha}{1+\theta}}$ is considered as the TFP of the social production function. In fact, the reduced form of the social production function is written as

$$Y = A^{\frac{1+\theta}{1+\theta-a}} \left(\frac{a}{\delta_0} \right)^{\frac{a}{1+\theta-a}} K^{\alpha \frac{1+\theta}{1+\theta-\alpha}} N^{\beta \frac{1+\theta}{1+\theta-\alpha}}, \tag{2.43}$$

implying that the aggregate return to scale of the reduced form of the social production function is higher than $\alpha + \beta$.

Again, we focus on condition (2.10). In this case, the condition, $CN^{\gamma} = w$, expressed as

$$CN^{\gamma} = A^{\frac{1+\theta}{1+\theta-a}} \left(\frac{a}{\delta_0} \right)^{\frac{a}{1+\theta-a}} K^{\alpha \frac{1+\theta}{1+\theta-\alpha}} N^{\beta \frac{1+\theta}{1+\theta-\alpha} - 1}.$$

Therefore, the log-linearized labor demand curve is steeper than the log-linearized Frisch labor supply curve, if the following condition is satified:

$$1 + \gamma < \frac{1+\theta}{1+\theta-\alpha} \beta.$$

In the case of indivisible labor $(\gamma = 0)$, if $\theta = 0.5$ and $a = 0.35$, then the above condition is satisfies if $\beta > 0.766$. Thus, if $\alpha = 0.4 \, (> a = 0.35)$, the return to scale of the social production function $(= \alpha + \beta)$ is higher than 1.2. Therefore, indeterminacy would hold under more plausible parameter values than those in the model with full utilization of capital.

2.4.1.2 Two-Sector Economy

Another popular approach that reduces the degree of external effect for generating indeterminacy is to assume that consumption and investment goods are produced by the use of different technologies. Following Benhabib and Farmer (1996), we consider a two-sector economy where one sector produces investment goods and the other sector produces pure consumption goods. The production function of each sector is

$$Y_i = A_i \bar{X}_i K_i^a N_i^{1-a}, \quad 0 < a < 1, \ \ i = 1, 2. \tag{2.44}$$

In the above, we assume that sector 1 produces investment goods, while sector 2 produces pure consumption goods. In (2.44), $\bar{X}_i$ represents sector-specific externality that is specified as

$$X_i = \bar{Y}_i^{\theta}, \quad 0 < \theta < 1, \ \ i = 1, 2,$$

where $\bar{Y}_i$ is the total output of sector i. Note that the production function of each sector has the same form.

The competitive factor prices are given by

$$r = a\frac{Y_1}{K_1} = pa\frac{Y_2}{K_2}, \tag{2.45}$$

$$w = (1-a)\frac{Y_1}{N_1} = p(1-a)\frac{Y_2}{N_2}. \tag{2.46}$$

Equations (2.45) and (2.46) mean that both sectors hold the same factor intensity as shown by

$$\frac{w}{r} = \frac{1-a}{a}\left(\frac{K_i}{N_i}\right), \quad i = 1, 2,$$

which leads to

$$\frac{K_2}{K_1} = \frac{N_2}{N_1}.$$

Letting $K_2/K_1 = N_2/N_1 = \lambda$ and using the full-employment conditions of capital and labor,

$$K = K_1 + K_2, \ \ N = N_1 + N_2,$$

we obtain $K_1 = \lambda K$,. $K_2 = (1-\lambda)K$, $N_1 = \lambda N$, and $N_2 = (1-\lambda)N$. As a consequence, the production function of each sector is expressed as

$$Y_1 = \lambda \bar{X}_1 K^a N^{1-a}, \quad Y_2 = (1-\lambda)\bar{X}_2 K^a N^{1-a}. \tag{2.47}$$

Thus, the relative price, p, is expressed as

$$p = \frac{Y_1/K_1}{Y_2/K_2} = \frac{\bar{X}_1}{\bar{X}_2} = \left(\frac{I}{C}\right)^{\theta},$$

meaning that the aggregate income (in terms of the investment good) is given by

$$Y = Y_1 + pY_2 = X_1 K^{\alpha} N^{1-a}.$$

Using $X_1 = Y_1 = I$ and $Y = I + pC$, we obtain

$$I^{1-\theta} + C^{1-\theta} = K^{\alpha} N^{1-a}. \tag{2.48}$$

This equation expresses the social production possibility frontier between consumption and investment goods.

Again, the household maximizes

$$U = \int_0^{\infty} e^{-\rho t}\left(\log C - \frac{N^{1+\gamma}}{1+\gamma}\right) dt$$

subject to

$$\dot{K} = rK + wN - pC - \delta K.$$

The optimal choice of C and N gives

$$1/C = pq, \tag{2.49}$$

$$CN^{\gamma} = w/p. \tag{2.50}$$

The implicit price, q, follows

$$\dot{q} = q(\rho + \delta - r). \tag{2.51}$$

Finally, the market equilibrium conditions for both goods are the following:

$$Y_1 = I = \dot{K} + \delta K, \quad Y_2 = C.$$

From (2.10) and (2.46), the familiar labor supply and demand relation is now given by

$$CN^{\gamma} = \frac{w}{p} = (1-a)\, C^{\theta} K^{a} N^{-a}. \tag{2.52}$$

Notice that due to the external effect, the labor demand depends on the level of consumption. Therefore, when C rises, not only the Frisch labor supply curve but also the labor demand curve shift upward. Condition (2.52) yields

$$N = (1-a)^{\frac{1}{a+\gamma}}\, C^{\frac{\theta-1}{a+\gamma}} K^{\frac{a}{a+\gamma}}. \tag{2.53}$$

To derive a complete dynamic system of K and C, we first rewrite (2.48) in the following manner:

$$I = \left(K^{a} N^{1-a} - C^{1-\theta}\right)^{\frac{1}{1-\theta}}.$$

Substituting (2.53) into the above, we relate I to K and C as follows:

$$I = I\,(K, C)\,. \tag{2.54}$$

Thus, capital stock follows

$$\dot{K} = I\,(K, C) - \delta K. \tag{2.55}$$

In addition, conditions (2.49) and (2.51) give

$$\begin{aligned} \frac{\dot{C}}{C} &= aK^{a-1}N^{1-a} - \rho - \delta - \theta\left(\frac{\dot{C}}{C} - \frac{\dot{I}}{I}\right) \\ &= aK^{a-1}N^{1-a} - \rho - \delta - \theta\left(1 - \frac{I_C C}{I}\right)\frac{\dot{C}}{C} - I_K\dot{K}. \end{aligned}$$

By use of (2.54), we obtain the following dynamic equation of C:

$$\frac{\dot{C}}{C} = \frac{1}{1+\theta[1-\varepsilon\,(C,K)]}\left[\left(K^{a-1}N^{1-a} - \rho - \delta\right) - \theta I_K \dot{K}\right], \tag{2.56}$$

where $\varepsilon\,(.) = I_K\,(K,C)\,C/I\,(K,C)$. To sum up, the dynamic behavior of the two-sector economy is described by (2.55) and (2.56).

It is easy to see that if $\theta = 0$, the dynamic system reduces to the baseline one-sector RBC model without external effects. Complexity of the two-sector model with social increasing returns stems from the fact that the social production possibility frontier is nonlinear: it is convex to the origin in (C, I) space, so that the relative price also depends on the scale parameter θ. Analyzing numerical examples of a discrete-time version of this model, Benhabib and Farmer (1996) reveal that when $a = 0.3$ and $\gamma = 0$, the steady state of the above dynamic system is a sink even though θ is sufficiently low at 0.06, so that the aggregate return to scale, $1+\theta$, is about 1.06.

2.4.2 *Preference Structure*

We have focused on the role of production technologies in discussing equilibrium indeterminacy. In this subsection, we turn our attention to the role of preference structure in the indeterminacy issue.

2.4.2.1 Non-separable Utility

As discussed in Sect. 2.3, the key conditions for indeterminacy in the one-sector RBC model is that the labor demand curve slopes up and is steeper than the Frisch labor supply curve. This condition ensures that a rise in consumption caused by a positive sunspot shock raises the equilibrium level of hours worked, which supports self-fulfilling expectations. One may conjecture that even though the labor demand curve has a negative slope, the same outcome can arise if the Frisch labor supply curve slopes down and is steeper than the labor demand curve. As Fig. 2.3 shows, in this situation, an upward shift of the Frisch labor supply curve increases the equilibrium level of hours worked.

Obviously, the additive separable utility used so far cannot bring about the situation such as in Fig. 2.3. To see when the Frisch labor curve has a negative slope, consider the following general utility function:

$$u = u(C, N).$$

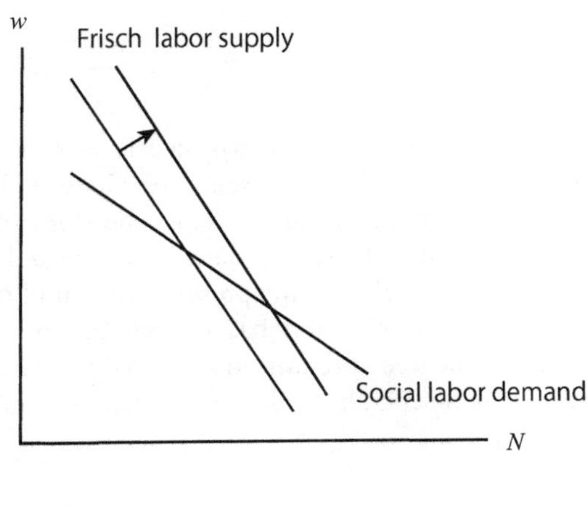

Fig. 2.3 A shift of the Frisch labor supply curve

Following the standard setting, we assume that $u_C > 0$, $u_N < 0$, $u_{CC} < 0$, and $u_{NN} < 0$. The household's optimal choice conditions for C and N are

$$u_C(C, N) = q, \tag{2.57}$$

$$u_N(C, N) = -wq, \tag{2.58}$$

where q is the utility price of capital. The Frisch labor supply function is derived under a fixed level of marginal utility. Keeping q constant, the first-order conditions (2.57) and (2.58) in the above give

$$u_{CC}\frac{dC}{dw} + u_{CN}\frac{dN}{dw} = 0,$$

$$u_{NC}\frac{\delta C}{dw} + u_{NN}\frac{dN}{dw} = -q.$$

Hence, we find that the slope of the Frisch labor supply is given by

$$\frac{dN}{dw} = \frac{u_{CC}\frac{u_N}{w}}{u_{CC}u_{NN} - (u_{CN})^2}. \tag{2.59}$$

As a result, if the utility function fails to satisfy strict concavity with respect to C and N (so the denominator in the right hand side of (2.59) is negative), then the Frisch labor supply curve has a negative slope.

Bennett and Farmer (2000) assume that the instantaneous utility function is

$$u(C, L) = \frac{\left(C \exp\left(-\frac{N}{1+\gamma}\right)\right)^{1-\sigma}}{1-\sigma}, \quad \sigma > 0, \quad \gamma > 0.$$

Hence, if $\sigma = 1$, we have $u(C, N) = \log C - N^{1+\gamma}/(1+\gamma)$. Bennett and Farmer (2000) find that the necessary condition for local indeterminacy is

$$\beta - 1 > \frac{\sigma - 1}{\sigma} N^{*1+\gamma} + \gamma,$$

where N^* denotes the steady state level of hours worked. The left hand side of the above inequality represents the slope of log-linearized labor demand curve, while the right hand side expresses the slope of Frisch labor supply curve linearly approximated at the steady state. Thus, when the external effects of labor are small enough to hold $\beta < 1$, the presence of equilibrium indeterminacy requires that the Frisch labor supply curve has a negative slope. This is possible if $\sigma < 1$, so that the necessary degree of returns to scale that generates indeterminacy can be small in the case of non-separable utility. However, as pointed out by Hintermaier (2003), this outcome holds only if the instantaneous utility function violates the usual concavity assumption.

2.4.2.2 The Role of the Income Effect

Regarding the intuitive implication of indeterminacy, we have discussed the case in which a positive sunspot shock raises the expected permanent income of the households, which generates an upward shift of the Frisch labor supply curve through an increase in the current consumption. To examine the role of the income effect for generating indeterminacy, it is useful to use the Greenwood-Hercowitz-Huffman (GHH) preferences under which the income (wealth) effect does not exist. Following Greenwood et al. (1988), suppose that the utility function is given by

$$u(C,N) = v(C - \Lambda(N)), \tag{2.60}$$

where $v(.)$ is a monotonically increasing and strictly concave function, and $\Lambda(N)$ is a monotonically increasing and strictly convex function. It is easy to see that the optimal choice of household with respect to C and N yields

$$\Lambda'(N) = w,$$

implying that the income effect that changes the current level of consumption will not affect labor supply. As a result, the optimal level of hours worked depends on the real wage alone, and it monotonically increases with the real wage rate.

In our baseline model, the GHH preference can be set as

$$u(C,N) = \log\left(C - \frac{N^{1+\gamma}}{1+\gamma}\right). \tag{2.61}$$

Given this specification, the household's optimization conditions (2.57) and (2.58) are respectively given by

$$\frac{1}{C - \frac{N^{1+\gamma}}{1+\gamma}} = q, \tag{2.62}$$

$$N^{\gamma}\left(\frac{1}{C - \frac{N^{1+\gamma}}{1+\gamma}}\right) = wq. \tag{2.63}$$

These conditions yield

$$N^{\gamma} = w. \tag{2.64}$$

Hence, N is related to Y as $N^{1+\gamma :} = (1-a)\,Y$. This means that from (2.62) we obtain

$$C = \frac{1}{q} + \frac{(1-\alpha)\,Y}{1+\gamma}. \tag{2.65}$$

In view of (2.64), we find

$$N = [(1-a)\,AK^{\alpha}]^{\frac{1}{1+\gamma-\beta}},$$

meaning that the social production function can be expressed as

$$Y = A^{\frac{2+\gamma}{1+\gamma-\beta}}\,(1-a)^{\frac{1}{1+\gamma-\beta}}\,K^{\frac{\alpha(1+\gamma)}{1+\gamma-\beta}}.$$

In sum, a complete dynamic system is given by the following:

$$\dot{K} = \left(\frac{1-\alpha}{1+\gamma}\right) A^{\frac{2+\gamma}{1+\gamma-\beta}}\,(1-a)^{\frac{1}{1+\gamma-\beta}}\,K^{\frac{\alpha(1+\gamma)}{1+\gamma-\beta}} - \frac{1}{q} - \delta K,$$

$$\dot{q} = q\left[aA^{\frac{2+\gamma}{1+\gamma-\beta}}\,(1-a)^{\frac{1}{1+\gamma-\beta}}\,K^{\frac{\alpha(1+\gamma)}{1+\gamma-\beta}-1} - \rho - \delta\right].$$

Inspecting the above dynamic system, we find that if

$$\frac{\alpha(1+\gamma)}{1+\gamma-\beta} < 1, \tag{2.66}$$

then the steady state is uniquely given. The coefficient matrix of the linearized system is given by

$$J_g = \begin{bmatrix} \alpha\left(\frac{1+\gamma}{1+\gamma-\beta}\frac{Y^*}{K^*}\right) & \frac{1}{q^{*2}} \\ -\alpha\left(\frac{\alpha(1+\gamma)}{1+\gamma-\beta}-1\right)\frac{Y^*}{K^{*2}} & 0 \end{bmatrix}.$$

Therefore, if (2.66) holds, the determinant of the above matrix is negative, so that the equilibrium path is locally determinate around the steady state, even if the degree of external increasing returns is high enough to fulfill $\beta > 1+\gamma$. It is easy to confirm that the same outcome holds in a more general GHH-type utility given by (2.60).

To clarify the role of the income effect in the indeterminacy issue, Jaimovich (2008) presents an interesting discussion. In a discrete time setting, Jaimovich (2008) sets up the following utility function:

$$u\,(C_t, N_t) = \frac{\left(C_t - \psi X_t N_t^{1+\gamma}\right)^{1-\sigma}}{1-\sigma}, \quad \psi > 0, \ \sigma > 0, \tag{2.67}$$

where X_t follows

$$X_t = C_t^{\chi} X_{t-1}^{1-\chi}, \quad \leq \chi \leq 1.$$

In this formulation, the utility function becomes

$$u(C_t, N_t) = \begin{cases} \dfrac{[C_t(1-\psi N_t^{1+\gamma})]^{1-\sigma}}{1-\sigma}, & \text{if } \gamma = 1, \\ \dfrac{\left(C_t - \psi \bar{X} N_t^{1+\gamma}\right)^{1-\sigma}}{1-\sigma} & \text{if } \gamma = 0. \end{cases}$$

Namely, (2.67) covers both the standard non-separable utility as well as the GHH preference structure. Assuming that the social production function is $Y_t = A_t K_t^{\alpha} N_t^{\beta}$ $(\alpha + \beta > 1)$, Jaimovich (2008) seeks the parameter space of $(\alpha + \beta, \gamma)$ that gives rise to equilibrium indeterminacy.

As anticipated, indeterminacy tends to emerge as $\alpha + \beta$ becomes large. However, indeterminacy will not emerge when γ is close to zero for any degree of return to scale between 0 and 2.0. The numerical experiment also shows that indeterminacy does not hold when γ is close to one, there is a minimum level of γ for generating indeterminacy, and the value of $\alpha+\beta \in [0, 2]$ if γ is relatively large. This experiment demonstrates that some level of income effect is necessary for the presence of equilibrium indeterminacy in the one-sector RBC model.

It is to be noted that the above conclusion is valid for one-sector models alone. In fact, Guo and Harrison (2010) reveal that in two-sector models with sector-specific externalities, indeterminacy emerges under the GHH preference if the external effect associated with the investment good sector is sufficiently large.

2.4.3 Consumption Externalities

2.4.3.1 Basic Idea

If the consumption behavior of each household is affected by other households' consumption decisions, then there are consumption externalities. This idea has been used in various fields of macroeconomics such as asset pricing, optimal taxation, and long-run economic growth.[4] Some authors have studied whether the consumption external effect can be a source of indeterminacy.

[4] A sample includes Abel (1990), Gali (1994), and Turnovsky and Monteiro (2007).

One popular formulations of consumption externalities is to assume that the instantaneous utility function is given by

$$u\left(C,\bar{C},N\right)=\frac{\left(C\bar{C}^{-\theta}\right)^{1-\sigma:}}{1-\sigma}-\frac{N^{1+\gamma}}{1+\gamma},\quad \sigma>0,\ <\theta<1. \tag{2.68}$$

Since the first term on the right hand side of the above can be rewritten as

$$\frac{\left(C\bar{C}^{-\theta}\right)^{1-\sigma:}}{1-\sigma}=\frac{\left[C^{1-\theta}\left(\frac{C}{\bar{C}}\right)^{\theta}\right]}{1-\sigma},$$

the felicity of the household depends on its private consumption as well as on its relative consumption, $C/\bar{C}$. According to the terminology in the literature, if $\partial u/\partial\bar{C}$ is negative (positive), consumers have jealousy (admiration) toward other consumers' consumption. In addition, if the marginal utility of private consumption, $\partial u/\partial C$ increases (decreases) with $\bar{C}$, then consumers' preferences exhibit conformism (anti-conformis). Therefore, in the above specification, if $\sigma>1$ and $\theta>0$, then the preference structure shows jealousy and conformism, which are standard assumptions in macroeconomic studies on the role of consumption externalities. In addition, under our assumption that the mass of households is one, it holds that $\bar{C}=C$ in equilibrium.

It is easy to see that in this popular formulation, the presence of consumption externalities will not yield indeterminacy. Noting that the household takes the sequence of external effects, $\left\{\bar{C}_t\right\}_{t=0}^{\infty}$, in deciding its optimal saving-consumption plan, we find that under (2.68), the optimal condition for C gives $C^{(1-\theta)(1-\sigma)-1}=q$. Therefore, the Euler equation for consumption is given by

$$\frac{\dot{C}}{C}=\frac{1}{\sigma\left(1-\theta\right)+\theta}\left[r-\rho-\delta\right],$$

implying that the (social) intertemporal elasticity in consumption is $1/\left[\sigma(1-\theta)+\theta\right]$. Except for the level of intertemporal substitutability of consumption, the optimization conditions are the same as in the standard one-sector model, the dynamic behavior of the economy essentially the same as the case of $\theta=0$. Therefore, without assuming external increasing returns, the economy never displays indeterminacy.

This outcome suggests that if consumption externalities yield indeterminacy, we should use a complex utility function. To see this clearly, let us consider a more general utility function such as

$$u=u\left(C,\bar{C},N\right),$$

where $\bar{C}$ is the average consumption in the economy at large. In this case, the first-order conditions for the household are the following:

$$u_c\left(C,\bar{C},N\right) = q, \tag{2.69}$$

$$u_N\left(C,\bar{C},N\right) = -wq. \tag{2.70}$$

Conditions (2.69) and (2.70) yield

$$(u_{CC} + u_{C\bar{C}})\frac{dC}{dw} + u_{CN}\frac{dN}{dw} = 0,$$

$$\left(u_{NC} + u_{N\bar{C}}\right)\frac{dC}{dw} + u_{NN}\frac{dN}{dw} = -q.$$

As a result, the effect of a change in the real wage on the hours worked is shown by

$$\frac{dN}{dw} = \frac{-\frac{u_{NN}}{w}\left(u_{CC} + u_{C\bar{C}}\right)}{(u_{CC} + u_{C\bar{C}})u_{NN} - u_{CN}\left(u_{NC} + u_{N\bar{C}}\right)}. \tag{2.71}$$

Although the concavity assumption regarding private consumption and labor is satisfied (so that $u_{CC}u_{NN} - u_{cN}u_{Nc} > 0$), the sign of the right hand of the above can be negative because of the effect of consumption externalities represented by $u_{C\bar{C}}$ and $u_{N\bar{C}}$. In fact, Alonso-Carrera et al. (2008) set up the following utility function:

$$u\left(C,\bar{C},N\right) = \frac{\left(C\bar{C}^{\psi}\right)^{1-\sigma}\left(1 - N + \mu\bar{C}^{2}\right)^{\theta(1-\sigma)}}{1-\sigma}.$$

These authors examined numerical examples that yield indeterminacy under this utility function, even in the absence of production externalities. In their examples, dN/dw in (2.71) is negative and the relation between the labor demand and supply functions is as shown in Fig. 2.3.

2.4.3.2 A Two-Sector Model

If there are two types of consumption goods, it is rather easy to identify examples in which consumption externality alone generates equilibrium indeterminacy. Chen et al. (2015) examine a two-sector economy where one sector produces pure consumption goods and the other sector produces general goods that can be either consumed or invested. There is no labor-leisure choice, and thus, the household supplies one unit of labor in each moment. The instantaneous utility function of the representative household is

$$u = u\left(C_1, C_2, \bar{C}_1, \bar{C}_2\right),$$

where C_1 (C_2) denotes consumption of general (pure consumption) goods. In addition, $\bar{C}_i$ $(i = 1, 2)$ represents external effects generated by each good. Here, the representative household solves the following problem:

$$\max \int_0^\infty e^{-\rho t} u\left(C_1, C_2, \bar{C}_1, \bar{C}_2\right) dt$$

subject to

$$\dot{K} = rK + w - C_1 - pC_2 - \delta K,$$

where p is the price of the pure consumption good in terms of the general good.

In solving the optimization problem, the household takes the sequences of external effects, $\left\{\bar{C}_{1,t},\ \bar{C}_{2,t}\right\}_{t=0}^{\infty}$, as given. Denoting q as the utility price of capital, the household's optimization gives the following conditions:

$$u_1\left(C_1, C_2, \bar{C}_1, \bar{C}_2\right) = q, \tag{2.72}$$

$$u_2\left(C_1, C_2, \bar{C}_1, \bar{C}_2\right) = pq, \tag{2.73}$$

$$\dot{q} = q\left(\rho + \delta - r\right). \tag{2.74}$$

Conditions (2.72) and (2.73) yield

$$\frac{u_2\left(C_1, C_2, \bar{C}_1, \bar{C}_2\right)}{u_1\left(C_1, C_2, \bar{C}_1, \bar{C}_2\right)} = p, \tag{2.75}$$

which implies that the private marginal substitution of good 1 for good 2 equals the relative price.

The formulation of production the side is the standard one. There is no production externalities, and each good is produced by the well-behaved, neoclassical production function with constant returns to scale:

$$Y_i = F\left(K_1, N_i\right), \quad i = 1, 2.$$

As usual, the production technology can be expressed as

$$y_i = f_i\left(k_i\right), \quad y_i = Y_i/N_i, \quad k_i = K_i/N_i, \quad i = 1, 2.$$

Then, the competitive factor prices satisfy

$$r = f_1'\left(k_1\right) = pf_2'\left(k_2\right),$$

$$w = f_1\left(k_1\right) - f_1'\left(k_1\right)k_1 = p\left[f_2\left(k_2\right) - f_2'\left(k_2\right)k_2\right].$$

It is well known that the capital intensity of each sector is a function of p. We also see that

$$\text{sign } k_i'(p) = \text{sign } [k_2(p) - k_1(p)], \quad i = 1, 2.$$

The market equilibrium conditions in commodity markets are

$$Y_1 = \dot{K} + \delta K + C_1, \ Y_2 = C_2, \tag{2.76}$$

and the full employment conditions in the factor markets are given by

$$K_1 + K_2 = K, \quad N_1 + N_2 = 1. \tag{2.77}$$

Using the full-employment conditions, we see that the supply function of each good is expressed as

$$Y_1 = \frac{K - k_2(p)}{k_1(p) - k_2(p)} f_1(k_1(p)) = Y^1(K, p),$$

$$Y_2 = \frac{k_1(p) - K}{k_1(p) - k_2(p)} f_2(k_2(p)) = Y^2(K, p).$$

To derive a complete dynamic system, from $Y_2 = C$ in (2.76) and the supply function given above, we first express C_2 as a function of K and p as follows:

$$C_2 = C^2(K, p).$$

Plugging this into (2.75), we obtain

$$\frac{u_2\left(C_1, C^2(K, p), C_1, C^2(K, p)\right)}{u_{12}(C_1, C^2(K, p), C_1, C^2(K, p))} = p.$$

This equation enables us to express C_1 as a function of K and p. Finally, substituting $C_2 = C^2(K, p)$ into (2.72) gives

$$u_1\left(C^1(K, p), C^2(K, p), C^1(K, p), C^2(K, p)\right) = q.$$

As a result, we can relate the relative price to K and q in such a way that

$$p = p(K, q).$$

To sum up, we obtain a complete dynamic system with respect to capital and its implicit price given by the following:

$$\dot{K} = Y^1(K.p(K, q)) - C^1(K, p(K, q)) - \delta K,$$

$$\dot{q} = q\left[\rho + \delta - f_1'(k_1(p(K, q)))\right].$$

Chen et al. (2015) specify the utility function in such a way that

$$u\left(C_1, C_2, \bar{C}_1, \bar{C}_2\right) = \frac{\left[\gamma\left(C_1 C_1^{-\theta_1}\right)^{\frac{\varepsilon-1}{\varepsilon}} + (1-\gamma)\left(C_2 \bar{C}_2^{-\theta_2}\right)^{\frac{\varepsilon-1}{\varepsilon}}\right]^{\frac{\varepsilon}{\varepsilon-1}}}{1-\sigma},$$
$$\sigma > 0,\ \varepsilon > 0.\ 0 < \gamma < 1.$$

Namely, each consumption good is associated with commodity-specific external effect, and θ_i denotes the degree of externalities of the social consumption of good i. In addition, ε denotes the elasticity of substitution between the felicity generated by the consumption of goods 1 and 2. The production function of each sector is given by

$$Y_i A_i K_i^{a_i} N_i^{1-a_i}, \quad 0 < a_i < 1, \quad i = 1, 2.$$

The Cobb-Douglas formulation means that the factor intensity of each sector is expressed as

$$k_1(p) = \left(\frac{A_1}{A_2}\right)^{\frac{1}{\alpha_2-\alpha_1}} \left(\frac{a_1}{a_2}\right)^{\frac{\alpha_2}{\alpha_2-\alpha_1}} \left(\frac{1-a_1}{1-a_2}\right)^{\frac{\alpha_2-1}{\alpha_1-\alpha_2}} p^{\frac{1}{\alpha_2-\alpha_1}},$$

$$k_2(p) = \left(\frac{A_1}{A_2}\right)^{\frac{1}{\alpha_2-\alpha_1}} \left(\frac{a_1}{a_2}\right)^{\frac{\alpha_1}{\alpha_2-\alpha_1}} \left(\frac{1-a_1}{1-a_2}\right)^{\frac{\alpha_2-1}{\alpha_1-\alpha_2}} p^{\frac{1}{\alpha_2-\alpha_1}}.$$

These expressions show that

$$\text{sign}\, k_i'(p) = \text{sign}\ (\alpha_2 - \alpha_1), \quad i = 1, 2.$$

Given the above specifications, Chen et al. (2015) analyze a calibrated version of the model and found the parameter spaces in which indeterminacy emerges. They revealed that the indeterminacy conditions critically depend on the magnitudes of θ_i, ε as well as on the factor-intensity raking, that is, sign $(a_1 - a_2)$. They demonstrated that the model can hold indeterminacy in a wide range of parameter space. In particular, indeterminacy tends to emerge easily if θ_i has a negative value.

2.4.4 *News Versus Sunspots*

Ever since the contribution of Beaudry and Portier (2004), news shocks have been considered to be useful driving forces of business cycles. The news-shock theory is based on an old idea in dynamic macroeconomics: if a future shock is anticipated, it may affect current decisions of households and firms. Since this theory considers that changes in expectations of agents generate business fluctuations, it is often called the expectations-driven business cycle theory. Although both the news-driven and sunspot-driven business cycle theories rely on the same idea that changes in expectations bring about economic fluctuations, there are two distinctive differences between these two approaches. First, the news-shock theory assumes that equilibrium is determinate. Second, news may or may not materialize: unlike the sunspot-shock theory, expectations in the news-shock models may not be self-fulfilled.

Intuitively speaking, if a positive technological shock in the future is anticipated, the current consumption, investment, hours worked, and output all rise. However, as pointed out by Beaudry and Portier (2004), the baseline RBC model with a separable utility function cannot produce the comovement of key macroeconomic variables. In the baseline model, the labor market condition is depicted by Fig. 2.1. When a future technological innovation is anticipated by the households, their expected permanent income will rise, which brings about an upward shift of the Frisch labor supply curve. Under a given level of capital stock, such a shift lowers the current levels of hours worked, output, and investment. To resolve this comovement puzzle, subsequent studies extended the baseline RBC model by introducing additional factors such as multi-sector settings, adjustment costs of investment, habit formation, and generalized preference structure with non-separability between consumption and labor.

While most subsequent investigations mentioned above assume that there is no market distortion, Eusepi (2009) proposes an alternative resolution of the comovement puzzle by introducing external increasing returns into the base model. As shown in Sect. 2.3, if labor externality is sufficiently large to hold $\beta > 1 + \gamma$, then the labor demand curve is positively sloped and is steeper than the Frisch labor supply curve. In this situation, a rise in the current consumption caused by a positive news shock shifts the labor supply curve upward, so that hours worked, consumption and output simultaneously increase.[5] Eusepi (2009) confirms that investment also rises, implying that a positive news shock produces positive comovement of consumption, hours, output, and investment. Based on this finding, Eusepi (2009) claims that there is a strong connection between the news-driven and the sunspot-driven business cycles at least in the baseline one-sector RBC model.

Guo et al. (2012), however, point out that while the presence of strong increasing returns brings about comovement of key macroeconomic variables, a positive news shock reduces those variables when the households receive the signal about the good news. This is because if the labor demand curve is steeper than the labor supply curve, an upward shift of the labor demand caused by a positive technological shock lowers the equilibrium levels of real wage and employment (see Fig. 2.4). Therefore, in the presence of strong increasing returns, when a positive shock materializes, it yields a negative impact on the households' income. Since the households anticipate

[5]Remember that $\beta > 1 + \gamma$ is necessary but not sufficient for indeterminacy. Eusepi (2009) implicitly assumed that determinacy holds even under $\beta > 1 + \gamma$.

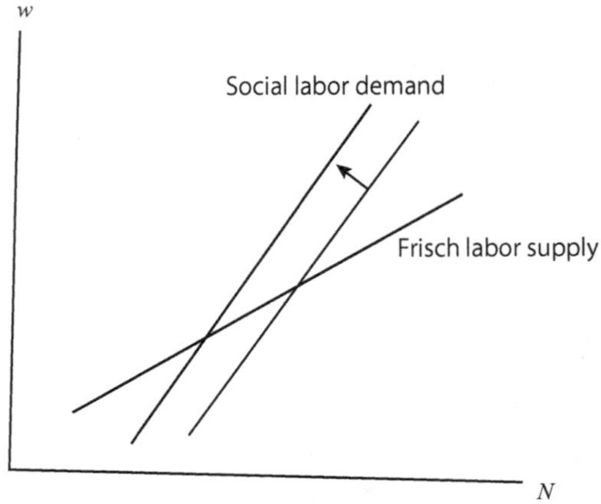

Fig. 2.4 The effect of a positive TFP shock

this fact, they reduce rather than increase their current labor supply when they receive the signal. Consequently, the current levels of hours worked, output, and investment decline as well. This contradicts the empirical fact of business booms generated by good news about future technology. Guo et al. (2012) confirm this outcome by analyzing impulse responses of the calibrated model of Eusepi (2009).

In sum, the foregoing research has suggested that there is no direct theoretical connection between the news-driven and sunspot-driven business cycle theories.

2.4.5 Local Versus Global Indeterminacy

Our discussion on equilibrium intermediacy so far has focused on local analysis. Some authors have revealed that even if the steady state of the Benhabib-Farmer model exhibits local saddle-point property (so that determinacy holds near the steady state), there may exist stable cycles around the steady state. For example, Coury and Wen (2009) re-examine a discrete time version of the Benhabib-Farmer model in which the production function is specified as

$$Y = AK^a N^{1-a} \left(\bar{K}^a \bar{N}^{1-a}\right)^{1+\theta}, \quad \theta > 0.$$

In this specification, the social production function is

$$Y = AK^{a(1+\theta)} N^{(1-a)(1+\theta)}.$$

Therefore, a higher θ enhances the external effects of aggregate capital and labor simultaneously.

In the absence of stochastic disturbance, the linearized deterministic dynamic system is written as

$$\begin{bmatrix} k_{t+1} \\ c_{t+1} \end{bmatrix} = M \begin{bmatrix} k_t \\ c_t \end{bmatrix},$$

where $k_t = \log(K_t/K^*)$, $c_t = \log(C_t/C^*)$, and M denotes 2×2 coefficient matrix. Coury and Wen (2009) first confirm that there is a critical level of $\theta = \hat{\theta}$: if $\theta < \hat{\theta}$, one characteristic root of M is in the unit circle, while the absolute value of the other root is higher than one. This means that the steady state is a saddle point and local determinacy holds. If $\theta > \theta^*$, then both characteristic roots are within the unit circle, implying that the steady state is a sink, thereby local indeterminacy emerges. They also show that if $\theta = \theta^*$, the absolute value of one characteristic root equals one, while the other root has an absolute value less than one. In this critical case, a flip bifurcation arises and there may exist a stable two-period cycle around the steady state. Since the presence of a stable cycle can also hold when θ is less than but close to θ^*, even if the steady state exhibits local determinacy, the economy can be on the stable cycle rather than the stable saddle path converging to the steady state. In this sense, local determinacy does not necessarily exclude the possibility of global indeterminacy.

In a similar vein, Guo and Lansing (2002) introduce factor income taxation into the above model. The flow budget constraint under income taxation is

$$K_{t+1} = (1 + \tau_k)\, r_t K_t + (1 + \tau_w)\, w_t N_t + (1 - \delta)\, K_t - C_t + T_t,$$

where τ_k is the rate of tax on capital income, τ_w the rate of tax on wages, and T_t denotes a lump-sum transfer from the government. The factor prices are determined by

$$r_t = a\frac{Y_t}{K_y}, \quad w_t = (1 - a)\frac{Y_t}{N_t}.$$

Assuming that $\tau_k = \tau_w = \tau$, Guo and Lansing (2002) focus on the relation between τ and equilibrium indeterminacy. They show that if $\tau < 0$, the steady state is a sink even if the degree of increasing returns, $1 + \theta$, is small. Then, as τ rises, there is a critical level of $\hat{\tau}$ under which a flip bifurcation emerges. After τ exceeds that critical level, the steady state becomes a saddle point. Then there is another critical value of τ at which the absolute values of both roots equal to one: at this point, a Hopf bifurcation emerges, and the steady state turns from a sink to a source (i.e., total instability of the dynamic system). Again, stable cycles exist around the steady state if τ is less than but close to this second critical level.

2.5 References and Related Studies

Besides the seminal works by Kydland and Prescott (1982) and Long and Plosser (1983), the real business cycle approach is popularized by Hansen (1985) and King et al. (1988a). The baseline RBC model in this book follows their formulations. It is to be noted that Altug (2009) presents an insightful evaluation of the RBC theory.

As mentioned in Sect. 2.2, the 1994 special issue of the *Journal of Economic Theory* contains early contributions to business cycle and endogenous growth models with equilibrium indeterminacy. Aiyagari (1995) presents a penetrating criticism of sunspot-driven business cycles from the viewpoint of empirical plausibility. Many subsequent studies attempt to construct models that yield indeterminacy under empirically plausible parameter values. A useful overview of the literature up to the late 1990s is given by Benhabib and Farmer (1999). Chapters 7 and 8 in Farmer (2004) also present a comprehensive exposition of indeterminacy in the baseline RBC models. Recent overviews of indeterminacy and sunspots in RBC models include Eusepi (2009) and Farmer (2016).

Following Farmer and Guo (1994 and 1995), several authors conduct quantitative evaluations of sunspot-driven business cycles. Among others, Schmitt-Grohé(1997 and 2000) and Thomas (Do sunspot produce business cycles? Unpublished manuscript, Department of Economics, Ohio State University, 2004) present detailed evaluations of calibrated models. As for the theoretical connection between sunspot-driven and the fundamental shock driven business cycle models, Kamihigashi (1996) and Christiano and Harrison (1999) show insightful results.

Benhabib and Farmer (1996) are the first to reveal that in a two-sector model, indeterminacy may arise under a weak degree of external increasing returns. Moreover, Benhabib and Nishimura (1998) demonstrate that equilibrium indeterminacy emerges in a two-sector model with social constant returns, so that the presence of increasing returns is not necessary for indeterminacy. (We refer to their finding in the next chapter.) For further studies on indeterminacy in two-sector models, see Harrison (2001, 2003), Guo and Harrison (2001b), and Drugeon and Venditti (2001). In addition to Guo and Harrison (2010) and Dufourt et al. (2015) give a detailed analysis of a two-sector RBC model without income effect.

The two-sector model with consumption externalities discussed in Section 2.4.4 is based on Chen et al. (2015). See also Chen and Hsu (2007), Chen et al. (2013), and Weder (2000) for further exploration on indeterminacy generated by the presence of consumption externalities. Regarding the news-driven business cycles, Beaudry and Portier (2014) provide a detailed and updated survey of this topic.

Note that in this chapter we focus on the standard RBC models with perfect competition in final goods and factor markets. Some authors consider equilibrium indeterminacy in models with monopolistic competition. A notable sample includes Gali (1995), Jaimovich (2007), and Pavlov and Weder (2012).

Chapter 3
Indeterminacy in Endogenous Growth Models

This chapter examines endogenous growth models in which equilibrium intermediacy may emerge. It is known that some endogenous growth models assume that there is no market distortion and that every production factor is reproducible under constant returns to scale technologies.[1] In this class of models, the perfect-foresight competitive equilibrium coincides with the optimal growth path of a social planning problem, so that equilibrium indeterminacy will not arise in those models. However, the majority of endogenous growth models assume the presence of technological spillover and external effects to sustain continuing growth in the absence of exogenous technical change. As a consequence, coordination problems and multiplicity of equilibria easily arise. In what follows, we mainly focus on the local indeterminacy of equilibrium around the balanced-growth path. As we have seen, the central concern of studies on real business cycle (RBC) models with multiple equilibria is to explore the conditions under which sunspot-driven fluctuations exist. On the other hand, endogenous growth models with multiple equilibria may explain not only fluctuations of the trajectory of a growing economy but also various patterns of long-run growth generated by self-fulfilling expectations. These models provide us with possible reasons for why two economies that have similar fundamentals can display different growth processes in the long run.

We start with one-sector endogenous growth models with external increasing returns. One key point in this type of models is the specification of the instantaneous utility function of the representative household. We see that indeterminacy conditions critically depend on whether or not the utility function is additively separable between consumption and labor. We then examine two-sector endogenous growth models with external increasing returns with or without endogenous labor-leisure choice. The final section of this chapter deals with a two-sector model with social

[1] Well known examples include Jones and Manuelli (1990), King et al. (1988b) and Rebelo (1991).

K. Mino, *Growth and Business Cycles with Equilibrium Indeterminacy*,
Advances in Japanese Business and Economics 13,
DOI 10.1007/978-4-431-55609-1_3

constant returns. This section demonstrates that the presence of increasing returns is not necessary to hold equilibrium indeterminacy.

While there are a variety of formulations of endogenous growth models, this chapter discusses a small set of models. However, it must be emphasized that the mathematical structure of the existing endogenous growth models have common features. The models in this chapter share these key features, and, hence, the main results in this chapter may apply to other models that sustain continuing growth in the absence of exogenous productivity growth.

3.1 A One-Sector Model with Social Increasing Returns

As mentioned above, endogenous growth models have a common mathematical structure. In particular, if a model establishes a balanced-growth equilibrium in which key macroeconomic variables grow at a common, constant rate, then the aggregate production function must be a linear function of key stock variables such as physical capital, human capital and knowledge capital. In addition, since consumption continues growing on the balanced-growth path, if labor-leisure choice is allowed, the instantaneous utility function of the representative household should take one of the following forms:

$$u(C,N) = \log C + \Lambda(N), \quad \Lambda' < 0, \ \Lambda'' < 0,$$

$$u(C,N) = \frac{C^{1-\sigma}}{1-\sigma}\Lambda(N), \quad \sigma > 0, \quad \frac{1}{1-\sigma}\Lambda' < 0, \ \frac{1}{1-\sigma}\Lambda'' < 0.$$

Here, when the total time available in each moment is unity, the leisure time is given by $L = 1 - N$. Thus, the assumptions on the $\Lambda(N)$ function mean that the instantaneous utility is an monotonically increasing and strictly concave function of leisure. Despite these restrictive conditions on preference and production structures, the endogenous growth models with market distortion easily yield equilibrium indeterminacy.

3.1.1 Separable Utility

In this section, the production function of an individual firm is specified as

$$Y = F(K, \bar{K}, N, \bar{N}) = f(K, \bar{K})\, G(N, \bar{N}),$$

where $f(K, \bar{K})$ is homogeneous of degree one with respect to private capital, K, and external effect associated with the aggregate capital, $\bar{K}$. It is also assumed that marginal products of private capital and labor are decreasing: $f_1 > 0$, $f_{11} < 0$,

$G_1 > 0$, and $G_{11} < 0$. Again, identical firms constitute a continuum with a unit measure, so that $\bar{K} = K$ and $\bar{N} = N$ in each moment. Consequently, the aggregate, social production function is

$$Y = AKG(N,N), \tag{3.1}$$

where $A = f(1,1)$. The factor markets are competitive and thus the factor prices are given by

$$r = aG(N,N), \quad a = f_1(1,1), \tag{3.2}$$

$$w = AKG_1(N,N). \tag{3.3}$$

Note that strict concavity of $f\left(K,\bar{K}\right)$ in K means that $A > a$.

We first assume that the instantaneous utility function of the representative household is additively separable between consumption and labor: the household maximizes

$$\int_0^\infty e^{-\rho t}\left[\log C + \Lambda(N)\right] dt, \quad \rho > 0, \ \gamma > 0$$

subject to $\dot{K} = rK + wN - C - \delta K$ and a given initial holding of capital, K_0. The optimization conditions for the household include

$$-C\Lambda'(N) = w, \tag{3.4}$$

$$\frac{\dot{C}}{C} = r - \rho - \delta, \tag{3.5}$$

together with the transversality condition: $\lim_{t\to\infty} e^{-\rho t}K_t/C_t = 0$. Equation (3.4) shows that the marginal rate of substitution of consumption for labor equals the real wage rate, while (3.5) is the Euler equation of consumption. From (3.3) and (3.4), we obtain

$$-\frac{C}{K}\Lambda'(N) = AG_1(N,N). \tag{3.6}$$

The market equilibrium condition for the final goods is $Y = C + \dot{K} + \delta K$. Hence, in view of (3.1) and (3.6), the growth rate of capital is given by

$$\frac{\dot{K}}{K} = AG(N,N) + \frac{AG_1(N,N)}{\Lambda'(N)} - \delta. \tag{3.7}$$

Additionally, from (3.2) and (3.5), the aggregate consumption follows

$$\frac{\dot{C}}{C} = aG(N,N) - \rho - \delta. \tag{3.8}$$

Using (3.6), (3.7) and (3.8), it is easy to derive the following differential equation of N that summarizes the dynamic behavior of the aggregate economy:

$$\frac{\dot{N}}{N} = \left[\frac{G_{11}(N,N) + G_{12}(N,N)}{G_1(N,N)} + \frac{\Lambda''(N)N}{\Lambda'(N)}\right]^{-1}\left(\frac{\dot{C}}{C} - \frac{\dot{K}}{K}\right) = \Gamma(N)\,\Omega(N), \tag{3.9}$$

where

$$\Gamma(N) = \left[\frac{G_{11}(N,N) + G_{12}(N,N)}{G_1(N,N)} + \frac{\Lambda''(N)N}{\Lambda'(N)}\right]^{-1},$$

$$\Omega(N) = (a-A)\,G(N,N) + \frac{G_1(N,N)}{\Lambda'(N)} - \rho.$$

We assume that $\Gamma(N) \neq 0$ for all feasible levels of N and that there is at least one stationary level of N satisfying $\Omega(N) = 0$ in (3.9). Denoting the steady state value of N by N^*, the balanced-growth rate is

$$g = aG\left(N^*, N^*\right) - \rho - \delta.$$

The sign of $d\dot{N}/dN$ evaluated at the steady state is given by

$$\left.\frac{d\dot{N}}{dN}\right|_{N=N^*} = \Gamma\left(N^*\right)\Omega'\left(N^*\right),$$

where

$$\Omega'\left(N^*\right) = (a-A)\,G_1\left(N^*,N^*\right) + \frac{G_{11}(N^*,N^*)\,\Lambda'(N^*) - G_1(N^*,N^*)\,\Lambda''(N^*)}{\Lambda'(N^*)^2}.$$

Since the initial value of N is not historically given, if $\Gamma(N^*)\,\Omega'(N^*) > 0\,(< 0)$, then the balanced-growth path is locally determinate (indeterminate).

To obtain a clear implication of the indeterminacy condition derived above we specify the forms of production and utility functions. Following Benhabib and

Farmer (1994), we set

$$\Lambda(N) = -\frac{N^{1+\gamma}}{1+\gamma}, \quad \gamma \geq 0,$$
$$F(K, \bar{K}) = AK^{\alpha}\bar{K}^{1-\alpha},$$
$$G(N, \bar{N}) = N^{1-\alpha}\bar{N}^{\beta-(1-\alpha)}, \quad 0 < \alpha < 1, \quad \beta > 1-\alpha.$$

Then, as seen in the previous chapter, the social production function and the competitive factor prices are respectively given by

$$Y = AKN^{\beta}, \quad r = \alpha AN^{\beta}, \quad w = (1-\alpha)AKN^{\beta}.$$

In this specified setting, we find that condition (3.6) becomes

$$\frac{C}{K}N^{\gamma} = (1-\alpha)AN^{\beta-1}, \tag{3.10}$$

and the dynamic equation (3.9) is expressed as

$$\frac{\dot{N}}{N} = \frac{1}{\beta-(1+\gamma)}\left[(1-a)AN^{\beta-(1+\gamma)} - \rho - (1-a)AN^{\beta}\right]. \tag{3.11}$$

The above equation shows that the steady state value of N fulfills

$$(1-a)AN^{\beta-(1+\gamma)} = (1-a)AN + \rho. \tag{3.12}$$

It is easy to see that equation (3.12) has a unique solution if $1+\gamma > \beta$. On the other hand, if $\beta > 1+\gamma$, then (3.12) may have either two solutions or no solutions (see Fig. 3.1).

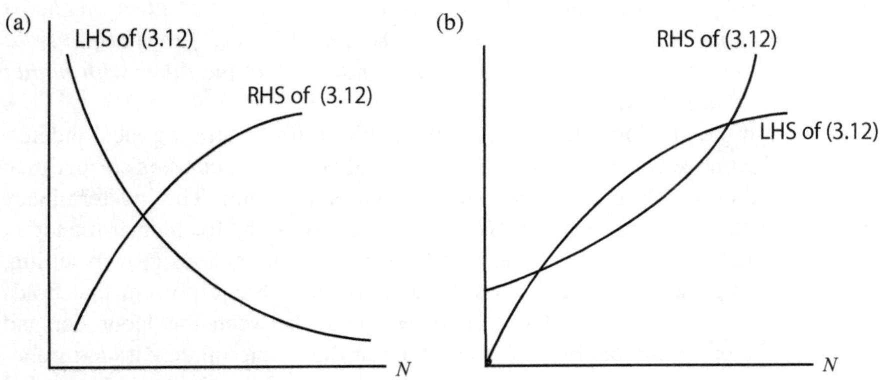

Fig. 3.1 (**a**) The case of $1+\gamma > \beta$. (**b**) The case of $\beta > 1+\gamma$

Evaluating $d\dot{N}/dN$ at the steady state, it holds that

$$\left.\frac{d\dot{N}}{dN}\right|_{N=N^*} = N^* \frac{(1-a)A}{\beta-(1+\gamma)}\left[(\beta-(1+\gamma))\,N^{*\beta-2-\gamma} - \beta N^{*\beta-1}\right]$$
$$= \frac{(1-a)A}{\beta-(1+\gamma)}\left[(\beta-(1+\gamma))\,N^{*\beta-1-\gamma} - \beta N^{*\beta}\right].$$

We see that if $\beta < 1+\gamma$, then $\left.\frac{d\dot{N}}{dN}\right|_{N=N^*} > 0$. Since in this case N^* is uniquely given and N is an unpredetermined variable, the economy always stays on the balanced-growth path: the economy exhibits not only local determinacy around the balanced-growth equilibrium but also satisfies global determinacy. In contrast, if $\beta > 1+\gamma$ and there are two steady state levels of N, then the balanced-growth path with a lower N shows $d\dot{N}/dN > 0$, while at the steady state with a higher N^* we have $d\dot{N}/dN < 0$. Therefore, the balanced-growth path with a lower steady state level of N is locally determinate, while that with a higher steady state level of N is locally indeterminate. Since the initial level of N can be chosen according to the expectations formation of the households, the economy exhibits global indeterminacy as well. Note that, unlike the RBC (exogenous growth) version of the Benhabib-Farmer model, the condition $\beta > 1+\gamma$ is necessary and sufficient for intermediacy in the endogenous growth setting.

The balanced-growth rate is given by

$$g = \alpha A N^{*\beta} - \rho - \delta,$$

so that it increases with the steady state level of N. Hence, if there are dual balanced-growth paths under $\beta > 1+\gamma$, then the balanced-growth path with higher growth rate is indeterminate, whereas that with lower growth rate is determinate. In sum, we have shown the following result shown by Benhabib and Farmer (1994):

Proposition 3.1 *Given our specified functional forms of the production and utility functions, if* $1+\gamma > \beta$, *the balanced-growth equilibrium is uniquely given and holds global determinacy. If* $\beta > 1+\gamma$, *there may exist dual balanced-growth equilibria: one with lower growth rate holds local determinacy, while the other with higher growth rate exhibits local indeterminacy.*

As seen in the previous chapter, the key condition for generating local indeterminacy in the one-sector RBC model is that the labor demand curve is steeper than the Frisch labor supply curve at the steady state equilibrium. The indeterminacy condition in the above proposition ($\beta > 1+\gamma$) is necessary for indeterminacy in the RBC model. However, it is to be noted that in our endogenous growth setting, if $\beta > 1+\gamma$, there may exist another balanced-growth equilibrium that holds local determinacy. Therefore, the relative steepness between the labor demand and Frisch labor supply curves is not essential in the indeterminacy issue in one-sector endogenous growth models. Instead, the key condition is the behaviors of the growth rates of capital and consumption near the balanced-growth equilibrium. Using (3.10), the growth rates of capital and consumption are respectively given by

$$\frac{\dot{K}}{K} = A\left[\frac{1}{(1-a)A}\left(\frac{C}{K}\right)\right]^{\frac{\beta}{\beta-(1+\gamma)}} - \frac{C}{K} - \delta,$$

$$\frac{\dot{C}}{C} = aA\left[\frac{1}{(1-a)A}\left(\frac{C}{K}\right)\right]^{\frac{\beta}{\beta-(1+\gamma)}} - \delta - \rho.$$

Suppose that the economy initially stays on the balanced-growth path. If a positive sunspot shock makes the household anticipate that its future income will increase, then the household raises its current consumption, so that C/K increases. If $\beta < 1+\gamma$, a higher C/K lowers growth rates of consumption and capital. As Fig. 3.2a shows, in this case, the behavior of C/K near the steady state is unstable, implying that the economy never diverges from the initial balanced-growth position. If $\beta > 1+\gamma$, there may exist two balanced-growth equilibria as shown in Fig. 3.2b. In this case the steady state with a lower C/K, which corresponds to the balanced growth path with a lower growth rate, is locally unstable. Therefore, in this case, as well as in the case of $\beta < 1+\gamma$, local determinacy is satisfied. However, in the steady state associated with a higher C/K (a higher balanced-growth rate), the dynamic behavior of C/K is stable, and thereby the economy may diverge from the initial position due to an extrinsic sunspot shock.

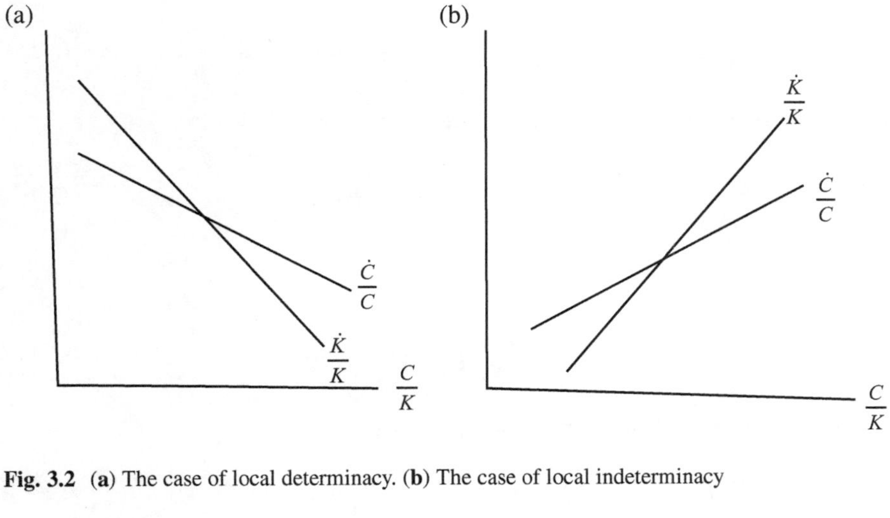

Fig. 3.2 (**a**) The case of local determinacy. (**b**) The case of local indeterminacy

3.1.2 Non-separable Utility

As shown above, the one-sector RBC model that allows endogenous growth needs a sufficiently high degree of labor externality with a separable utility function. Such a restrictive condition for indeterminacy may be weakened if the utility function is not additively separable between consumption and labor. To confirm this, let us assume that the instantaneous utility function is

$$u(C,N) = \frac{1}{1-\sigma} C^{1-\sigma} \Lambda(N).$$

Pelloni and Waldmann (1998, 2000) examine the models with the non-separable utility function given above. To ensure that $u(C,N)$ monotonically decreases with labor N and is strictly concave in C and N, we assume the following:

$$\begin{gathered} \Lambda(N) > 0, \quad \tfrac{1}{1-\sigma}\Lambda'(N) < 0, \quad \tfrac{1}{1-\sigma}\Lambda''(N) < 0, \\ -\tfrac{\sigma}{1-\sigma}\Lambda''(N)\Lambda(N) > (\Lambda'(N))^2. \end{gathered} \tag{3.13}$$

We still assume that the production function is $Y = AK^{\alpha}N^{1-\alpha}\bar{K}^{1-\alpha}N^{\beta-(1-a)}$.

In this setting the first-order conditions of the household's optimization with respect to C and N are respectively given by

$$C^{-\sigma}\Lambda(N) = q, \tag{3.14}$$

$$\frac{1}{1-\sigma} C^{1-\sigma}\Lambda'(N) = -qw, \tag{3.15}$$

where q is the utility price of capital that follows

$$\frac{\dot{q}}{q} = \rho + \delta - r = \rho + \delta - \alpha A N^{\beta}. \tag{3.16}$$

Conditions (3.14), (3.15), and $w = (1-\alpha)AN^{\beta-1}K$ present

$$-\frac{1}{1-\sigma}\frac{\Lambda'(N)}{\Lambda(N)}\frac{C}{K} = (1-a)AN^{\beta-1}. \tag{3.17}$$

As a result, the capital stock changes according to

$$\frac{\dot{K}}{K} = \frac{Y}{K} - \frac{C}{K} - \delta = AN^{\beta} - (\sigma-1)(1-a)A\frac{\Lambda(N)N^{\beta-1}}{\Lambda'(N)} - \delta = \Delta(N).$$

Using (3.14), (3.16), and (3.17), we obtain the following equations:

$$\sigma\frac{\dot{C}}{C}-\frac{\Lambda'(N)\,N}{\Lambda(N)}\frac{\dot{N}}{N}=AN^{\beta}-\rho-\delta,$$

$$\frac{\dot{C}}{C}+\frac{\Lambda''(N)\,N}{\Lambda'(N)}\frac{\dot{N}}{N}=\Delta(N)+(\beta-1)\frac{\dot{N}}{N}.$$

Eliminating $\dot{C}/C$ from the above two equations leads to the following:

$$\frac{\dot{N}}{N}=\left[\sigma(1-\beta)+\sigma\frac{\Lambda''(N)\,N}{\Lambda'(N)}+\frac{\Lambda'(N)\,N}{\Lambda(N)}\right]^{-1}$$
$$\times\left[\rho+(1-\sigma)+\sigma(1-\sigma)(1-a)A\frac{\Lambda(N)}{\Lambda'(N)}N^{\beta-1}\right],\qquad(3.18)$$

which gives a complete dynamic system of the aggregate economy.

First, assume that $\sigma>1$. In this case, conditions in (3.13) mean that $\Lambda'(N)>0$ and $\Lambda''(N)>0$. Evaluating $d\left(\dot{N}/N\right)/dN$ at the steady state where $\dot{N}=0$, it easy to see that if $\sigma>1$ and $\beta<1$, then $d\left(\dot{N}/N\right)/dN>0$, so that local determinacy holds. Next, suppose that $\sigma<1$. In this case, from (3.13) it holds that $\Lambda'(N)<0$ and $\Lambda''(N)<0$. Inspecting (3.18) demonstrates that when $\Lambda'(N)<0$ and $\Lambda''(N)<0$, $d\left(\dot{N}/N\right)/dN<0$ may hold even if $\beta<1$. Hence, the non-separable utility function can be a source of indeterminacy even in the absence of strong increasing returns.

Again, the (in)determinacy condition depends on the behavior of C/K near the balanced-growth equilibrium. When the utility function is non-separable, the growth rates of capital and consumption are expressed as

$$\frac{\dot{K}}{K}=A\left[\frac{1}{(1-a)A}\Gamma\left(\frac{C}{K}\right)\right]^{\beta}-\frac{C}{K}-\delta,$$

$$\frac{\dot{C}}{C}=aA\left[\frac{1}{(1-a)A}\frac{1}{(1-a)A}\Gamma\left(\frac{C}{K}\right)\right]^{\beta}-\delta-\rho,$$

where $\Gamma(C/K)$ represents the relation between N and C/K satisfying (3.17). As well as the model with separable utility, the equilibrium indeterminacy requires the $\dot{K}/K$ curve be steeper than the $\dot{C}/C$ curve at the steady state, but it can hold even though β is not high enough. It is also easy to confirm that indeterminacy holds under weaker restrictions on the utility function if the production function does not take a Cobb-Douglas form. For example, consider the following production function:

$$Y = A\left[\mu K^{\frac{\varepsilon-1}{\varepsilon}} + (1-\mu)\left(\bar{K}N\right)^{\frac{\varepsilon-1}{\varepsilon}}\bar{N}^{\theta}\right]^{\frac{\varepsilon}{\varepsilon-1}}, \quad \varepsilon > 0, \quad 0 < \mu, \quad \theta > 0.$$

Given this specification, we can show that the indeterminacy condition depends not only on the magnitude of the externality parameter, θ, but also on the elasticity of substitution between capital and labor, ε.

3.2 A Two-Sector Model with Intersectoral Externalities

We now turn our attention to the indeterminacy of equilibrium in two-sector endogenous growth models with social increasing returns. In this section, we explore a two-sector version of the *AK* growth model with fixed labor supply.

3.2.1 Model

Suppose that the production side of the economy consists of two production sectors. We assume that the first sector produces investment goods, while the second sector produces pure consumption goods. The production function of each sector is

$$Y_i = F_i\left(K_i, A_i(K)N_i\right), \quad i = 1, 2,$$

where Y_i is the output, K_i is the capital stock, N_i is the labor input, and K denotes the aggregate stock of capital. Here, $A_i(K)$ represents positive externalities generated by capital stock of the economy at large and it is assumed to be an increasing function of K. The implication of this formulation is the same as that of Romer (1986). It is assumed that function $F_i(.)$ is linearly homogenous, increasing and strictly quasi concave with respect to private capital K_i and effective labor $A_i(K)N_i$. Since the aggregate capital stock affects the labor efficiency of both sectors, our formulation assumes that there are intersectoral externalities of knowledge capital.

We also assume that labor and capital are perfectly mobile across sectors and that capital does not depreciate. Due to the assumptions made above, the production function is expressed as

$$Y_i = A_i(K)N_i f_i(x_i), \quad i = 1, 2,$$

where $x_i \equiv K_i/A_i(K)N_i$, $f_i(x_i) \equiv F_i(K_i/A_i(K)N_i, 1)$, $f_i'(x_i) > 0$, and $f_i''(x_i) < 0$. Furthermore, it is assumed that $f_i(x_i)$ satisfies the Inada conditions: $\lim_{x_i \to 0} f_i'(x_i) = \infty$ and $\lim_{x_i \to \infty} f_i'(x_i) = 0$.

The commodity markets are competitive, so that the profit maximization of firms equates the marginal product of each private input to its price. The profit maximization conditions are thus given by

$$
\begin{aligned}
r &= A_1(K) f_1'(x_1), \quad & w &= A_1(K)\left[f_1(x_1) - x_1 f_1'(x_1)\right], \\
r/p &= A_2(K) f_2'(x_2), \quad & w/p &= A_2(K)\left[f_2(x_2) - x_2 f_2'(x_2)\right],
\end{aligned}
\tag{3.19}
$$

where r, w and p respectively denote real rent, real wage and the price of consumption good. We take the investment good as the numèraire. Using (3.19), we obtain

$$\frac{w}{r} + x_i = \frac{f_i(x_i)}{f_i'(x_i)}, \quad i = 1, 2. \tag{3.20}$$

In order to keep the AK structure of the model, we assume that the externality effects are expressed by linear functions of the aggregate capital as follows:

$$A_i(K) = a_i K, \quad a_i > 0, \quad i = 1, 2.$$

Given this specification, in view of (3.20), we can express x_i in the following manner:

$$x_i = x_i(\omega), \quad x_i'(\omega) = -a_i f_i'^2 / f_i'' f_i > 0, \quad i = 1, 2,$$

where $\omega = w/rK$. As a result, the relative price of consumption good is expressed as

$$p = \frac{f_1'(x_1(\omega))}{f_2'(x_2(\omega))} \equiv p(\omega). \tag{3.21}$$

It is easy to show that the relation between ω and p satisfies the following:

$$\operatorname{sign} p'(\omega) = \operatorname{sign}\left[\frac{a_2}{x_2(\omega) + \omega} - \frac{a_1}{x_1(\omega) + \omega}\right]. \tag{3.22}$$

Hence, if the externality effects are symmetric (i.e., $a_1 = a_2$), the sign of $p'(\omega)$ is determined by the magnitudes of private factor intensities, K_1/L_1 and K_2/L_2.

As for consumers' side of the economy, we use the standard representative family model with fixed labor supply. Each household provides one unit of labor in each moment and maximizes a discounted sum of utilities

$$U = \int_0^\infty \frac{C^{1-\sigma} - 1}{1 - \sigma} e^{-\rho t} dt, \quad \sigma > 0, \quad \rho > 0,$$

subject to the flow budget constraint:

$$\dot{K} = rK + w - pC. \quad K_0 = \text{given}.$$

Letting q be the implicit price of capital, the necessary conditions for optimization are given by

$$C^{-\sigma} = pq, \tag{3.23}$$

$$\dot{q} = q(\rho - r). \tag{3.24}$$

It is assumed that the number of households is normalized to unity; C also denotes the aggregate consumption, and the total labor supply is one.

Finally, the market clearing conditions for goods and factor inputs are given by the following:

$$\dot{K} = Y_1 - \delta K, \qquad C = Y_2, \tag{3.25}$$

$$K_1 + K_2 = K, \qquad N_1 + N_2 = 1. \tag{3.26}$$

3.2.2 Dynamic System

Observe that the full-employment conditions in (3.25) and the definition of x_i yield

$$a_1 N_1 x_1(\omega) + a_2(1 - N_1) x_2(\omega) = 1.$$

Thus, the labor devoted to investment good production is written as

$$N_1 = \frac{1 - a_2 x_2(\omega)}{a_1 x_1(\omega) - a_2 x_2(\omega)} \equiv N_1(\omega),$$

and the production function of both sectors is expressed as

$$Y_i = y_i(\omega) K, \quad i = 1, 2, \tag{3.27}$$

where

$$y_1(\omega) \equiv a_1 L_1(\omega) f_1(x_1(\omega)),$$

$$y_2(\omega) \equiv a_2[1 - L_1(\omega)] f_2(x_2(\omega)).$$

Keeping our assumptions in mind, we can show that

$$\begin{aligned}\text{sign } y_1'(\omega) &= \text{sign } [a_2 x_2(\omega) - a_1 x_1(\omega)], \\ \text{sign } y_2'(\omega) &= \text{sign } [a_1 x_1(\omega) - a_2 x_2(\omega)].\end{aligned} \tag{3.28}$$

Remember that $a_i x_i = K_i/KN_i$, which represents the ratio of capital allocation rate, K_i/K, and labor allocation rate, N_i, in sector i. Again, if $a_1 = a_2$, then the sign of $y_i'(\omega)$ is determined by the relative magnitude of private input ratio, K_i/N_i.

The commodity market equilibrium conditions (3.25) and (3.27) present the following:

$$\frac{\dot{K}}{K} = y_1(\omega) - \delta, \tag{3.29}$$

$$C/K = y_2(\omega). \tag{3.30}$$

Note that the optimization conditions for the household's consumption plan gives

$$-\sigma\frac{\dot{C}}{C} = \rho - f_1'(x_1(\omega)) + \frac{\dot{p}}{p}. \tag{3.31}$$

Equations (3.21) and (3.31) respectively yield $\dot{p}/p = [p'(\omega)/p(\omega)]\dot{\omega}$ and $\dot{C}/C - \dot{K}/K = [y_2'(\omega)/y_2(\omega)]\dot{\omega}$. Hence, by use of (3.29) and (3.31), we obtain the following dynamic equation that summarizes the entire model:

$$\dot{\omega} = \Omega(\omega)\left\{\frac{1}{\sigma}\left[f_1'(x_1(\omega)) - \rho - \delta\right] - y_1(\omega)\right\}, \tag{3.32}$$

where

$$\Omega(\omega) \equiv \frac{\sigma y_2(\omega)p(\omega)}{\sigma y_2'(\omega)p(\omega) + y_2(\omega)p'(\omega)}.$$

In the balanced-growth equilibrium, ω stays constant. Thus, the steady state value of ω^*, if it exists, should satisfy

$$f_1'\left(x_1\left(\omega^*\right)\right) = \sigma y_1\left(\omega^*\right) + \rho. \tag{3.33}$$

When $\omega = \omega^*$, $\dot{K}/K$ and C/K also stay constant. Consequently, letting g be the balanced-growth rate, the long-run equilibrium of our model is characterized by $\dot{C}/C = \dot{K}/K = \dot{Y}_i/Y_i = \dot{w}/w = g$. Furthermore, ω, r, p, and x_i do not change in the long-run equilibrium.

3.2.3 Indeterminacy Conditions

The dynamic behavior of our model, as well as that of the standard two-sector neoclassical growth models (e.g., Uzawa 1963), depends on the relative magnitude of factor intensity used in both production sectors. For analytical simplicity, the following discussion assumes that the externality effects in both sectors are symmetric ($a_1 = a_2$). Given this assumption, from (3.22) and (3.28) we find the following relations:

$$\begin{aligned}\operatorname{sign} p'(\omega) &= \operatorname{sign}\left[x_1(\omega) - x_2(\omega)\right],\\ \operatorname{sign} y_1'(\omega) &= \operatorname{sign}\left[x_2(\omega) - x_1(\omega)\right],\\ \operatorname{sign} y_2'(\omega) &= \operatorname{sign}\left[x_1(\omega) - x_2(\omega)\right].\end{aligned} \tag{3.34}$$

We also assume that no factor intensity reversal condition globally holds, so that $x_1(\omega) > x_2(\omega)$ or $x_2(\omega) < x_1(\omega)$ for all feasible values of ω. Note that by definition, $0 \leq L_1(\omega) \leq 1$. Since L_1 is a monotonic function of ω under the no factor intensity reversal condition, there exist the minimum and the maximum levels of ω. Thus, the full-employment condition of labor means that

$$p \in \left[p(\omega_{\min}), p(\omega_{\max})\right] \text{ if } x_1 > x_2,$$

$$p \in \left[p(\omega_{\max}), p(\omega_{\min})\right] \text{ if } x_1 < x_2.$$

First, suppose that $x_1(\omega) < x_2(\omega)$ for all $\omega \in [\omega_{\min}, \omega_{\max}]$. In this case, conditions in (3.34) mean that $p'(\omega) < 0$, $y_1'(\omega) > 0$ and $y_2'(\omega) < 0$, so that $\Omega(\omega) < 0$. Furthermore, since in this case the left hand side of (3.33) decreases with ω, while its right hand side increases with ω, there exists a unique ω^*. Hence, we find that (3.32) yields

$$\left.\frac{d\dot{\omega}}{d\omega}\right|_{\omega=\omega^*} = \Omega(\omega^*)\left[(1/\sigma) f_1'' x_1'(\omega^*) - y_1'(\omega^*)\right] > 0.$$

Because the initial value of $\omega\,(= W/KR)$ is not predetermined under perfect foresight, the above means that a competitive equilibrium is uniquely determined around the steady state value of ω^*. Furthermore, since ω^* is unique, the above inequality is satisfied for all $\omega \in [\omega_{\min}, \omega_{\max}]$. Thus, the global determinacy holds, and the economy should always stay in the balanced-growth equilibrium. Accordingly, we obtain the same conclusion as in the standard AK model.

In contrast, if we assume a more plausible condition under which the investment good sector uses a more capital intensive technology than the consumption good sector, that is, $x_1(\omega) > x_2(\omega)$, then we may have various possibilities. In this case, from (3.34) we find that $p'(\omega) > 0$. $y_1'(\omega) < 0$, $y_2'(\omega) > 0$, and $\Omega(\omega) > 0$. As a result, if $f_1''x_1'(\omega^*) < \sigma y_1'(\omega^*)$, we obtain

$$\left.\frac{d\dot{\omega}}{d\omega}\right|_{\omega=\omega^*} = \Omega(\omega^*)\left[(1/\sigma)f_1''x_1'(\omega^*) - y_1'(\omega^*)\right] < 0,$$

which means that there exists locally a continuum of conversing equilibria around the balanced-growth equilibrium. Moreover, in this case, the right and left hand sides of (3.33) are decreasing functions of ω, and thus there may exist multiple balanced-growth equilibria. The intermediacy condition displayed above means that under $x_1(\omega) > x_2(\omega)$, equilibrium indeterminacy tends to emerge if the intertemporal elasticity in consumption, $1/\sigma$, is high. Therefore, the specification of household's preference partially affects the (in)determinacy condition in this model. As we will see in Sect. 3.4, if external effects are sector specific, then the indeterminacy conditions in the two-sector model with fixed labor supply solely depend on the factor intensity ranking.

To sum up, we have found the following:

Proposition 3.2 *In the two-sector endogenous growth model with intersectoral production externalities, the balanced-growth path is unique and locally determinate if the consumption good sector uses more capital-intensive technology than the investment good sector. The balanced-growth path may be indeterminate if the consumption good sector uses less capital-intensive technology than the investment good sector.*

3.3 A Two-Sector Model with Flexible Labor Supply

The simple two-sector model examined in the previous section emphasizes that the production technology and industry structure may play a relevant role for equilibrium determinacy of endogenous growth models. In this section, we mainly focus on the role of the preference structure in the two-sector model. In what follows, we introduce endogenous labor-leisure choice in a two-sector endogenous growth model with sector specific production externalities.

3.3.1 Model

In this section we consider a growth model in which production activities use human capital alone. Production structure of the economy consists of two sectors. The first sector produces pure consumption goods by using human capital. The production technology is specified as

$$C = H_1^{\beta_1}\bar{H}_1^{\phi_1}, \quad \beta_1 > 0, \ \phi_1 > 0,$$

where C denotes consumption good, H_1 is the stock of human capital devoted to consumption good production, and $\bar{H}_1^{\phi_1}$ expresses sector-specific externalities associated with human capital employed in this sector. At this stage, we do not specify whether or not $\beta_1 + \phi_1$ is larger than one.

Human capital formation is determined by

$$\dot{H} = \gamma H_2^{\beta_2} \bar{H}^{\phi_2} - \eta H, \quad \gamma > 0,\ \beta_2 > 0,\ \phi_2 > 0, \quad \beta_2 + \phi_2 = 1,\ 0 < \eta < 1,$$

where H_2 is human capital used in the education sector, $\bar{H}_2^{\phi_2}$ stands for sector-specific externalities, and η denotes the depreciation rate of human capital. Here, the production function of new human capital exhibits social constant returns.

It is assumed that the total time available to the representative household is unity. Thus denoting the time length devoted to leisure by $l \in [0, 1]$, the full-employment condition for human capital is $H_1 + H_2 = (1 - l) H$. As a result, if we define $v = H_2/H$, the production technology of the first and second sectors are respectively written as

$$C = [(1 - v - l) H]^{\beta_1} \bar{H}_1^{\phi_1}, \tag{3.35}$$

$$\dot{H} = \gamma (vH)^{\beta_2} \bar{H}_E^{\phi_2} - \eta H. \tag{3.36}$$

The objective function of the representative household is

$$U = \int_0^{\infty} u(C, l) e^{-\rho t} dt, \quad \rho > 0,$$

where the instantaneous utility function is given by the following:

$$u(C, l) = \begin{cases} \dfrac{C^{1-\sigma}}{1-\sigma} h(l), & \sigma \in (0, 1), \\ \log C + h(l), & \text{for } \sigma = 1. \end{cases}$$

Function $h(l)$ is assumed to be increasing and strictly concave in l. We also assume that

$$\frac{\sigma h''(l)}{(1-\sigma) h'(l)} + \frac{h'(l)}{h(l)} < 0. \tag{3.37}$$

Given conditions $\sigma \in (0, 1)$, $h'(l) > 0$ and $h''(l) < 0$, (3.37) ensures that $u(C, l)$ is strictly concave in C and l.

The current value Hamiltonian for the optimization problem can be set as

$$\mathcal{H} = \frac{C^{1-\sigma}}{1-\sigma} h(l) + p_1 \left[(1 - v - l)^{\beta_1} H^{\beta_1} \bar{H}_1^{\phi_1} - C \right] + p_2 \left[\gamma v^{\beta_2} H^{\beta_2} \bar{H}_2^{\phi_2} - \eta H \right],$$

where p_1 and p_2 are respectively denote implicit prices of consumption good and new human capital, and v, l and C are control variables. Taking the sequences of external effects, $\left\{\bar{H}_i^{\phi_i}(t)\right\}_{t=o}^{\infty}$, as given, the necessary conditions for an optimum are the following:

$$C^{-\sigma}h(l) = p_1, \tag{3.38}$$

$$\frac{C^{1-\sigma}}{1-\sigma}h'(l) = \beta_1 p_1 (1-v-l)^{\beta_1 - 1} H^{\beta_1}\bar{H}_1^{\phi_1}, \tag{3.39}$$

$$p_2\beta_2\gamma v^{\beta_2 - 1}H^{\beta_2}\bar{H}_2^{\phi_2} = \beta_1 p_1 (1-v-l)^{\beta_1 - 1} H^{\beta_1}\bar{H}_1^{\phi_1}, \tag{3.40}$$

$$\dot{p}_2 = p_2\left[\rho + \eta - \gamma\beta_2(1-l)\right], \tag{3.41}$$

together with (3.35), (3.36), the initial value of H, and the transversality condition such that $\lim_{t\to\infty} p_2 H e^{-\rho t} = 0$. Notice that in deriving (3.41), we use (3.40).

3.3.2 *Dynamic System*

In equilibrium, it holds that $\bar{H}_i = H_i$ $(i = 1, 2)$ for all $t \geq 0$. Therefore, keeping in mind that $\beta_2 + \phi_2 = 1$, (3.39) and (3.40) respectively become

$$\frac{C^{1-\sigma}}{1-\sigma}h'(l) = \beta_1 p_1 (1-v-l)^{\beta_1+\phi_1-1} H^{\beta_1+\phi_1}, \tag{3.42}$$

$$p_2\beta_2\gamma H = \beta_1 p_1 (1-v-l)^{\beta_1+\phi_1-1} H^{\beta_1+\phi_1}. \tag{3.43}$$

From (3.38) and (3.42), we obtain

$$\frac{Ch'(l)}{(1-\sigma)h(l)} = \beta_1 (1-v-l)^{\beta_1+\phi_1-1} H^{\beta_1+\phi_1}.$$

Substituting (3.35) into the above and using $\bar{H}_1 = H_1$, we find

$$1 - v - l = \frac{\beta_1(1-\sigma)h(l)}{h'(l)}. \tag{3.44}$$

In addition, (3.42) and (3.43) yield

$$\frac{C^{1-\sigma}}{1-\sigma}h'(l) = p_2\beta_2\gamma H. \tag{3.45}$$

Hence, from (3.42), (3.43), and (3.44), we obtain the following equation:

$$x = B\left[h'(l)\right]^{1-(\beta_1+\phi_1)(1-\sigma)}\left[h(l)\right]^{(\beta_1+\phi_1)(1-\sigma)} \equiv \chi(l), \tag{3.46}$$

where

$$x = p_2 H^{1-(\beta_1+\phi_1)(1-\sigma)},$$
$$B = \left[\beta_1(1-\sigma)\right]^{(\beta_1+\phi_1)(1-\sigma)}\left[\gamma\beta_2(1-\sigma)\right]^{-1}(>0).$$

It can be verified that

$$\operatorname{sign}\chi'(l) = \operatorname{sign}\left[\frac{1-(\beta_1+\phi_1)(1-\sigma)}{(\beta_1+\phi_1)(1-\sigma)}\left(\frac{h''(l)}{h'(l)}\right)+\frac{h'(l)}{h(l)}\right].$$

Consequently, if technology of the consumption good sector also satisfies social constant returns (i.e., $\beta_1+\phi_1=1$), then condition (3.37) means that $\chi'(l)<0$.

For analytical simplicity, the following argument assumes that

$$h(l) = l^{\theta}, \quad 0<\theta<1.$$

Note that in this case condition (3.37) reduces to $\sigma>\theta$. Under this specification, it is easy to see that the sign of $\chi'(l)$ is determined as

$$\operatorname{sign}\chi'(l) = \operatorname{sign}\left[\theta-1+(\beta_1+\phi_1)(1-\sigma)\right]. \tag{3.47}$$

Since function $\chi(l)$ is invertible unless $\theta-1+(\beta_1+\phi_1)(1-\sigma)=0$, (3.46) yields $\dot{l}=\left[\chi(l)/\chi'(l)\right](\dot{x}/x)$. By definition of x, the rate of change in x is given by $\dot{x}/x=\dot{p}_2/p_2+\left[1-(\beta_1+\phi_1)(1-\sigma)\right]\dot{H}/H$. As a result, using (3.36) and (3.41), we obtain the following differential equation of l:

$$\dot{l} = \frac{\chi(l)}{\chi'(l)}\Delta(l),$$

where

$$\Delta(l) = \rho+\eta+\gamma\left[1-\beta_2-(\beta_1+\phi_1)(1-\sigma)\right](1-l)$$
$$-\left[1-(\beta_1+\phi_1)(1-\sigma)\right]\left[\frac{\beta_1(1-\sigma)l}{\theta}+\eta\right],$$

This differential equation is a complete dynamic system that summarizes the behavior of the entire model.

3.3.3 *Conditions for Indeterminacy*

The balanced-growth equilibrium is attained when v and l stay constant over time and H and C grow at constant rates. In view of (3.44), l should be smaller than $\hat{l}$ that satisfies $1 = \hat{l} + \left[\beta(1-\sigma)\hat{l}/\theta\right]$. When $l = \hat{l}$, all the available time is used for consumption good production and leisure. If there exists $l^* \in [0, \hat{l}]$ that fulfills $\Delta(l^*) = 0$, then we obtain a feasible steady state. Once $\bar{l}$ is given, the time fraction used for human capital formation, v, is determined by (3.44). Hence, the balanced-growth rate of human capital is

$$g = \gamma\left[1 - l^* - \frac{\beta(1-\sigma)l^*}{\theta}\right] - \eta.$$

Note that since C grows at the rate of $\beta_1 g$ in the balanced-growth equilibrium, the transversality condition requires the following condition:

$$\beta_1(1-\sigma)g < \rho.$$

Additionally, $x\left(= p_2 H^{1-(\beta_1+\phi_1)(1-\sigma)}\right)$ stays constant in the steady state, and hence p_2 changes at the rate of $[(\beta_1+\phi_1)(1-\sigma)-1]g$. Equation (3.43) shows that the relative price between the consumption good and new human capital changes according to $\dot{p}_1/p_1 - \dot{p}_2/p_2 = (1-\beta_1)g$ in the balanced growth equilibrium. Thus the steady state rate of change in p_1 is $[\phi_1(1-\sigma) - \sigma\beta_1]g$.

Since l is a non-jump variable, local indeterminacy of the balanced-growth equilibrium is established if $d\dot{l}/dl\big|_{l=\bar{l}} = [\chi(l^*)/\chi'(l^*)]\Delta'(l^*) < 0$, where the sign of $\Delta'(l^*)$ is given by

$$\text{sign}\,\Delta'\left(l^*\right) = \text{sign}\left[\beta_2 - [1-(\beta_1+\phi_1)(1-\sigma)]\left(\frac{\beta_1(1-\sigma)}{\theta} + 1\right)\right]. \tag{3.48}$$

Indeterminacy holds if $\chi'\left(\bar{l}\right)\Delta'\left(\bar{l}\right) < 0$, so that from (3.47) and (3.48), we find the following:

Proposition 3.3 *Suppose that the utility function is not additively separable between consumption and leisure time. Then the balanced-growth equilibrium is globally indeterminate if and only if*

$$\theta - 1 + (\beta_1+\phi_1)(1-\sigma) \text{ and } \beta_2 - [1-(\beta_1+\phi_1)(1-\sigma)]\left[\frac{\beta_1(1-\sigma)}{\theta} + 1\right]$$

have opposite signs.

Three special cases deserve to be mentioned. First, as was pointed out, if $\beta_1 + \phi_1 = 1$, then $\chi'(l) < 0$. Therefore, from (3.60) indeterminacy holds if

$$\beta_2 > \sigma\left[1 + \frac{\beta_1(1-\sigma)}{\theta}\right]. \tag{3.49}$$

Remember that the first-order conditions for optimization require that $0 < \sigma < 1$, while strict concavity of utility function means that $\sigma > \theta$. For example, suppose that $\sigma = 0.5$, $\beta_1 = 0.2$ and $\theta = 0.4$. Then, the right hand side of (3.49) is 0.65. Thus if $\beta_2 > 0.65$, indeterminacy is established. If we choose more plausible values such that $\sigma = 0.7$, $\beta_1 = 0.95$ and $\theta = 0.68$, the right hand side of (3.49) is 0.99338. Therefore, if there are externality effects that satisfy $\phi_1 = 1 - 0.95 = 0.05$ and $\phi_2 = 1 - 0.99338 = 0.00662$, then the long-run equilibrium is indeterminate. These examples clearly demonstrate that non-convexity of technologies is not indispensable to hold indeterminacy. It is also shown that the degree of external effect can be arbitrary small in order to satisfy the indeterminacy condition.

Second, assume that the utility function is additively separable between consumption and leisure. In this case $\sigma = 1$, so that

$$\text{sign } \chi'(l) = \text{sign } (\theta - 1) < 0,$$

$$\text{sign } \Delta'(l) = \text{sign } (\beta_2 - 1) < 0.$$

As a result, the system is determinate. Third, if there is no labor-leisure choice, we can set $\theta = 0$. Obviously, under this condition, both $\chi'(l)$ and $\Delta'(l)$ have negative values, so that the system is again determinate.

Finally, consider the general case in which $\beta_1 + \phi_1 \neq 1$, $\sigma \neq 1$ and $\theta > 0$. It is easy to find plausible set of parameter values that satisfy the indeterminacy conditions under constant or decreasing returns to scale in the consumption good sector. For example, assume that $\sigma = 0.8$, $\theta = 0.75$, $\beta_1 = 0.85$, ‘, and $\phi_1 = 0.1$. Then, we have $\chi'(l)\,\Delta'(l) < 0$ if $\beta_2 > 0.9936$. In this example, it holds that $\chi'(\bar{l}) < 0$ and $\Delta'(\bar{l}) > 0$. In order to satisfy $\chi'(\bar{l}) > 0$ and $\Delta'(\bar{l}) < 0$, (3.47) indicates that

$$\frac{1-\theta}{1-\sigma} < \beta_1 + \phi_1.$$

Strict concavity of the utility function needs that $\sigma > \theta$, and hence the above condition cannot be satisfied unless technology of the consumption good sector satisfies social increasing returns ($\beta_1 + \phi_1 > 1$).

3.3.4 An Alternative Formulation

So far, we have assumed that the utility function involves consumption and pure leisure time. An alternative formulation suggested by Becker (1975) assumes that leisure activity needs human capital as well as time.[2] The simplest form of utility function capturing this idea is the following:

$$u(C, lH) = \begin{cases} \dfrac{\left[C^{\alpha}(lH)^{1-\alpha}\right]^{1-\sigma}}{1-\sigma}, & \sigma > 0, \ \sigma \neq 1, \ \alpha \in (0,1), \\ \alpha \log C + (1-\alpha)\log(lH), & \text{for } \sigma = 1, \ \alpha \in (0,1). \end{cases}$$

Given this specification, the necessary conditions for an optimum include the following:

$$\alpha C^{\alpha-1}(lH)^{1-\alpha}\left[C^{\alpha}(lH)^{1-\alpha}\right]^{-\sigma} = p_1, \tag{3.50}$$

$$(1-\alpha)C^{\alpha}(lH)^{-\alpha}\left[C^{\alpha}(lH)^{1-\alpha}\right]^{-\sigma} = p_1\beta_1\left[(1-v-l)H\right]^{\beta_1-1}\bar{H}_1^{\phi_1}, \tag{3.51}$$

$$p_2\beta_2\gamma(vH_2)^{\beta_2-1}\bar{H}_2^{\phi_2} = p_1\beta_1\left[(1-v-l)H\right]^{\beta_1-1}\bar{H}_1^{\phi_1}. \tag{3.52}$$

The dynamic motion of p_2 still follows (3.41).

In what follows, we restrict our argument to the case that technology of the consumption good sector satisfies social constant returns ($\beta_1 + \phi_1 = 1$). This condition, together with (3.50), (3.51), and $\bar{H}_i = H_i \ (i = 1, 2)$, yields

$$\frac{C}{lH} = \frac{\beta_1\alpha}{1-\alpha}. \tag{3.53}$$

Using $\beta_1 + \phi_1 = \beta_2 + \phi_2 = 1$, (3.64) becomes

$$p_1 = \frac{\beta_2\gamma}{\beta_1}p_2.$$

Equation (3.53) means that

$$[\alpha(1-\sigma)-1]\dot{C}/C + (1-\alpha)(1-\sigma)\left[(\dot{l}/l) + (\dot{H}/H)\right] = \dot{p}_1/p_1.$$

[2]Milesi-Ferretti and Roubini (1998) point out that the formulation of leisure activity may affect policy outcomes in endogenous growth model. Our discussion consider the same issue in the context of equilibrium (in)determinacy.

In addition, (3.53) shows that $\dot{C}/C = \dot{l}/l + \dot{H}/H$. Thus, by use of (3.53), we obtain

$$\frac{\dot{l}}{l} = \frac{1}{\sigma}\left[\gamma\beta_2(1-l) - \rho - \eta\right] - \frac{\dot{H}}{H}. \tag{3.54}$$

Because of $\beta_1 + \phi_1 = 1$, the social production function of consumption good is $C = (1 - v - l)H$. Therefore, it holds that

$$\frac{C}{lH} = \frac{1 - v - l}{l}. \tag{3.55}$$

Accordingly, by (3.55) we find that

$$v = 1 - l - \frac{\beta_1\alpha}{1-\alpha}.$$

Substituting the above into $\dot{H}/H = \gamma v - \eta$, (3.54) gives a complete dynamic system such that

$$\frac{\dot{l}}{l} = \gamma\left[1 + \frac{\beta_1 a}{1-\alpha} - \frac{\beta_2}{\sigma}\right]l + \frac{1}{\sigma}(\beta_2\gamma - \rho - \eta) - \gamma.$$

This equation reveals the following result:

Proposition 3.4 *When leisure activity depends on human capital as well as on time, the balanced-growth equilibrium is globally indeterminate if and only if*

$$\sigma\left(1 + \frac{\beta_1\alpha}{1-\alpha}\right) < \beta_2. \tag{3.56}$$

Note that externality parameters, ϕ_1 and ϕ_2, do not appear in (3.56). Unlike (3.49), condition (3.56) is hard to be satisfied if σ close to one. Again, if the utility function is additively separable ($\sigma = 1$), (3.56) cannot be met, and thus indeterminacy will not emerge.

3.4 Indeterminacy Under Social Constant Returns

In this section, we introduce sector-specific externalities into the two-sector endogenous growth model with physical and human capital analyzed by Bond et al. (1996), Mino (1996), and Ladrón-de-Guevara et al. (1997).[3] The key assumption in this

[3]An early study on this type of model is King et al. (1988b). Bond et al. (1996) and Mino (1996) analyze the local uniqueness and stability of equilibrium of the model, while Ladrón-de-Guevara et al. (1997) explore its global stability.

section is that the social technology that involves external effects satisfies constant returns to scale. The model in this section demonstrates that the presence of social increasing returns to scale is not necessary for generating indeterminacy in two-sector endogenous growth models with production externalities.

3.4.1 Setup

Consider a competitive economy with two production sectors. We assume that the first sector produces a final good that can be used either for consumption or for investment on physical capital. The second sector produces new human capital. Both sectors produce by use of physical as well as human capital. The production technology of each sector is specified as

$$Y_i = K_i^{\alpha_i} H_i^{\beta_i} \bar{K}_i^{\varepsilon_i} \bar{H}_i^{\phi_i}, \qquad i = 1, 2, \tag{3.57}$$

where Y_i is output of the i-th sector, and K_i and H_i respectively denote physical and human capital used by that sector. As before, $\bar{K}_i^{\varepsilon_i}$ and $\bar{H}_i^{\phi_i}$ express the sector-specific externalities associated with physical and human capital employed by the i-th sector. The parameters involved in the production functions are assumed to satisfy the following:

$$0 < \alpha_i, \ \beta_i, \ \varepsilon_i, \ \phi_i < 1, \quad \alpha_i + \beta_i + \varepsilon_i + \phi_i = 1, \quad i = 1, 2.$$

The key assumption here is that production technology of each sector exhibits social constant returns to scale, while the private technology satisfies decreasing returns to scale.

The market equilibrium conditions for the first and second goods are

$$Y_1 = C + \dot{K} + \delta K, \tag{3.58}$$

$$Y_2 = \dot{H} + \eta H, \tag{3.59}$$

where δ and η respectively denote the depreciation rates of physical and human capital. We focus on the interior equilibrium, and thus we assume that both physical and human capital are fully employed in each moment of time, so that

$$K = K_1 + K_2, \tag{3.60}$$

$$H = H_1 + H_2. \tag{3.61}$$

Since private technology exhibits decreasing returns to scale, competitive firms may earn positive profits.[4] We assume that the profits are distributed back to the households who own physical and human capital. The instantaneous utility of the representative household depends on consumption alone. The objective of the household is to maximize a discounted sum of utilities

$$U = \int_0^\infty \frac{C^{1-\sigma} - 1}{1-\sigma} e^{-\rho t} dt, \qquad \sigma > 0, \ \sigma \neq 1.$$

subject to the flow budget constraint,

$$\dot{A} = (r + \dot{p}_1 - p_1 \delta) K + (w + \dot{p}_2 - p_2 \eta) H + \pi - p_1 C,$$

and the wealth constraint,

$$A = p_1 K + p_2 H,$$

where A is the nominal wealth, p_1 and p_2 are prices of the final good and new human capital, r and w are the nominal rates of return to physical and human capital, and π is the profits distributed to the household. When selecting the optimal consumption plan, the representative household takes the sequences of prices and profits, $\{p_i(t), r(t), w(t), \pi(t)\}_{t=0}^{\infty}$, as given. Notice that from (3.58) through (3.61), it holds that $A = p_1 K + p_2 H$, and from the flow budget constraint given above, we obtain the definition of distributed profits: $\pi = p_1 Y_1 + p_2 Y_2 - rK - wH$.

3.4.2 The Dynamic System

We can confirm that the market equilibrium can be characterized directly by solving a pseudo-planning problem in which the planner maximizes U under the constraints of (3.58) through (3.61). Here, the planner is assumed to take the sequences of external effects, $\left\{\bar{K}_i(t), \bar{H}_i(t)\right\}_{t=0}^{\infty}$ $(i = 1, 2)$, as given. To solve this optimization problem, we set up a Hamilton-Lagrange function such that

$$\mathcal{H} = \frac{C^{1-\sigma} - 1}{1-\sigma} + p_1 \left(K_1^{\alpha_1} H_1^{\beta_1} \bar{K}_1^{\varepsilon_1} \bar{H}_1^{\phi_1} - C - \delta K \right) + p_2 \left(K_2^{\alpha_2} H_2^{\beta_2} \bar{K}_2^{\varepsilon_2} \bar{H}_2^{\phi_2} - \eta H \right)$$
$$+ r(K - K_1 - K_2) + w(H - H_1 - H_2).$$

[4] The presence of positive profits means that fixed costs should be present to prevent entry, unless the number of firms is fixed. In this sense, we must assume some type of increasing returns in the private technology even when the social technologies satisfy constant returns to scale.

In the above, the costate variables, p_1 and p_2, and Lagrange multipliers, r and w, respectively correspond to the market prices in the competitive economy. The necessary conditions for an optimum include the following:

$$r = p_i \alpha_i K_i^{\alpha_i - 1} H_i^{\beta_i} \bar{K}_i^{\varepsilon_i} \bar{H}_i^{\phi_i}, \qquad i = 1, 2, \tag{3.62}$$

$$w = p_i \beta_i K_i^{\alpha_i} H_i^{\beta_i} \bar{K}_i^{\varepsilon_i} \bar{H}_i^{\phi_i} \qquad i = 1, 2, \tag{3.63}$$

$$C^{-\sigma} = p_1, \tag{3.64}$$

$$\dot{p}_1 = (\rho + \delta) p_1 - r, \tag{3.65}$$

$$\dot{p}_2 = (\rho + \eta) p_2 - w, \tag{3.66}$$

and the transversality conditions: $\lim_{t\to\infty} p_1 e^{-\rho t} K = \lim_{t\to\infty} p_2 e^{-\rho t} H = 0$.

We assume that the number of producers in each sector is normalized to one. Thus the market equilibrium requires that the external effects satisfy $\bar{K}_i = K_i$ and $\bar{H}_i = H_i$ for all $t \geq 0$. Taking externalities into account, conditions (3.62) and (3.63) are respectively written as

$$r = p_i \alpha_i k_i^{\alpha_i + \varepsilon_i - 1}, \quad i = 1, 2,$$

$$w = p_i \beta_i k_i^{\alpha_i + \varepsilon_i}, \quad i = 1, 2,$$

where $k_i = K_i / H_i$. Denoting the rental ratio as $w/r = \omega$, the above two equations yield

$$k_i = (\alpha_i / \beta_i)\, \omega, \quad i = 1, 2, \tag{3.67}$$

where $\omega = w/r$. Moreover, the price of new human capital in terms of the final good can be expressed as

$$p = \frac{p_2}{p_1} = \theta \omega^{\alpha_1 + \varepsilon_1 - (\alpha_2 + \varepsilon_2)}, \tag{3.68}$$

where $\theta = \left[\alpha_1^{\alpha_1 + \varepsilon_1} \beta_1^{1 - (\alpha_1 + \varepsilon_1)}\right] / \left[\alpha_2^{\alpha_2 + \varepsilon_2} \beta_2^{1 - (\alpha_2 + \varepsilon_2)}\right]$. Using (3.65) and (3.66), together with (3.67) and (3.68), we find that the relative price changes according to

$$\begin{aligned} \frac{\dot{p}}{p} &= \alpha_1 k_1^{\alpha_1 + \varepsilon_1 - 1} - \beta_2 k_2^{\alpha_2 + \varepsilon_2} + \eta - \delta \\ &= \alpha_1 \left(\frac{\alpha_1 \omega}{\beta_1}\right)^{\alpha_1 + \varepsilon_1 - 1} - \beta_2 \left(\frac{\alpha_2 \omega}{\beta_2}\right)^{\alpha_2 + \varepsilon_2} + \eta - \delta. \end{aligned}$$

As a result, provided that $\alpha_1 + \varepsilon_1 \neq \alpha_2 + \varepsilon_2$, dynamic behavior of the rental ratio, ω $(= w/r)$, is given by

$$\dot{\omega} = \frac{\omega}{\alpha_1 + \varepsilon_1 - (\alpha_2 + \varepsilon_2)} \left[\alpha_1 \left(\frac{\alpha_1 \omega}{\beta_1} \right)^{\alpha_1 + \varepsilon_1 - 1} - \beta_2 \left(\frac{\alpha_2 \omega}{\beta_2} \right)^{\alpha_2 + \varepsilon_2} + \eta - \delta \right]. \tag{3.69}$$

Note that the full-employment conditions for physical and human capital yield

$$\frac{H_1}{H} = \frac{k - k_2}{k_1 - k_2}, \quad \frac{H_2}{H} = \frac{k_1 - k}{k_1 - k_2},$$

where $k = K/H$. Using these expressions, from (3.58) and (3.59), the growth rates of physical and human capital are in such a way that

$$\frac{\dot{K}}{K} = \frac{1}{k} \left(\frac{k - k_2}{k_1 - k_2} k_1^{\alpha_1 + \varepsilon_1} \right) - \frac{C}{K} - \delta, \tag{3.70}$$

$$\frac{\dot{H}}{H} = \frac{k_1 - k}{k_1 - k_2} k_2^{\alpha_2 + \varepsilon_2} - \eta. \tag{3.71}$$

In addition, the optimal growth rate of consumption is

$$\frac{\dot{C}}{C} = \frac{1}{\sigma} \left(\frac{r}{p} - \rho - \delta \right) = \frac{1}{\sigma} \left(\alpha_1 k_1^{\alpha_1 + \varepsilon_1 - 1} - \rho - \delta \right). \tag{3.72}$$

Now define $c = C/H$. Then, from (3.70), (3.71), and (3.72), dynamic behaviors of k and c are respectively given by

$$\begin{aligned} \dot{k} = & \left(k - \frac{\alpha_2}{\beta_2} \omega \right) \frac{(\alpha_1/\beta_1)^{\alpha_1 + \varepsilon_1}}{\Delta} \omega^{\alpha_1 + \varepsilon_1 - 1} - c - k(\delta - \eta) \\ & - k \left(\frac{\alpha_1}{\beta_1} \omega - k \right) \frac{(\alpha_2/\beta_2)^{\alpha_2 + \varepsilon_2}}{\Delta} \omega^{\alpha_2 + \varepsilon_2 - 1}, \end{aligned} \tag{3.73}$$

$$\begin{aligned} \frac{\dot{c}}{c} = & \frac{1}{\sigma} \left[\alpha_1 \left(\frac{\beta_1}{\alpha_2} \right)^{\alpha_1 + \varepsilon_1} \omega^{\alpha_1 + \varepsilon_1 - 1} - \delta - \rho \right] \\ & - \frac{1}{\Delta} \left(\frac{\alpha_1}{\beta_1} \omega - k \right) \left(\frac{\beta_2}{\alpha_2} \right)^{\alpha_2 + \varepsilon_2} \omega^{\alpha_2 + \varepsilon_2 - 1} + \eta, \end{aligned} \tag{3.74}$$

where

$$\Delta = \frac{\alpha_1}{\beta_1} - \frac{\alpha_2}{\beta_2}.$$

The sign of Δ expresses the relative magnitude of private capital intensities.

Consequently, we obtain a complete dynamic system constituted by a set of differential equations (3.69), (3.73) and (3.74) that describe behaviors of $k\,(= K/H)$, $c\,(= C/H)$, and $\omega\,(= w/r)$.

3.4.3 Local Dynamics

We denote the right-hand sides in (3.73), (3.74), and (3.69) as $\Omega\,(\omega)$, $\Lambda\,(k, c, \omega)$, and $\Gamma\,(k, \omega)$, respectively. Then, the dynamic system is expressed as

$$\begin{aligned} \dot{k} &= \Lambda\,(k, c, \omega)\,, \\ \dot{c} &= c\Gamma\,(k, \omega)\,, \\ \dot{\omega} &= \Omega\,(\omega)\,. \end{aligned} \tag{3.75}$$

The balanced-growth equilibrium can be defined recursively. First, $\dot{\omega} = \Omega\,(\omega) = 0$ presents

$$\alpha_1 \left(\frac{\alpha_1 \omega}{\beta_1} \right)^{\alpha_1 + \varepsilon_1 - 1} - \delta = \beta_2 \left(\frac{\alpha_2 \omega}{\beta_2} \right)^{\alpha_2 + \varepsilon_2} - \eta. \tag{3.76}$$

This gives the steady state value of ω. Equation (3.76) is the non-arbitrage condition between holding physical and human capital in the steady state. The left hand side of the above decreases monotonically with ω, while the right hand side is a monotonic increasing function of ω. Therefore, the steady state value of $\bar{\omega}$ is uniquely determined. Given $\bar{\omega}$, the long-run equilibrium level of k satisfies $\dot{c} = c\Gamma\,(k, \bar{\omega}) = 0$, that is,

$$\alpha_1 \left(\frac{\beta_1}{\alpha_1} \right)^{\alpha_1 + \varepsilon_1} \bar{\omega}^{\alpha_1 + \varepsilon_1 - 1} - \delta - \rho = \frac{1}{\Delta} \left(\frac{\alpha_1}{\beta_1} \bar{\omega} - k \right) \left(\frac{\beta_2}{\alpha_2} \right)^{\alpha_2 + \varepsilon_2} \bar{\omega}^{\alpha_2 + \varepsilon_2 - 1} - \eta.$$

Thus the steady-state value of k is also unique. Finally, condition $\dot{k} = \Lambda\left(\bar{k}, c, \bar{\omega}\right) = 0$ yields:

$$\begin{aligned} &\left(\bar{k} - \frac{\alpha_2}{\beta_2} \bar{\omega} \right) \frac{(\alpha_1/\beta_1)^{\alpha_1 + \varepsilon_1}}{\Delta} \bar{\omega}^{\alpha_1 + \varepsilon_1 - 1} - c - \bar{k}\,(\delta - \eta) \\ &\quad = \bar{k} \left(\frac{\alpha_1}{\beta_1} \omega - \bar{k} \right) \frac{(\alpha_2/\beta_2)^{\alpha_2 + \varepsilon_2}}{\Delta} \bar{\omega}^{\alpha_2 + \varepsilon_2 - 1}. \end{aligned}$$

This equation presents the steady state value of c, which is uniquely determinate as well. Note that in the balanced-growth equilibrium, C, K, and H grow at a common rate such as

$$g = \frac{1}{\sigma}\left[\alpha_1\left(\frac{\beta_1\bar{\omega}}{\alpha_2}\right)^{\alpha_1+\varepsilon_1-1} - \delta - \rho\right].$$

We should assume that $\bar{\omega}$ fulfills $g(1-\sigma) < \rho$, which establishes the transversality conditions in the balanced-growth equilibrium.

The coefficient matrix of the dynamic system (3.75) linearized around the steady state equilibrium is as follows:

$$J = \begin{bmatrix} \Lambda_k & -1 & \Lambda_\omega \\ \bar{c}\Gamma_k & 0 & \bar{c}\Gamma_\omega \\ 0 & 0 & \Omega' \end{bmatrix},$$

where

$$\Lambda_k = \frac{1}{\Delta}\left[\left(\frac{\alpha_1}{\beta_1}\right)^{\alpha_1+\varepsilon_1}\bar{\omega}^{\alpha_1+\varepsilon_1-1} - \left(\frac{\alpha_1}{\beta_1}\right)\left(\frac{\alpha_2\bar{\omega}}{\beta_2}\right)^{\alpha_2+\varepsilon_2} + 2\bar{k}\left(\frac{\alpha_1}{\beta_1}\right)\left(\frac{\alpha_2}{\beta_2}\right)^{\alpha_2+\varepsilon_2}\bar{\omega}^{\alpha_2+\varepsilon_2-1}\right],$$

$$\Gamma_k = \frac{1}{\Delta}\left(\frac{\alpha_2}{\beta_2}\right)^{\alpha_2+\varepsilon_2}\bar{\omega}^{\alpha_2+\varepsilon_2-1},$$

$$\Omega' = \frac{\bar{\omega}}{\alpha_1+\varepsilon_1-(\alpha_2+\varepsilon_2)}\left[\alpha_1(\alpha_1+\varepsilon_1-1)\left(\frac{\alpha_1}{\beta_1}\right)^{\alpha_1+\varepsilon_1-1}\bar{\omega}^{\alpha_2+\varepsilon_2-2}\right.$$
$$\left. -\beta_2(\alpha_2+\beta_2)\left(\frac{\alpha_2}{\beta_2}\right)^{\alpha_2+\varepsilon_2}\bar{\omega}^{\alpha_2+\varepsilon_2-1}\right].$$

Letting λ be the eigenvalue of J, the characteristic equation is

$$(\lambda - \Omega')\left[\lambda^2 - \Lambda_k + \bar{c}\Gamma_k\right] = 0.$$

The eigenvalues of J are thus given by

$$\lambda = \Omega'(\bar{\omega}) \text{ and } (1/2)\left[\Lambda_k \pm \left(\Lambda_k^2 - 4\bar{c}\Gamma_k\right)^{1/2}\right]. \tag{3.77}$$

Since the dynamic system involves one non-jump variable, k, and two jump variables, c and ω, the balanced-growth equilibrium is locally indeterminate if the number of stable roots in (3.77) is either two or three.

3.4.4 Conditions for Local Indeterminacy

The dynamic behavior of this model, as well as that of the two-sector model of exogenous growth with constant returns, depends upon the relative factor intensity conditions.

Case (i): $\alpha_2 + \varepsilon_2 > \alpha_1 + \varepsilon_1$

In this case, the social technology of the new human capital producing sector is more physical capital intensive than that of the final good sector. Notice that

$$\text{sign } \Omega'(\omega) = \text{sign } [\alpha_2 + \varepsilon_2 - \alpha_1 - \varepsilon_1],$$

so that $\Omega'(\bar{\omega}) > 0$ under our assumption. Thus, (3.77) indicates that the dynamic system involves one negative eigenvalue if and only if $\Gamma_k < 0$. This is equivalent to the condition that $\Delta = (\alpha_1/\beta_1) - (\alpha_2/\beta_2) < 0$: that is, the private capital intensity is also more physical capital intensive in the new human capital good sector. When $\Delta > 0$ (so that $\Gamma_k > 0$), we find that the dynamic system has two stable roots if $\Lambda_k < 0$; or it has no stable root if $\Lambda_k > 0$. From the steady state conditions, it holds that

$$\bar{k} = \frac{\alpha_1}{\beta_1}\bar{\omega} - \frac{\Delta(g+\eta)}{(\alpha_2/\beta_2)^{\alpha_2+\varepsilon_2}\bar{\omega}^{\alpha_2+\varepsilon_2-1}}.$$

Hence, we obtain

$$\Lambda_k = \frac{1}{\Delta}\left[\left(\frac{\alpha_1}{\beta_1}\right)^{\alpha_1+\varepsilon_1}\bar{\omega}^{\alpha_1+\beta_1-1} + \left(\frac{\alpha_1}{\beta_1}\right)\left(\frac{\alpha_2\bar{\omega}}{\beta_2}\right)^{\alpha_2+\varepsilon_2} - 2\Delta(g+\eta)\right].$$

In view of the steady state conditions, we can confirm that if g, $\bar{k}$, and $\bar{c}$ have positive values, then $\Lambda_k > 0$ if $\Delta > 0$. As a result, the feasible balanced-growth equilibrium is totally unstable for $\alpha_2 + \varepsilon_2 > \alpha_1 + \varepsilon_1$ and $\Delta > 0$.

To sum up, if the production technology of the new human capital sector is more capital intensive than the general good sector from the social perspective, we have found the following:

Proposition 3.5 *Suppose that the social technology of the new human capital producing sector is more physical capital intensive than that of the final good sector. Then, if the private capital intensity is also more physical capital intensive in the new human capital producing sector than in the final good sector, the balanced-growth equilibrium is locally determinate. If the private technology of the final good sector is more physical capital intensive than that of the new human capital good sector, then a feasible balanced-growth equilibrium with a positive growth rate is totally unstable.*

The above demonstrates that if the technology is more physical capital intensive in the education sector than in the final good sector from the social perspective and if the balanced-growth path is saddle stable, we do not find local indeterminacy. Consequently, when $\alpha_2 + \varepsilon_2 > \alpha_1 + \varepsilon_1$ and $\Delta < 0$, the dynamic behavior of the two-sector endogenous growth model with sector specific externalities is essentially the same as that of the model without externalities.[5]

Case (ii): $\alpha_1 + \varepsilon_1 > \alpha_2 + \varepsilon_2$

In this case, it holds that $\Omega'(\bar{\omega}) < 0$. Hence, (3.77) indicates that the dynamic system has at least one stable root. If $\Delta < 0$, then $\Gamma_k < 0$. Thus, the subsystem that consists of the dynamic equations of k and c has one stable and one unstable root. This shows that the whole dynamic system involves two stable roots, and therefore the system displays local indeterminacy. In contrast, if $\Delta > 0$, according to the feasibility conditions mentioned in Proposition 3.1, we see that $\Lambda_k > 0$ and $\Gamma_k > 0$. If this is the case, the dynamic system has only one stable root, $\Omega'(\bar{\omega})$, under which uniqueness of the equilibrium path is established. Consequently, we obtain the following:

Proposition 3.6 *Suppose that the social technology of the final good sector is more physical capital intensive than that of the new human capital production sector and that the balanced growth equilibrium is feasible with a positive growth rate. Then, indeterminacy emerges if and only if private technology is more physical capital intensive in the new human capital sector than in the final good sector.*

This result is analogous to a finding by Benhabib and Nishimura (1998) in the context of exogenous growth models. This proposition makes two points. First, the magnitudes of externalities associated with human capital (i.e., values of ϕ_i) do not appear in the indeterminacy condition. Second, the above result demonstrates that indeterminacy will emerge even if external effects are sufficiently small. For example, if $\alpha_1 < \alpha_2$ but close enough each other, then the presence of small-degree externalities can establish that $\alpha_1 + \varepsilon_1 > \alpha_2$. Hence, indeterminacy would emerge even if $\phi_1 = \phi_2 = \varepsilon_2 = 0$.

3.4.5 Intuitive Implication

In the dynamic general equilibrium framework, it is generally difficult to obtain clear intuition as to why indeterminacy holds. It is, however, rather easy to give an economic implication of the indeterminacy conditions derived above. First, remember that in our economy, if the social planner controls the economy and

[5] If we follow Ladrón-de-Guevara et al. (1997), in this case, we can demonstrate that uniqueness and stability of equilibrium path hold globally.

internalizes externalities, the model coincides with the standard two-sector model of endogenous growth examined by Bond et al. (1996) and others. Therefore, the capital intensity chosen by the producers is written as $k_i = \frac{\alpha_1+\varepsilon_1}{1-\alpha_1-\omega_1}\omega$. In this standard case, if $k_1 > k_2$ (i.e., $\alpha_1 + \varepsilon_1 > \alpha_2 + \varepsilon_2$), Rybczynski's theorem gives

$$\frac{\partial (Y_1/H)}{\partial k} > 0, \quad \frac{\partial (Y_2/H)}{\partial k} < 0.$$

Now assume that the economy initially stays in the balanced-growth equilibrium and that the aggregate capital intensity, k, increases unanticipatedly. If ω is fixed at the original level $\bar{\omega}$, then (3.70), (3.71), and (3.72) show that $\dot{C}/C$ stays constant, whereas $\dot{K}/K$ increases and $\dot{H}/H$ decreases. Hence, both k $(= K/H)$ and c $(= C/H)$ continue to increase. To recover the stability, the value of c should be re-selected to make k decreasing. However, since the growth rate of c is independent of the level of c, it is generally impossible to determine c that may attain balanced growth if ω is fixed and the initial values of k diverge from the steady state level of $\bar{k}$. Accordingly, in order to return the economy to the balanced-growth equilibrium, the factor price ratio (and the relative price) should be adjusted to keep the economy on the stable manifold converging to the steady state. This means that the standard model ensures determinacy of equilibrium around the steady state.

When the market economy does not attain the social optimum because of externalities, the social and private capital intensities diverge. If $\alpha_1 + \varepsilon_1 > \alpha_2 + \varepsilon_2$ but $\alpha_1/\beta_1 < \alpha_2/\beta_2$, then the Rybczynski condition becomes

$$\frac{\partial (Y_1/H)}{\partial k} < 0, \quad \frac{\partial (Y_2/H)}{\partial k} > 0.$$

Again, assume that the initial position of the economy is in the balanced-growth equilibrium and that there is an unanticipated rise in k. Given these conditions, in contrast to the social planning economy, $\dot{K}/K$ starts to decrease and $\dot{H}/H$ starts to increase. Hence, if ω stays at a fixed level of $\bar{\omega}$, then both k and c are lowered. In this case, the transition process of k exhibits self-stabilizing behavior, so that the appropriate choice of the initial value of c may eventually attain the balanced-growth equilibrium without adjusting ω. This property can be obtained even if the fixed value of ω does not equal $\bar{\omega}$. In other words, the saddle point stability in c-k space can be established for any fixed level of ω. Since the initial value of ω is not predetermined, this result means that we may find a continuum of converging equilibrium around the balanced-growth equilibrium.

In a more formal manner, the above intuition can be stated as follows. First, consider the case of unique equilibrium. In this case the linearized system has one dimensional stable manifold around the steady state on which k_t and ω_t satisfy the following relation:

$$\omega_t - \bar{\omega} = \frac{\Gamma_k - \Omega'(\Lambda_k - \Omega')}{\Lambda_\omega \Omega' - \Gamma_\omega}\left(k_t - \bar{k}\right).$$

As was shown, $\Omega' < 0$, $\Lambda_k > 0$, and $\Gamma_\kappa > 0$ for $k_1 > k_2$. Additionally, when $k_1 > k_2$, we can show that $\Lambda_\omega < 0$ and $\Gamma_\omega < 0$.[6] Therefore, the stable manifold projected on the k-ω space has a positive slope. This means that if the initial level of k is higher than $\bar{k}$, the initial value of ω is also higher than $\bar{\omega}$. Once the appropriate level of ω is selected on the saddle path given above, the capital ratio, k, returns to its steady state level in accordance with the dynamic equation such that $k_t = \bar{k} + \exp\left[\Omega'(\bar{\omega})\right]\left(k_0 - \bar{k}\right)$. Thus, the rental ratio, ω, also decreases monotonically during the transition.

When there are multiple equilibria, we should first examine the behavior of the subsystem consisting of $\dot{k} = \Lambda(k, c, \omega)$ and $\dot{c} = c\Gamma(k, \omega)$. Since the matrix J has one stable root under the assumption that $\alpha_1 + \varepsilon_1 > \alpha_2 + \varepsilon_2$,, this subsystem exhibits saddle-point stability in the k-c space if ω is fixed. Under a given level of ω, the relation between k and c on the stable saddle path can be written as $c = \hat{c}(k, \omega)$. Using the phase diagram of $\dot{k} = \Lambda(k, c, \omega)$ and $\dot{c} = c\Gamma(k, \omega)$ with a fixed level of ω, we find that $\hat{c}(k, \omega)$ is strictly increasing in c and ω. Substituting $c = \hat{c}(k, \omega)$ into the dynamic equation describing the motion of k, we obtain the following complete system:

$$\dot{k} = \Lambda\left(k, \hat{c}(k, \omega), \omega\right),$$
$$\dot{\omega} = \Omega(\omega).$$

We find that the slope of $\dot{k} = 0$ locus in the k-ω space is ambiguous without imposing further restrictions on the model. The phase diagram depicts the case that $\dot{k} = 0$ locus has a negative slope. As the figure shows, the singular point of the dynamic system is a sink, and hence the initial value of ω (and the initial value of c) is indeterminate.

Indeterminacy of the initial value of ω does not, however, imply that the destiny of the economy is uncertain. Since the steady state in our dynamic system is uniquely given, once the initial value of ω is selected, the equilibrium path converging to the balanced-growth equilibrium becomes determinate. In particular, if there is no extrinsic uncertainty, we do not observe sunspot fluctuations during the converging process. For example, assume that the initial level of k is historically given at k_0 in Fig. 3.3. If the initial value of ω is set at ω_a, the economy monotonically converges to the balanced-growth path. On the other hand, if the initial level of ω is ω_b, the aggregate capital ratio, k, first decreases and then increases before reaching the steady state level of $\bar{k}$. On the other hand, if ω starts

[6]For more detailed discussion on the characterization of the transition process of the model with unique equilibrium, see Mino (1996).

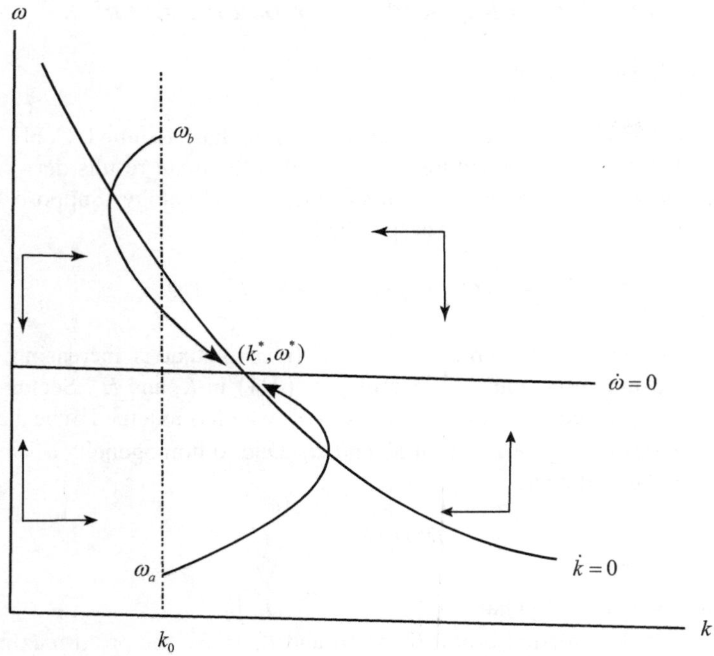

Fig. 3.3 Dynamics in (k, ω) *space*

from ω_c, then k overshoots its steady state value during the converging process. As a result, even starting from the same initial level of k, the economy may display various patterns of growth in the transition toward the balanced-growth equilibrium

Furthermore, the speed of convergence also depends on the selection of the initial value of ω. Existing studies on the converging speed of growing economies usually assumed that the converging path of the economy is uniquely given. In contrast, multiplicity of the growth trajectory will generate different convergent speeds in a single model. These arguments imply that indeterminacy would present useful implications not only for the endogenous business cycle theory based on the sunspot hypothesis but also for explaining diverging long-run patterns of growing economies.[7]

[7]The literature on the convergent speed of growing economies usually focused the dynamic systems that involve a one-dimensional stable manifold. In analyzing an exogenous growth model, Eicher and Turnovsky (1999) explored the transition speed of the system in which the stable manifold is two dimensional, that is,having two stable roots. (Their model, however, does not exhibit indeterminacy.) They show that converging speed is highly sensitive to selection of the initial position of the economy.

3.4.6 General Technology and Factor Income Taxation

3.4.6.1 A Generalization

For analytical simplicity, the foregoing discussion has assumed Cobb-Douglas production functions. In this section, we show that the main results derived above may hold for a more general class of production technology. Suppose that the production function of each sector is specified as

$$Y_i = F_i(K_i, H_i)\,\Theta_i\left(\bar{K}_i, \bar{H}_i\right), \quad i = 1, 2,$$

where private technology is presented by $F_i(K_i, H_i)$ that is increasing, strictly quasi-concave and homogenous of degree $\gamma \in (0, 1)$ in K_i and H_i. Sector-specific externality is expressed by a function, $\Theta_i\left(\bar{K}_i, \bar{H}_i\right)$, which is assumed to be increasing and homogenous of degree $1 - \gamma$ in $\bar{K}_i$ and $\bar{H}_i$. Due to homogeneity assumptions, the above can be written as

$$Y_i = H_i^{\gamma}\bar{H}_i^{1-\gamma} f_i(k_i)\,\theta_i\left(\bar{k}_i\right),$$

where $f_i(k_i) = F_i(K_i/H_i, 1)$ and $\theta(k_i) = \Theta\left(\bar{K}_i/\bar{H}_i, 1\right)$.

Considering that in equilibrium $\bar{H}_i = H_i$ and $\bar{K}_i = K_i$, the profit maximization conditions for the firm yield:

$$r = p_i f_i'(k_i)\,\theta_i(k_i),$$
$$w = p_i\left[\gamma f_i(k_i) - k_i f'(k_i)\right]\theta_i(k_i).$$

Hence, the factor price ratio is related to the capital intensity of each production sector in such a way that

$$k_i + \omega = \frac{\gamma f_i(k_i)}{f_i'(k_i)}. \tag{3.78}$$

This equation gives

$$k_i = k_i(\omega), \quad k_i'(\omega) = -f_i'^2/\gamma f_i f_i'' > 0, \quad i = 1, 2. \tag{3.79}$$

The relative price $p\,(= p_2/p_1)$ is thus expressed by

$$p(\omega) = \frac{\theta_1(k_1(\omega))f_1'(k_1(\omega))}{\theta_2(k_2(\omega))f_2'(k_2(\omega))}. \tag{3.80}$$

Consequently, in view of (3.78) and (3.79), it is easy to see that logarithmic differentiation of (3.80) yields the following: where $\hat{\theta}_i\left(= \hat{\theta}_i k_i/\theta_i\right)$ and $\hat{f}_i'\left(= -f_i'' k_i/f_i'\right)$ denote the elasticities of the θ_i and f_i' functions.

Given the production technologies specified above, the growth rates of consumption, and physical and human capital are respectively given by

$$\frac{\dot{C}}{C} = \frac{1}{\sigma}\left[f_1'\left(k_1\left(\omega\right)\right)\theta_1\left(k_1\left(\omega\right)\right) - \rho - \delta\right],$$

$$\frac{\dot{K}}{K} = \frac{k - k_1\left(\omega\right)}{k_1\left(\omega\right) - k_2\left(\omega\right)} f_1\left(k_1\left(\omega\right)\right)\theta\left(k_1\left(\omega\right)\right) - \frac{c}{k} - \delta,$$

$$\frac{\dot{H}}{H} = \frac{k_2\left(\omega\right) - k}{k_1\left(\omega\right) - k_2\left(\omega\right)} f_2\left(k_2\left(\omega\right)\right)\theta_2\left(k_2\left(\omega\right)\right) - \eta.$$

In addition, the factor price ratio changes in accordance with

$$\dot{\omega} = \frac{p'\left(\omega\right)\omega}{p\left(\omega\right)}\left\{f_1'\left(k_1\left(\omega\right)\right)\theta_1\left(k_1\left(\omega\right)\right)\right.$$
$$\left. -\gamma f_2\left(k_2\left(\omega\right)\right) - k_2\left(\omega\right) f_2'\left(k_2\left(\omega\right)\right)\theta_2\left(k_2\left(\omega\right)\right) + \eta - \delta\right\}.$$

Accordingly, the dynamics of the economy can be summarized as a set of differential equations with respect to k, c, and ω. Given the concavity assumption on $f_i\left(k_i\right)\theta_i\left(k_i\right)$, there exists a unique balanced-growth equilibrium. Inspecting the characteristic roots of the linearized dynamic system, it is easy to confirm that indeterminacy may emerge if $p'\left(\omega\right)\left[k_1\left(\omega\right) - k_2\left(\omega\right)\right] < 0$. Again, if a feasible balanced-growth rate is positive, the case in which $p'\left(\omega\right) < 0$ and $k_1\left(\omega\right) > k_2\left(\omega\right)$ cannot hold. Therefore, local indeterminacy is observable if and only if $k_2\left(\omega\right) > k_1\left(\omega\right)$ and $p'\left(\omega\right) > 0$ around the balanced-growth equilibrium.

In the case of Cobb-Douglas technologies, $f_i\left(k_i\right) = k_i^{\alpha_i}$, $\theta_i\left(k_i\right) = k_i^{\varepsilon_i}$, and $\gamma_i = \alpha_i + \beta_i$. As a result, $k_i = \alpha_i\omega/\beta_i$, $.\hat{\theta}_i = \varepsilon_i$ and $\hat{f}_i' = 1 - \alpha_i$, and, hence, sign $\left(dp/d\omega\right) =$sign $\left[\alpha_1 + \varepsilon_1 - \left(\alpha_2 + \varepsilon_2\right)\right]$.

Using the relations derived above, we can show the following:

Proposition 3.7 *Suppose that the social productivity function $f_i\left(k_i\right)\theta_i\left(k_i\right)$ satisfies strict concavity. Then, a feasible balanced-growth equilibrium with a positive growth rate exhibits local indeterminacy if and only if $k_2\left(\omega\right) > k_1\left(\omega\right)$ and*

$$\left(1 - \frac{\hat{\theta}_2}{\hat{f}_2'}\right)\frac{1}{k_2 + \omega} > \left(1 - \frac{\hat{\theta}_1}{\hat{f}_1'}\right)\frac{1}{k_1 + \omega}.$$

For example, suppose that $F_i\left(K_i, H_i\right) = \left(K_i^{\nu_i} + a_i H_i^{\nu_i}\right)^{\frac{1-\varepsilon_i-\phi_i}{\nu_i}}$ and $\Theta_i\left(K_i, H_i\right) = K_i^{\varepsilon_i} H_i^{\phi_i}$. This means that

$$f_i\left(k_i\right) = \left(k_i^{\nu_i} + a_i\right)^{\frac{1-\varepsilon_i-\phi_i}{\nu_i}}, \quad \theta_i\left(k_i\right) = k_i^{\varepsilon_i}.$$

Using these functions, we find that $k_i = (\lambda_i \omega)^{\frac{1}{\nu_i - 1}}$. Hence, the condition in the above proposition is expressed as

$$\left(1-\frac{\varepsilon_2}{1-\alpha_2}\right)\frac{1}{(\lambda_2\omega)^{\frac{\nu_2}{\nu_2-1}}+1} > \left(1-\frac{\varepsilon_1}{1-\alpha_1}\right)\frac{1}{(\lambda_1\omega)^{\frac{\nu_1}{\nu_1-1}}+1}.$$

3.4.6.2 Factor Income Taxation

Now assume that the government levies sector-specific factor income. Let τ_{K_i} and τ_{H_i} respectively denote the rate of tax (subsidies if they have positive values) on physical and human capital employed in sector i. We assume that the government neither consumes nor invests and that the government budget is balanced by adjusting lump-sum transfer for the households. If we denote the after-tax rate of return to capital by r and w, the profit maximization conditions yield

$$r = (1-\tau_{Ki})\, p_i f_i'(k_i)\, \theta_i(k_i),$$
$$w = (1-\tau_{H_i})\, p_i \left[f_i(k_i) - k_i f_i'(k_i)\right] \theta_i(k_i).$$

These equations present the relation between k_i and ω as follows:

$$k_i + \lambda_i \omega = \frac{f_i(k_i)}{f'(k_i)}, \quad \lambda_i = \frac{1-\tau_{K_i}}{1-\tau_{H_i}},$$

which yields a function $k_i = k_i(\lambda_i \omega)$. It is easy to see that in this case, the relation between p and ω is shown by

$$p'(\omega) = p\left[\left(1-\frac{\hat{\theta}_2}{\hat{f}_2'}\right)\frac{\lambda_2}{k_2+\lambda_2\omega} - \left(1-\frac{\hat{\theta}_1}{\hat{f}_1'}\right)\frac{\lambda_1}{k_1+\lambda_1\omega}\right]. \tag{3.81}$$

The dynamics of ω are given by

$$\begin{aligned}\dot{\omega} &= \frac{p'(\omega)\,\omega}{p(\omega)}\left\{(1-\tau_{K_1}) f_1'(k_1)\,\theta_1(k_1) - (1-\tau_{H_2})\left[f_2(k_2) - k_2 f_2'(k_2)\right]\theta_2(k_2) + \eta - \delta\right\} \\ &= \Omega\left(\omega; \tau_{K_1}, \tau_{K_2}, \tau_{H_1}, \tau_{H_2}\right),\end{aligned}$$

where $k_i = k_i(\lambda_i \omega)$ and $k_i' > 0 (i = 1, 2)$.

As pointed out by Bond et al. (1996), even in the absence of externalities, indeterminacy may emerge if taxation distorts the relation between the relative price and capital intensity in each production sector. In our formulation, if there is no externality, we obtain

$$\operatorname{sign} p'(\omega) = \operatorname{sign}\left[\lambda_1 k_2 - \lambda_2 k_1\right].$$

Thus, if $k_1 > k_2$ and $\lambda_1 k_2 > \lambda_2 k_1$, there is local indeterminacy around the balanced-growth equilibrium. Obviously, if taxation is symmetric between the two sectors (i.e., $\lambda_1 = \lambda_2$), the rates of tax will not affect the indeterminacy condition. It is also to be noted that, if the production technologies are of Cobb-Douglas type, sector-specific distortionary taxation do not generate indeterminacy either. In fact, if $f_i(k_i) = k_i^{\alpha_i}$ and $\theta_i(k_i) = k_i^{\varepsilon_i}$, then $k_i = \lambda_i \left(\frac{1}{\alpha_i} - 1\right)\omega$,.so that λ_1 and λ_2 do not appear in (3.81). To sum up, we obtain the following:

Proposition 3.8 *Unless the production technology in each sector is of Cobb-Douglas type, sector specific factor income taxation may generate indeterminacy if and only if* $k_2 > k_1$ *and*

$$\left(1 - \frac{\hat{\theta}_2}{\hat{f}_2'}\right) \frac{1 - \tau_{K_2}}{(1 - \tau_{H_2}) k_2 + (1 - \tau_{K_2}) \omega} > \left(1 - \frac{\hat{\theta}_1}{\hat{f}_1'}\right) \frac{1 - \tau_{K_1}}{(1 - \tau_{H_1}) k_1 + (1 - \tau_{K_1}) \omega}.$$

3.5 References and Related Studies

The *AK* growth model with variable labor supply has been frequently used in the literature. The applied studies generally employ the model with equilibrium determinacy: see, for example, Turnovsky (1999, 2000). The model with indeterminacy discussed in Sect. 3.1 is based on Benhabib and Farmer (1994). The *AK* growth model with non-separable utility is examined by Pelloni and Waldmann (1998, 2000). The two-sector *AK* growth model in Sect. 3.2 depends on Mino (1999) and Naito and Ohdoi (2008). Naito and Ohdoi (2011) apply the similar setting to the two-country Heckscher-Ohlin model. The two-sector model with variable labor-leisure choice in Sect. 3.4 follows Mino (1999).

Indeterminacy in the two sector model with social constant returns is first discussed by Benhabib and Nishimura (1998) in the context of neoclassical growth model. The endogenous growth version examined in Sect. 3.5 is based on Mino (2001). Benhabib et al. (2000) discuss a more general model. It is to be noted that Mino et al. (2008) reexamine the model in Mino (2001) in the discrete time setting. The authors find that the indeterminacy conditions also depend on the rates of depreciation of physical and human capital stocks, which is not seen in the continuous-time model. The two-sector models with physical and human capital without external effects have been analyzed by a large number of authors and applied for discussing a variety of issues. As to the baseline model, see Bond et al. (1996) and Mino (1996) for local indetermiacy, and Ladrón-de-Guevara et al. (1997) for global analysis. Mulligan and Sala-i-Martin (1993) introduce external increasing returns into the base model and analyze transition dynamics through numerical experiments. The model in Sect. 3.5 focuses on the case in which indeterminacy arises.

This chapter has discussed equilibrium indeterminacy in a small set of endogenous growth models. The foregoing studies have found the presence of indeterminacy in alternative types of models of endogenous growth. For example, Benhabib and Perli (1994), Xie (1994), and Mitra (1998) derive indeterminacy conditions in the Lucas-Uzawa model with external effects of human capital. Chamley (1993) also investigates indeterminacy in the Lucas-Uzawa model in which learning technology of the representative household is associated with external effects. Ben-Gad (2003) provides a detailed discussion on transition dynamics and equilibrium (in)determinacy in the Lucas-Uzawa model with externalities. In addition, Mattana et al. (2009) and Antoci et al. (2014) present detailed discussions on the global dynamics of endogenous growth models with physical and human capital.

Moreover, several authors examined indeterminacy in the R&D based models of endogenous growth. Among others, Benhabib et al. (1994) find indeterminacy conditions in a variety-expansion model of endogenous growth à la (Romer 1990). Greiner and Semmler (1995, 1996) and Chen and Chu (2010) also reveal the conditions under which the Romer-type, R&D-based model of endogenous growth involves multiple steady states and equilibrium indeterminacy. On the other hand, Benhabib (2014) examines indeterminacy in a quality ladder model of innovation based on Aghion and Howitt (1992).

Chapter 4
Growth Models with Multiple Steady States

This chapter examines growth models in which there are multiple steady states. This class of models can explain why two countries with similar initial conditions sometimes display very different patterns of growth and development. We start with a well-known two-sector model of economic development that involves multiple steady states. We then examine a one-sector neoclassical growth model with threshold externalities and a two-sector endogenous growth model with human capital accumulation. Although this chapter considers a sample of the large body of literature on growth and development models that involve multiple long-run equilibria, our discussion focuses on the central issues in this literature.

4.1 History Versus Expectations

We first summarize a well-cited contribution by Krugman (1991). Krugman's paper shows a simple example in which the economy's destiny depends not only on the initial conditions but also on expectations of agents. While the model is highly stylized, it provides us with basic concepts that are relevant to understand this class of models.

The economy consists of two production sectors: agricultural and manufacturing. The agricultural sector uses a linear production technology such as

$$Y_a = AN_a, \quad A > 0, \tag{4.1}$$

where Y_a and N_m are output and labor input of the agricultural sector, respectively. The manufacturing sector also uses labor alone, but its technology is associated

K. Mino, *Growth and Business Cycles with Equilibrium Indeterminacy*,
Advances in Japanese Business and Economics 13,
DOI 10.1007/978-4-431-55609-1_4

with sector-specific, external increasing returns. We assume that its production function is

$$Y_m = AN_m G(\bar{N}_m), \tag{4.2}$$

where Y_m is the output of manufacturing goods, N_m is the labor input, and $\bar{N}_m$ denotes the sector-specific external effect generated by the total labor input employed by the manufacturing good firms. We also assume that $G'\left(\bar{N}_m\right) > 0$, $G(1) > 1$ and there is a unique level of $\bar{N}_m^* \in (0, 1)$ that satisfies $G\left(\bar{N}_m^*\right) = 1$.

The aggregate labor supply is fixed and normalized to one. Hence, the full employment condition of labor is given by

$$N_a + N_m = 1. \tag{4.3}$$

We also assume that the number of manufacturing good firms is normalized to one, implying that $\bar{N}_m = N_m$ in equilibrium. The equilibrium levels of real wage in each production sector is competitively determined. Hence, in view of (4.1) and (4.2), we obtain

$$w_a = A \ \text{and}\ w_m = AG\left(N_m\right), \tag{4.4}$$

where w_a and w_m denote real wage rates held in the agricultural and manufacturing sectors, respectively.

First, suppose that the sectoral shift of labor takes time and workers are myopic in the sense that they simply compare the current levels of w_a and w_m to select a sector where they work. Shifting labor between the two production sectors takes time, so that N_m changes according to

$$\dot{N}_m = \phi\left(w_m - w_a\right), \quad \phi > 0.$$

Using (4.3) and (4.5), the above equation is written as

$$\dot{N}_m = \phi A\left[G\left(N_m\right) - 1\right]. \tag{4.5}$$

We assume that $\dot{N}_m = 0$ when $N_m = 0$ or 1. This dynamic system invoices three steady state levels of N_m: $N_m = 0$, N_m^*, and 1. Given our assumptions, the interior steady state that establishes $G\left(N_m^*\right) = 1$ is unstable, while the boundary steady states $N_m = 0$ and $N_m = 1$ are stable. Thus, as shown by Fig. 4.1, if the initial level of N_m is less than N_m^*, the economy converges to the steady state with $N_m = 0$. Otherwise, the economy converges to the steady state with $N_m = 1$. In the former, the economy's destiny is a poverty trap in which all of the labor force is allocated to the less productive agricultural sector. Thus, using Krugman's (1991) terminology, the destiny of the economy depends on history alone.

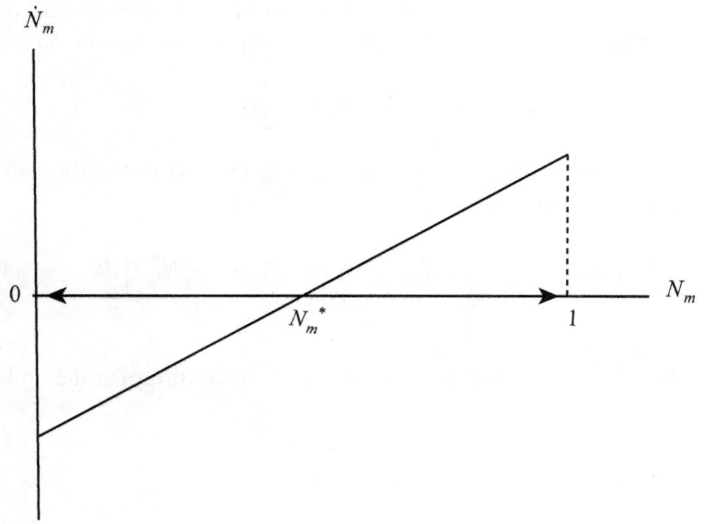

Fig. 4.1 Dynamics of $\dot{N}_m$

Next, consider the other extreme situation in which workers are rational and have perfect foresight. In addition, labor can shift between the two sectors instantaneously. The workers' objective is to maximizes a discounted sum of their income by controlling N_m:

$$\max_{N_m \in [0,1]} \int_0^\infty e^{-rt} Y dt,$$

where

$$Y = w_m N_m + w_a (1 - N_m).$$

If the external effect in the manufacturing sector, $G(\bar{N}_m)$, is internalized, the optimal solution of this problem is $N_m = 1$ for all $t \geq 0$. However, since the workers take $\{\bar{N}_{m,t}\}_0^\infty$, as given when they solve the above problem, there are two perfect foresight equilibria: $N_m = 0$ and $N_m = 1$. To see this, suppose that the initial level of $N_m = N_m^*$ so that $w_a = w_m$. However, this state is "unstable" in the sense that if some workers deviate from this equilibrium by reducing N_m, then w_a becomes higher than w_m, so that all the workers move to the agricultural sector. Similarly, if some workers to choose to work at the manufacturing sector, the equilibrium wage of w_m exceeds w_a, and, hence, all workers choose to work in the manufacturing sector. Consequently, in this setting the selection of the equilibrium totally depends upon expectations formed by the workers.

To avoid such an extreme outcome, let us assume that the sectoral shift of labor is associated with adjustment costs. The real income of workers is now replaced with

$$Y = w_m N_m + w_a (1 - N_m) - \frac{\gamma}{2}\dot{N}_m^2, \quad \gamma > 0.$$

Here, $(\gamma/2)(\dot{L}_m)^2$ represents the costs of shifting labor between the two sectors. Then the workers' problem is written as

$$\max_{\dot{N}_m} \int_0^\infty e^{-rt} \left[w_m N_m + w_a (1 - N_m) - \frac{\gamma}{2}\dot{N}_m^2, \right] dt,$$

where $w_a = A$ and $w_m = AG(\bar{L}_m)$.

Letting the shadow value of N_m be λ, it is easy to confirm that the optimization conditions involve the following:

$$\dot{N}_m = \frac{1}{\gamma}\lambda, \tag{4.6}$$

$$\dot{\lambda} = r\lambda + w_a - w_m = r\lambda + A[1 - G(N_m)]. \tag{4.7}$$

Figure 4.2 depicts the phase diagram of the dynamic system consisting of (4.6) and (4.7). As the figure shows, there are three steady state levels of

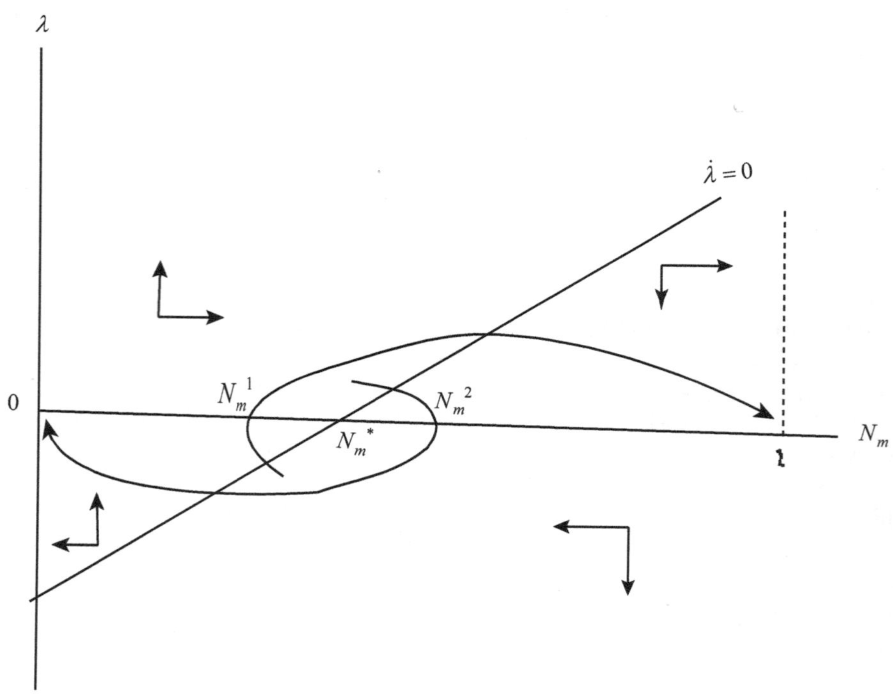

Fig. 4.2 Phase diagram of $N_m = \lambda$

N_m $(= 0, N_m^*$, and $1)$.[1] Again, the interior steady state is totally unstable, while there are paths converging to the boundary steady states: $N_m = 0$ and 1.

Figure 4.2 reveals that if the initial level of N_m is less that N_m^1, then the economy converges to $N_m = 0$ where the entire labor is devoted to the agricultural sector; that is, the economy ultimately falls into the poverty trap. Conversely, if the initial level of N_m exceeds N_m^2, then the destination of the economy is the steady state with $N_m = 1$: the manufacturing sector employs whole labor. If the initial level of N_m is stays between N_m^1 and N_m^2, the destination of the economy fully depends on the expectations of agents. Therefore, if the initial N_m is either less than N_m^1 or higher than N_m^2, then the initial condition (history) determines the destiny of the economy. In contrast, if the initial N_m is in between N_m^1 and N_m^2, the long-run equilibrium of the economy totally depends on the expectations of households.

4.2 A Neoclassical Growth Model with Threshold Externalities

This section considers the "history versus expectations" problem in the context of a one-sector neoclassical growth model. In this section, we modify the standard Ramsey model by adding threshold external effects of aggregate capital. We first review the one-sector optimal growth mode with non-convex technology in which the optimal path is uniquely determined. Then we, see that the same type of technology may generate complex dynamics if agents fail to internalize external effects in a decentralized economy.

4.2.1 Optimal Growth Under a Concave-Convex Production Function

In his well-cited paper, Skiba (1978) examines a one-sector optimal growth model with a convex-concave production function. The social planning problem is the standard one in which the planner maximizes the social welfare represented by

$$U = \int_0^\infty e^{-\rho t} u(c)\, dt$$

subject to

$$\dot{k} = f(k) - c - \delta k. \tag{4.8}$$

[1]Figure 4.2 follows Fukao and Benabou (1993) who pointed out that the phase diagram in Krugman (1991) was imprecise.

The production function, $f(k)$, satisfies

$$f(0) - 0, \quad f'(k) > 0, \quad f''(k) > 0 \ \text{ for } 0 < k < \hat{k}, \quad f''(k) < 0 \ \text{ for } k > \hat{k},$$

together with $f'(0) < \infty$ and $f'(\infty) = 0$. It is easy to see that under this production function there are two interior steady state levels of k that establish the modified golden-rule condition: $f'(k) = \rho + \delta$ (see Fig. 4.3). It is also shown that the upper interior steady state satisfies saddle-point stability, whereas the lower interior steady state is locally unstable. Skiba (1978) showed that there may exist two kinds of optimal paths: one converges to the steady state with $k = 0$ and the other converges to the upper interior steady state. Analyzing the discrete version of this model, Dechert and Nishimura (1983) conduct a rigorous analysis and reveal that there may exist a threshold level of capital, k_s. Under some conditions, if the initial level of capital, k_0, is less than k_s, the optimal path of capital accumulation is the trajectory that converges to the steady state with $k = 0$. In contrast, if $k_0 > k_s$, the planner selects the path converging to the upper interior steady state.

Following Akao et al. (2011) who characterize the threshold level of capital in a continuous-time model, the above discussion can be summarized as follows. The value function of this planning problem is given by

$$V(k_0) = \max \int_0^\infty e^{-\rho t} u(c)\, dt \ \text{ subject to (4.8).}$$

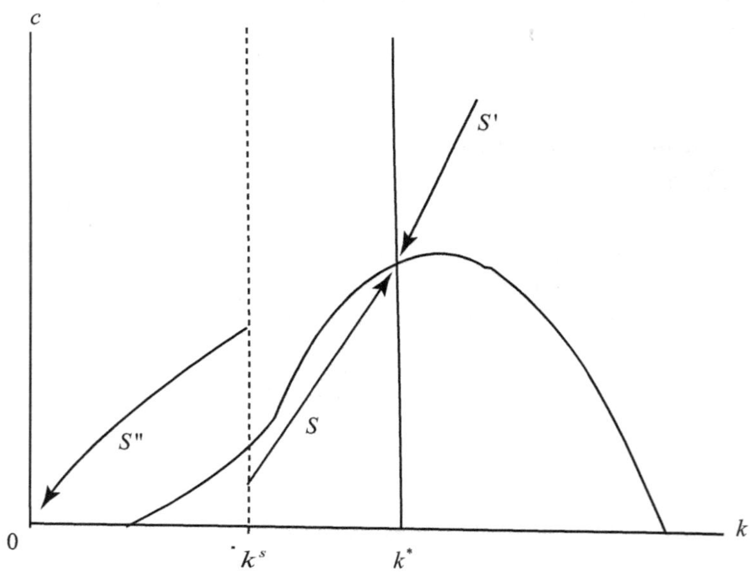

Fig. 4.3 Optimal paths under a concave-conves production function

Let us define the value obtained by following the path that converges to a steady state as

$$V^i(k_0) = \int_0^\infty e^{-\rho t} u\left(c_t^i\right) dt, \quad i = a, b.$$

Here, $V^a(.)$ $(V^b(.))$ denotes the value function corresponding to the path that coverages to $k = 0$ (the upper interior steady state). Then, if the discount rate, ρ, satisfies some restrictions, there exists a unique level of $k = k^s$ that satisfies the following:

$$V^a(k^s) = V^b(k^s),$$

$$V^a(k_0) > V^b(k_0) \quad \text{for } 0 < k_0 < k^s,$$

$$V^a(k_0) < V^b(k_0) \quad \text{for } k_0 > k^s.$$

Namely, in this case, the planner can select a unique optimal trajectory for any level of initial capital stock, k_0. Therefore, unless $k_0 = ks$, the optimal path is determinate even though there are two feasible steady states.

However, if the presence of the external effect of aggregate capital gives rise to a convex-concave social production function, then the competitive equilibrium of the economy diverges from the optimal solution of the planning problem. Hence, equilibrium determinacy established in the social planning problem may fail to hold in the corresponding decentralized economy. The central concern of the next subsection is to characterize the competitive equilibrium when the economy has a convex-concave social production technology.

4.2.2 A Model with Threshold Externalities

Azariadis and Drazen (1990) introduce the concept of threshold externalities into a two-period lived overlapping generations model. Here, we first consider a simple example of threshold externalities in the context of the Solow growth model. The production technology is given by

$$y = A\left(\bar{k}\right) f(k),$$

where y is per capita output and k is per capita capital stock. The productivity function $f(k)$ is assumed to satisfy the standard neoclassical properties. The total factor productivity $A\left(\bar{k}\right)$ represents the external effect generated by the aggregate capital, where $\bar{k}$ is the average capita in the economy. Here, we assume that the external effects are expressed as

$$A\left(\bar{k}\right) = \begin{cases} A_H & \text{for } \bar{k} \geq \hat{k}, \\ \underline{A}_L & \text{for } 0 < k < \hat{k}. \end{cases}$$

This assumption means that there is a threshold level of capital, $\hat{k}$ where the total factor productivity jumps up from A_L to $A_H(> A_L)$.

We assume that population stays constant. As a result, keeping the consistency condition, $\bar{k} = k$ in mind, we obtain the basic Solow equation that describes capital formation as follows:

$$\dot{k} = sA\left(k\right)f\left(k\right) - \delta k, \tag{4.9}$$

where s is an exogenously given saving rate.

Figure 4.4 depicts the graph of (4.9) under our assumption on external effects of capital. There are three steady state levels of per capita capital: high, middle, and low. The middle steady state, $\hat{k}$, is unstable, whereas the high and low steady states are stable. Using Krugman's (1991) terminology, in this model, the long-run equilibrium of this economy is determined by history alone. In what follows, we introduce threshold externalities shown above into the standard Ramsey model.

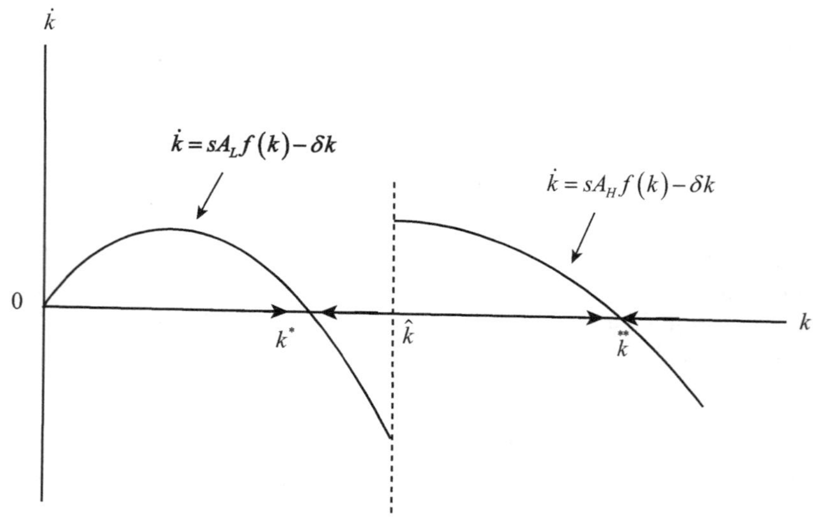

Fig. 4.4 The Solow model with threshold externalities

4.2.3 Model

Let us assume that the production function of the entire economy is given by

$$Y = A\left(\bar{K}\right) F(K, N).$$

Letting $k = K/N$ and $y = Y/N$. Using the equilibrium condition $\bar{K} = K$, the social production function is thus expressed as

$$y = A(k) f(k).$$

In this model, we assume that the population stays constant.

As to the characterization of external effects, we assume that there are two critical levels of per-capita capital, k_1 and k_2, that satisfy the following conditions:

$$\begin{gathered} A(k_1) f'(k_1) = A(k_2) f'(k_2) \quad 0 < k_1 < k_2 < +\infty, \\ A'(k) > 0 \ \text{ for } k_1 < k < k_2, \\ \lim_{k \to 0} A(k) = A_L, \quad \lim_{k\infty} = A_H, \quad 0 < \underline{A_L} < A_H < \infty. \end{gathered} \tag{4.10}$$

These restrictions mean that the external effects of capital are positive, but they have threshold properties: positive effects stay constant if capital stock is either sufficiently low or high. Under these assumptions, the social production function with $\bar{k} = k$ is depicted as in Fig. 4.5.

The representative household solves

$$\max \int_0^{\infty} e\rho^{-\rho t} u(c)\, dt$$

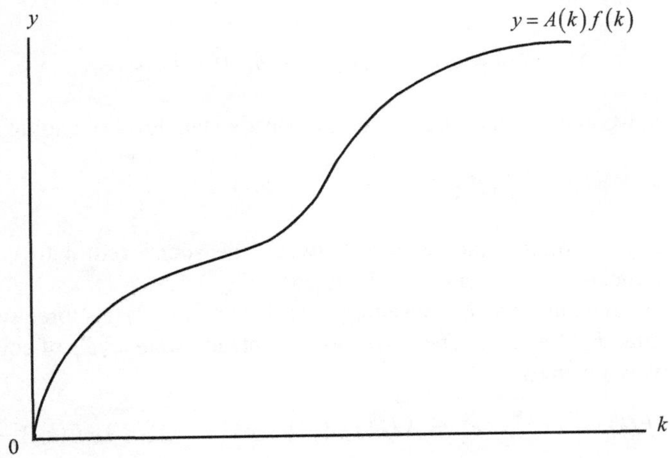

Fig. 4.5 Social productiion function

subject to

$$\dot{k} = rk + w - c - \delta k.$$

In equilibrium, the competitive factor prices equal the marginal productivity of private capital and labor, so that

$$r = A(k) f'(k), \quad w = A(k) \left[f(k) - f'(k) k \right].$$

In sum, a complete dynamic system consists of the following:

$$\dot{k} = A(k) f(k) - c - \delta k, \tag{4.11}$$

$$\dot{c} = \frac{c}{\sigma(c)} \left[A(k) f'(k) - \rho - \delta \right], \tag{4.12}$$

where $\sigma(c) = -u''(c) / u'(c) c > 0$. If $A(k)$ is a positive constant, then this system is the same as the standard Ramasey model.

4.2.4 Steady State Equilibria and Local Dynamics

Assumptions made in (4.10) mean that the private rate of return to capital, $A(k) f'(k)$, is close to$\underline{A}_L f'(k)$ for small k and close to $A_H f'(k)$ for large k. Hence, the private rate of return to capital decreases with k for small or large k. In contrast, $A(k) f'(k)$ may increase with k for intermediate levels of capital as long as the positive external effect of capital is strong enough to offset the decreasing return of private capital. Here, we assume that there are two steady state levels of capital, k_L and k_H, that fulfill

$$\underline{A}_L f'(k_L) = A_H f'(k_H) = \rho + \delta, \; 0 < k_L < A_H. \tag{4.13}$$

Additionally, we assume that there is another steady state level of capital satisfying

$$A\left(k^*\right) f'\left(k^*\right) = \rho + \delta, \qquad k_L < k^* < k_H. \tag{4.14}$$

Given these assumptions, the relation between the social return to capital that involves external effects and $\rho + \delta$ is depicted in Fig. 4.6.

In sum, the dynamic system consisting of (4.11) and (4.12) has three steady state levels of capital, $k_L k^*$ and k_H. The corresponding steady state levels of consumption are respectively given by

$$c_L = \underline{A} f(k_L) - \delta \underline{k_L}, \quad c^* = A\left(k^*\right) f\left(k^*\right) - \delta k^*, \quad c_H = A_H f(k_H) - \delta k_H.$$

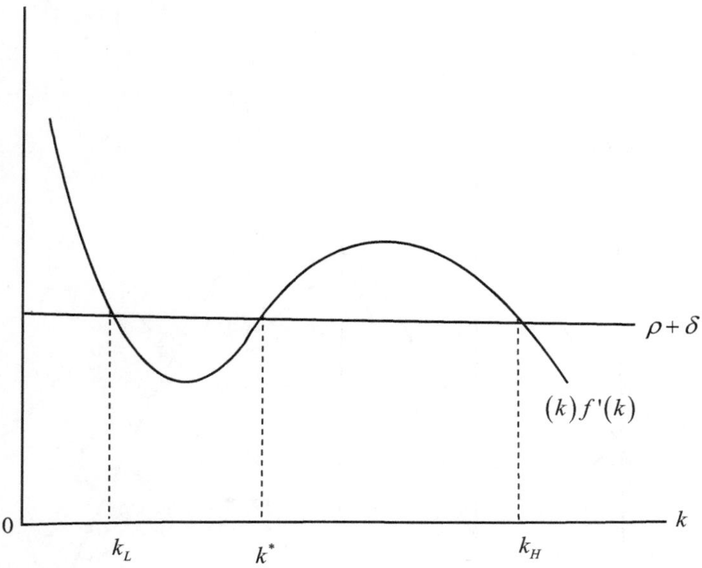

Fig. 4.6 Steady state levels of capital

The coefficient matrices of the dynamic system linearized at (k_L, c_L) and (k_H, c_H) are the standard ones and, hence, those steady state exhibit local saddle-point properties. On the other hand, the coefficient matrix evaluated at the middle steady state is

$$J = \begin{bmatrix} A'(k^*) + \rho + \delta & -1 \\ \frac{c^*}{\delta(C^*)} \left[A(k^*) f''(k^*) + A'(k^*) f'(k^*)\right] & 0 \end{bmatrix}.$$

Since both the trace and determinant of this matrix are positive, (k^*, c^*) is totally unstable. The discriminant of the characteristic equation of the coefficient matrix evaluated at the middle steady state is

$$D = \left[\rho + A'(k^*) f(k^*)\right]^2 - 4\left[c^*/\sigma(c^*)\right]\left[A'(k^*) f'(k^*) + A(k^*) f''(k^*)\right].$$

Since $A'(k^*) f'(k^*) + A(k^*) f''(k^*)$ is strictly positive under our assumptions, D may have both signs. If $D > 0$, the middle steady state (k^*, c^*) is an unstable node, while it is an unstable focus so that the equilibrium path exhibits cyclical motion around (k^*, c^*).

4.2.5 *Patterns of Global Dynamics*

Typical examples of the phase diagram of dynamic equations (4.11) and (4.12) are depicted in Fig. 4.7. Given our assumptions, there exist three $\dot{c} = 0$ loci on which

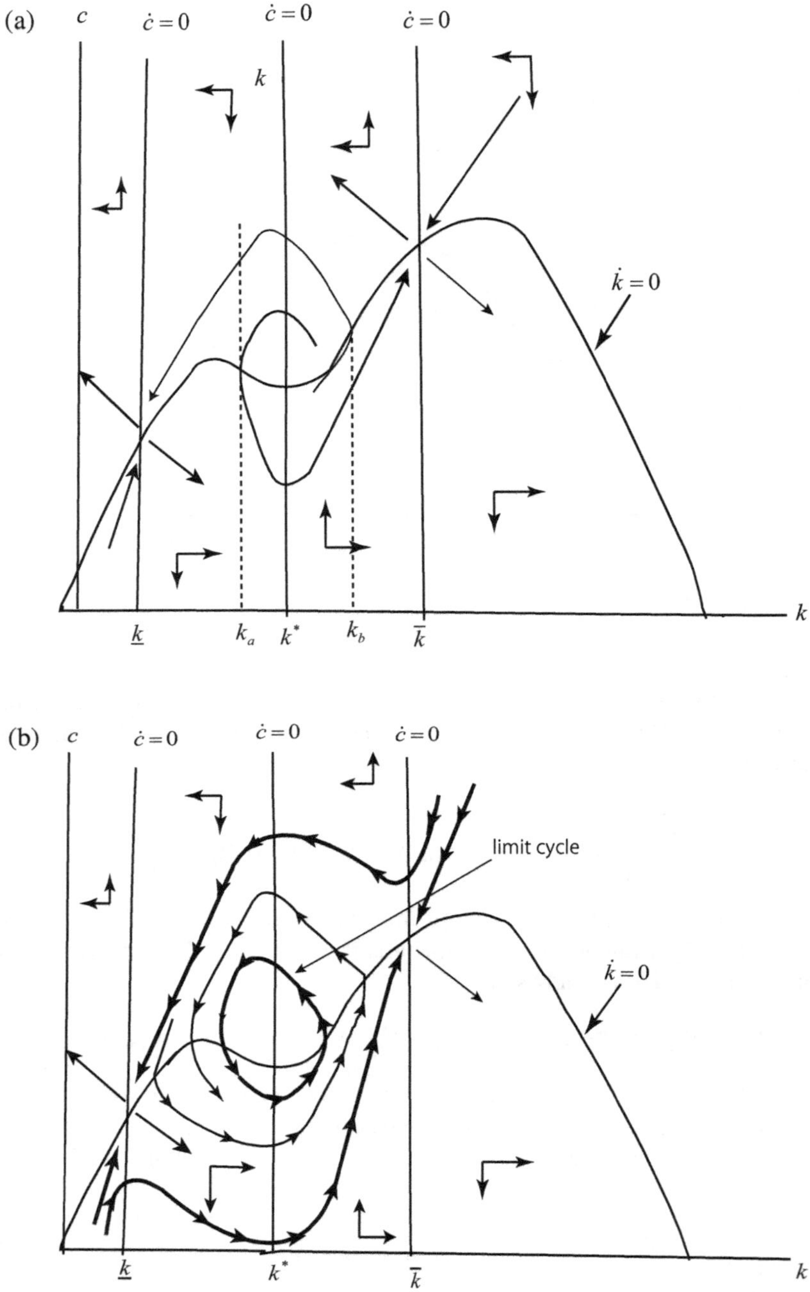

Fig. 4.7 (**a**) Pattern of dynamics (I). (**b**) Pattern of dynamics (II)

$A(k)f'(k) = \rho + \delta$ holds. On the other hand, the $\dot{k} = 0$ locus that fulfills $c = A(k)f(k) - \delta k$ has two local maxima and one local minimum. Corresponding values of k that give those extremes are denoted by k_1, k_2, and k_3 and shown in Fig. 4.6. We see that $k_L < k_1 < k_2 < k^* < k_H < k_3$, and thus the position of the $\dot{c} = 0$ loci can be located as in Fig. 4.7. In panel (a) of this figure, if the initial value of k is less than k_a, then there is a unique equilibrium path that converges to (k_L, c_L). By contrast, if the initial k exceeds k_b, then the economy converges to (k_H, c_H). However, if the initial k is between k_a and k_b, there exist two equilibrium paths: one converges to (k_L, c_L) and the other converges to (k_H, c_H), meaning that indeterminacy holds if $k_a < k_0 < k_b$. Therefore, according to Krugman's (1991) classification,if either $k_0 < k_a$ or $k_0 > k_b$, the equilibrium path is determined by history, while it depends on expectations if $k_a < k_0 < k_b$.

The pattern of growth is more complex in the situation given by panel (b) of Fig. 4.7. In this figure, it is seen that if the initial position of the economy is inside the thick line, then the economy continues staying in this area. However, the interior steady state, (k^*, c^*), is locally unstable, so that the economy cannot converge to this point. As a result, in view of Poincarè-Bendixson theorem, there is at least one stable limit cycle around (k^*, c^*). This means that the economy starting with a point inside the thick line will converge to one of those stable limit cycles. Consequently, if the initial capital is in between k_L and k_L, then the final destiny of the economy is either (k_L, c_L), (k_H, c_H) or a limit cycle around (k^*, c^*). In this case, the equilibrium of the economy exhibits global indeterminacy, and quite different patterns of growth may emerge depending on the expectations of households.

4.3 Global Indeterminacy in an Endogenous Growth

In this section, we examine an endogenous growth model with multiple balanced-growth equilibria. Our main concern is to demonstrate that growth models with multiple converging paths may present a useful analytical framework to consider various growth patterns among the countries that have similar economic environments. Of course, it is not novel to use endogenous growth models with multiple equilibria for describing diverse growth patterns. A common feature in this class of studies is that indeterminacy holds under the assumption of strong degree of increasing returns. However, recent empirical investigations suggest that the degree of increasing returns may not be so large as many theoretical studies have assumed. This implies that the exposition of non-convergence of per capita income and diverse patterns of growth based on indeterminacy of equilibrium would be empirically dubious.

The model in this section demonstrates that the presence of increasing returns is not necessary for generating indeterminacy of equilibrium. Using one of the prototype models of endogenous growth, we show that multiple equilibria and complex patterns of transitional dynamics can emerge even under social constant returns. The main purpose of examining such a model is to emphasize that we do not need extreme assumptions to show diverse growth performances among the countries with similar technologies and preferences. If we make a small modification of the base model in which equilibrium should be unique, the model will display various patterns of growth dynamics.

More specifically, we analyze a generalized version of the two-sector endogenous growth models à la Lucas (1988). We show that if the utility function of the representative family is not additively separable between consumption and leisure and if there are sector-specific externalities, then the Lucas model may produce indeterminacy of equilibrium even if technologies of the final good and the new human capital production sectors satisfy social constant returns. In order to clarify the analysis, we impose specific conditions on the parameter values involved in the model. This enables us to examine global dynamic behavior of the model.

4.3.1 Model

Consider a competitive economy with two production sectors. The first sector produces a final good that can be used either for consumption or for investment on physical capital. The production technology is given by

$$Y_1 = K^{\alpha} H_1^{\beta_1} \bar{K}_1^{\varepsilon} \bar{H}_1^{\phi_1}, \quad \alpha,\ \beta_1 > 0,\ \alpha + \beta_1 + \varepsilon + \phi_1 = 1, \tag{4.15}$$

where Y_1 denotes the final good, K is the stock of physical capital, and H_1 is human capital devoted to the final good production. $\bar{K}^{\varepsilon}$ and $\bar{H}_1^{\phi_1}$ represent sector-specific externalities associated with physical and human capital employed in this sector.[2] The key assumption in (4.15) is that the production technology is socially constant returns to scale. The second sector is an education sector that produces new human capital. Following the Lucas-Uzawa setting, we assume that new human capital production needs human capital alone, and its technology is specified as

$$Y_2 = \gamma H_1^{\beta_2} \bar{H}_2^{\phi_2}, \quad \gamma, \beta_2, \phi_2 > 0, \quad \beta_2 + \phi_2 = 1. \tag{4.16}$$

Here, Y_2 is newly produced human capital, H_2 is the stock of human capital used in the education sector, and $\bar{H}_2^{\phi_2}$ stands for sector-specific externalities. Again, the production technology of new human capital exhibits social constant returns.

The firms in each sector maximize their profits under given external effects. Thus, the value of the marginal product of each private capital equals its nominal rent:

$$R = p_1 \alpha K^{\alpha-1} H_1^{\beta_1} \bar{K}_1^{\varepsilon} \bar{H}_1^{\phi_1}, \tag{4.17}$$

$$W = p_1 \beta_1 K^{\alpha} H_1^{\beta_1 - 1} \bar{K}_1^{\varepsilon} \bar{H}_1^{\phi_1} = p_2 \gamma \beta_2 H_2^{\beta_2 - 1} \bar{H}_2^{\phi_2}, \tag{4.18}$$

---

[2]The role of sector-specific externalities was first analyzed by Benhabib and Farmer (1996).

where R, W, p_1, and p_2 respectively denote the nominal rent on physical capital, nominal rent on human capital, price of the final good and price of the new human capital. Note that since the private technologies exhibit decreasing returns, the firms may earn positive profits. We assume that entire stocks of physical and human capital are owned by the households so that the profits are distributed back to them.

The representative household maximizes a discounted sum of utilities

$$U = \int_0^{\infty} u(C, l)\, e^{-\rho t} dt, \quad \rho > 0,$$

where C is consumption and l is the time length spent for leisure. We specify the instantaneous utility function as follows:

$$u(C, l) = \begin{cases} \dfrac{[C\Lambda(l)]^{1-\sigma} - 1}{1-\sigma}, & \sigma > 0,\ \sigma \neq 1, \\ \ln C + \ln \Lambda(l), & \text{for } \sigma = 1. \end{cases}$$

Function $\Lambda(l)$ is assumed to be monotonically increasing and strictly concave in l. We also assume that

$$\sigma\Lambda(l)\,\Lambda''(l) + (1 - 2\sigma)\,\Lambda'(l)^2 < 0. \tag{4.19}$$

This assumption, along with strict concavity of $\Lambda(l)$, ensures that $u(C, l)$ is strictly concave in C and l.

Since the lH unit of human capital is not used for production activities, the wage income of the household is $W(1 - l)H$. Hence, the flow budget constraint for the household is given by

$$p_1\left(\dot{K} + \delta K\right) + p_2\left(\dot{H} + \eta H\right) + p_1 C = RK + W(1 - l)H + \pi_1 + \pi_2,$$

where δ and η are depreciation rates of physical and human capital, and π_i $(i = 1, 2)$ denotes the distributed profits earned by the i-th sector. We define the total wealth of the household as

$$A = p_1 K + p_2 H. \tag{4.20}$$

Then the flow budget constraint can be written as

$$\dot{A} = \left(\frac{R}{p_1} + \frac{\dot{p}_1}{p_1} - \delta\right) p_1 K + \left(\frac{W(1-l)}{p_2} + \frac{\dot{p}_2}{p_2} - \eta\right) p_2 H + \pi_1 + \pi_2 - p_1 C. \tag{4.21}$$

The household maximizes U subject to (4.20), (4.21) and the given initial level of wealth (A_0) by controlling $C, l,\ K$ and H. In so doing, the household takes sequences of prices and profits, $\{p_1(t), p_2(t), R(t), W(t), \pi_1(t), \pi_2(t)\}_{t=o}^{\infty}$, as given.

The current value Hamiltonian for the household's optimization problem can be set as

$$\mathcal{H} = \frac{\left[C\Lambda(l)\right]^{1-\sigma}-1}{1-\sigma} + q\left[\left(\frac{R}{p_1}+\frac{\dot{p}_1}{p_1}-\delta\right)p_1K + \left(\frac{W(1-l)}{p_2}+\frac{\dot{p}_2}{p_2}-\eta\right)p_2H + \pi_1 + \pi_2 - p_1C\right] + \lambda\left(A - p_1K - p_2H\right).$$

Under the given sequences of prices and distributed profits, the necessary conditions for an optimum are the following:

$$C^{-\sigma}\Lambda(l)^{1-\sigma} = qp_1, \tag{4.22}$$

$$C^{1-\sigma}\Lambda'(l)\Lambda(l)^{-\sigma} = qWH, \tag{4.23}$$

$$q\left(\frac{R}{p_1}-\frac{\dot{p}_1}{p_1}-\delta\right) = \lambda, \tag{4.24}$$

$$q\left(\frac{W(1-l)}{p_2}-\frac{\dot{p}_2}{p_2}-\eta\right) = \lambda, \tag{4.25}$$

$$\dot{q} = q\rho - \lambda, \tag{4.26}$$

together with (4.20), (4.21) and the transversality condition,

$$\lim_{t\to\infty} e^{-\rho t}qA = 0. \tag{4.27}$$

Note that (4.24) and (4.25) yield

$$\frac{R}{p_1}+\frac{\dot{p}_1}{p_1}-\delta = \frac{W(1-l)}{p_2}+\frac{\dot{p}_2}{p_2}-\eta, \tag{4.28}$$

which shows the non-arbitrage condition between holding physical and human capital.

4.3.2 Market Equilibrium Conditions

The equilibrium conditions in product markets are given by

$$Y_1 = C + \dot{K} + \delta K, \tag{4.29}$$

$$Y_2 = \dot{H} + \eta H. \tag{4.30}$$

The full-employment condition for human capital is

$$H_1 + H_2 + lH = H. \tag{4.31}$$

Denoting $H_1/H = v$, (4.15), (4.16), (4.29), (4.30), and (4.31) give the accumulation equations of physical and human capital as follows:

$$\dot{K} = K^{\alpha} (vH)^{\beta_1} \bar{K}^{\varepsilon} \bar{H}_1^{\phi_1} - C - \delta K, \tag{4.32}$$

$$\dot{H} = \gamma (1 - v - l)^{\beta_2} H^{\beta_2} \bar{H}_2^{\phi_2} - \eta H. \tag{4.33}$$

4.3.3 Growth Dynamics

For analytical simplicity, the following discussion assumes that $\Lambda(l)$ is specified as

$$\Lambda(l) = \exp\left(\frac{l^{1-\theta} - 1}{1-\theta}\right), \quad \theta > 0, \ \theta \neq 1, \tag{4.34}$$

where $\Lambda(l) = l$ for $\theta = 1$. Given this specification, when $\sigma = 1$, the instantaneous utility function becomes

$$u(C, l) = \ln C + \frac{l^{1-\theta}}{1-\theta}.$$

Under this specification, the concavity condition (4.19) reduces to

$$(1-\sigma) l^{1-\theta} - \sigma\theta < 0. \tag{4.35}$$

If we assume that the number of households is normalized to one, in equilibrium it holds that $\bar{K}(t) = K(t)$ and $\bar{H}_i(t) = H_i(t)$ $(i = 1, 2)$ for all $t \geq 0$. Thus, keeping in mind that $\alpha + \beta_1 + \varepsilon + \phi_1 = 1$ and $\beta_2 + \phi_2 = 1$, (4.17), (4.18), (4.32), and (4.33) respectively become

$$R = p_1 \alpha K^{\alpha+\varepsilon-1} (vH) H^{1-(\alpha+\varepsilon)}, \tag{4.36}$$

$$W = p_1 \beta K^{\alpha+\varepsilon} (vH)^{-(\alpha+\varepsilon)} = p_2 \gamma \beta_2 [(1 - v - l) H]^{-(\alpha+\varepsilon)}, \tag{4.37}$$

$$\dot{K} = K^{\alpha+\varepsilon} (vH)^{1-(\alpha+\varepsilon)} - C - \delta K, \tag{4.38}$$

$$\dot{H} = \gamma (1 - v - l) H. \tag{4.39}$$

Similarly, (4.22) and (4.23) yield:

$$\frac{C\Lambda'(l)}{\Lambda(l)} = \frac{p_2\gamma\beta_2 H}{p_1}.$$

Given (4.34), the above becomes

$$C = (p_2/p_1)\,\gamma\beta_2 l^{\theta} H. \tag{4.40}$$

Let us denote the factor intensity in the final good sector as $x = K/vH$. From (4.18) we obtain:

$$\frac{p_2}{p_1} = \frac{\beta_1}{\gamma\beta_2}x^{\alpha+\varepsilon}. \tag{4.41}$$

Equations (4.40) and (4.41) give $C = \beta_1 l^{\theta} x^{\alpha+\varepsilon} H$. Hence, using $x = K/vH$ and denoting the capital ratio by $K/H = k$, the commodity market equilibrium conditions (4.38) and (4.40) yield the following growth equations of capital stocks:

$$\frac{\dot{K}}{K} = x^{\alpha+\varepsilon-1} - \frac{\beta_1 l^{\theta} x^{\alpha+\varepsilon}}{k} - \delta, \tag{4.42}$$

$$\frac{\dot{H}}{H} = \gamma\left(1 - l - \frac{k}{x}\right) - \eta. \tag{4.43}$$

Equations (4.36) and (4.37) are respectively written as follows:

$$R/p_1 = \alpha x^{\alpha+\varepsilon-1},$$

$$W/p_2 = \gamma\beta_2(1-l).$$

Using the expressions derived above and keeping in mind that $\delta = \eta$, (4.28) leads to

$$\frac{\dot{p}_2}{p_2} - \frac{\dot{p}_1}{p_1} = \alpha x^{\alpha+\varepsilon-1} - \gamma\beta_2(1-l). \tag{4.44}$$

As a result, in view of (4.41) and (4.44), we find that $x (= K/vH)$ changes according to

$$\frac{\dot{x}}{x} = \frac{1}{\alpha+\varepsilon}\left[\eta - \delta + \alpha x^{\alpha+\varepsilon-1} - \beta_2\gamma(1-l)\right]. \tag{4.45}$$

From (4.34), equation (4.22) is expressed as

$$C^{-\sigma}\exp\left((1-\sigma)\frac{l^{1-\theta}-1}{1-\theta}\right) = qp_1.$$

Substituting (4.40) into the above and taking time derivatives of both sides, we obtain

$$\left[(1-\sigma)\,l^{1-\theta}-\sigma\theta\right]\frac{\dot{l}}{i}=(1-\sigma)\,\frac{\dot{p}_1}{p_1}+\sigma\left(\frac{\dot{p}_2}{p_2}+\frac{\dot{H}}{H}\right)+\frac{\dot{q}}{q}.$$

This equation, together with (4.24), (4.26), and (4.44), yields the dynamic equation of leisure time, l:

$$\frac{\dot{l}}{l}=\Delta\,(l)\left\{\alpha\,(1-\sigma)\,x^{\alpha+\varepsilon-1}+\sigma\gamma\frac{k}{x}-\sigma\gamma\,(1-\beta_2)\,(1-l)-\rho-(1-\sigma)\,\delta\right\}, \tag{4.46}$$

where $\Delta\,(l)\;=\;\left[\sigma\theta-(1-\sigma)\,l^{1-\theta}\right]^{-1}$, which has a positive value under the concavity assumption given by (4.35). Finally, (4.42) and (4.43) mean that the dynamic equations for the behavior of $k\;(=K/H)$ is expressed as

$$\frac{\dot{k}}{k}=x^{\alpha+\varepsilon-1}-\frac{\beta_1 l^{\theta}x^{\alpha+\varepsilon}}{k}-\delta+\eta-\gamma\left(1-l-\frac{k}{x}\right). \tag{4.47}$$

Consequently, we find that (4.45), (4.46), and (4.47) constitute a complete dynamic system with respect to $k\,(=K/H)$, $x\,(=K/vH)$, and l.

4.3.4 A Simplified System

Since the complete dynamic system derived above is a rather complex, three-dimensional one, it is difficult to conduct a precise analysis of transition dynamics. A conventional strategy to deal with such a situation is to linearize the system around the steady state and to focus on the local behavior of the model. In what follows, rather than concentrating on the local analysis, we impose specific conditions on parameter values in order to clarify the global dynamics of the model. First, we assume that $\theta=1$ (so that $\Lambda\,(l)=l$). Second, following Xie's (1994) idea, we focus on the special case in which $\sigma=\alpha$. As shown below, these assumptions enable us to reduce the three-dimensional dynamic system to a two-dimensional one.[3] Finally, we also assume that $\delta=\eta$; that is, physical and human capital depreciate at an identical rate. This assumption is made only for notational simplicity, and the main results obtained below are not altered when $\delta\neq\eta$.

[3]The key condition for simplification of the dynamic system is that $\sigma=\alpha$. The assumption $\theta=1$ is not essential for our results,but it is useful for analytical convenience.

Given our assumptions, $\sigma = \alpha$ and $\theta = 1$, we can verify that C/K stays constant over time even without the balanced-growth path. To see this, let us define $z = \beta_1 x^{\alpha+\varepsilon} l/k \,(= C/K)$. If $\sigma = \alpha,\ \delta = \eta$ and $\theta = 1$, then (4.47) becomes

$$\frac{\dot{k}}{k} = x^{\alpha+\varepsilon-1} - z - \gamma(1-l) + \gamma\frac{k}{x}. \tag{4.48}$$

Therefore, keeping in mind that $\delta = \eta$, from (4.45) and (4.46) we obtain

$$\frac{\dot{z}}{z} = (\alpha+\varepsilon)\frac{\dot{x}}{x} + \frac{\dot{l}}{l} - \frac{\dot{k}}{k} = z - \frac{\alpha + (1-\alpha)\delta}{\alpha}.$$

Since this system is completely unstable, on the perfect foresight competitive equilibrium path the following should hold for all $t \geq 0$:

$$z\left(=\frac{C}{K}\right) = \frac{\rho + (1-\alpha)\delta}{\alpha}.$$

Hence, consumption and physical capital always change at the same rate during the transition process.

The above result means that on the equilibrium path, x is related to k and l in such a way that

$$x = \left[\left(\frac{\alpha + (1-\alpha)\delta}{\alpha}\right)\frac{k}{l}\right]^{\frac{1}{\alpha+\varepsilon}}. \tag{4.49}$$

Substituting this into (4.46) and (4.48), we obtain the following set of differential equations:

$$\frac{\dot{k}}{k} = \left(\lambda\frac{k}{l}\right)^{1-\frac{1}{\alpha+\varepsilon}} + \frac{\gamma}{\lambda}\left(\lambda\frac{k}{l}\right)^{1-\frac{1}{\alpha+\varepsilon}} l - \gamma(1-l) - \lambda,$$

$$\frac{\dot{l}}{l} = (1-\alpha)\left(\lambda\frac{k}{l}\right)^{1-\frac{1}{\alpha+\varepsilon}} + \frac{\gamma}{\lambda}\left(\lambda\frac{k}{l}\right)^{1-\frac{1}{\alpha+\varepsilon}} l - \gamma(1-\beta_2)(1-l) - \lambda,$$

where $\lambda = [\rho + (1-\alpha)\delta]/\alpha$. To simplify further, we denote

$$q = (\lambda k/l)^{1-\frac{1}{\alpha+\varepsilon}}. \tag{4.50}$$

Then, the above system may be rewritten in the following manner:

$$\frac{\dot{q}}{q} = \left(\frac{1-\alpha-\varepsilon}{\alpha+\varepsilon}\right)[\gamma\beta_2(1-l) - \alpha q], \tag{4.51}$$

$$\frac{\dot{l}}{l} = \left(1-\alpha+\frac{\gamma}{\lambda}l\right)q - \gamma(1-\beta_2)(1-l) - \lambda. \tag{4.52}$$

Under the conditions under which $\sigma = \alpha$, $\delta = \eta$ and $\theta = 1$, this system is equivalent to the original dynamic equations given by (4.45), (4.46), and (4.47).

4.3.5 *Local Dynamics*

First, consider the steady state in (4.51) and (4.52). When $\dot{q} = \dot{l} = 0$, (4.50) shows that k stays constant over time. Thus from (4.49) x does not change in the steady state, which means that $v = x/k$ stays constant as well. Accordingly, in the steady state K, H, C, and Y grow at a common, constant rate of

$$g = \gamma \left(1 - l^* - v^*\right) - \delta,$$

where l^* and v^* respectively denote steady state values of l and v.

To examine the existence of the balanced- growth path, we first observe that when $\dot{q} = 0$, (4.51) yields $q = (\gamma\beta_2 l\alpha)(1 - l)$. Thus, conditions $\dot{l} = \dot{q} = 0$ are established if the following equation is satisfied:

$$\xi(l) = \frac{\gamma\beta_2}{\alpha}\left(1 - \alpha + \frac{\gamma}{\lambda}l\right)(1 - l) - \gamma(1 - \beta_2)(1 - l) - \lambda = 0.$$

Note that

$$\begin{aligned}\xi(0) &= (\gamma\beta_2/\alpha)(1 - \alpha) - \gamma(1 - \beta_2) - \lambda \\ &= (1/\alpha)\left[\gamma(\beta_2 - \alpha) - \rho - (1 - \alpha)\delta\right], \\ \xi(1) &= -(1/\alpha)\left[\rho + (1 - \alpha)\delta\right] < 0.\end{aligned}$$

We see that if

$$\gamma(\beta_2 - \alpha) - \rho - (1 - \alpha)\delta > 0, \tag{4.53}$$

then $\xi(0) > 0$ and $\xi(l)$ is monotonically decreasing with l for $l \in [0, 1]$. Hence, $\xi(l) = 0$ has a unique solution between 0 and 1. Conversely, if

$$\gamma(\beta_2 - \alpha) - \rho - (1 - \alpha)\delta < 0, \tag{4.54}$$

then $\xi(0) < 0$. Since $\xi(l) = 0$ is a quadratic equation, if $\xi(l) = 0$ has solutions for $l \in [0, 1]$, there are two solutions, meaning that there are dual balanced-growth equilibria. To sum up, the following holds:

Proposition 4.1 *Under* $\sigma = 1$ *and* $\theta = 1$, *there exists a unique, feasible balanced-growth equilibrium if and only if* (4.53) *holds, while there may exist dual balanced-growth equilibria if* (4.54) *is fulfilled.*

To consider numerical examples, suppose that $\alpha = \sigma = 0.3$, $\varepsilon = 0.1$, $\beta_2 = 0.7$, $\rho = 0.03$, $\delta = \eta = 0.04$, and $\gamma = 0.2$. These parameter magnitudes satisfy (4.53) so that the balanced-growth equilibrium is uniquely determined. Given these values, we find that the steady state level of leisure time is $\bar{l} = 0.3731$, and the balanced-growth rate is $\bar{g} = 0.0151$. If we set β_2 and γ as 0.6 and 0.15 respectively and keep the other parameter values at the same levels shown above, we see that condition (4.54) is met. In this case, the steady state values of l are 0.118 and 0.512. In the steady state with the lower l, the balanced growth rate is 0.083, while it is 0.0021 at the steady state with the higher l.[4]

Before analyzing the dynamic properties of (4.51), and (4.52), let us relate the stability conditions of the simplified system to those of the original system consisting of (4.45), (4.46), and (4.47). First, note that (4.50) gives the relationship between q, l and k. Since the initial value of k $(= K/H)$ is predetermined, (4.50) implies that the initial levels of q and l cannot be freely selected. For example, if the steady state of (4.51) and (4.52) where $\dot{q} = \dot{l} = 0$ is a source, then the original system is totally unstable. This is because, in view of (4.50), there is no way to select the initial values of q and l at their steady state levels simultaneously, unless the initial value of k happen to be its steady-state level, $\bar{k}$. If (4.51) and (4.52) exhibit a saddle-point property, there (at least locally) exists a one-dimensional stable manifold around the steady state. Hence, the relation between q and l on the stable manifold can be expressed as $q = q(l)$. By depicting phase diagrams of (4.51) and (4.52), it is easy to confirm that if the stationary equilibrium is a saddle point, the stable arms have negative slopes. Thus we find that $q'(l) < 0$ (see Figs. 4.7 and 4.8 below). Substituting $q = q(l)$ into (4.50), we obtain

$$k = lq(l)^{\frac{\alpha+\varepsilon}{\alpha+\varepsilon-1}}.$$

Since the right hand side of the above monotonically increases with l, the above relation is invertible, and thus we have

$$l = l(k), \quad l'(k) > 0. \tag{4.55}$$

Using (4.46), (4.47), and (4.55), we obtain a two-dimensional system with respect to x and k. It is easy to confirm that this reduced system has a saddle-point property, which means that the original system exhibits determinacy around the steady state equilibrium.

In contrast, suppose that the steady state of (4.51) and (4.52) is a source, and, hence there is a continuum of converging paths. In this case, unlike (34), the relation between k and l on the converging trajectories is not uniquely determined. This

[4]Ladrón-de-Guevara et al. (1997) show that if labor-leisure choice is allowed in the in the Lucas model, multiple steady states could be obtained even without externalities. However, the Lucas model without externalities is an optimal growth model, and therefore indeterminacy is not the issue in their study.

shows that, under a given initial value of k, a unique converging path cannot be selected in the original system either.

To sum up, if (4.51) and (4.52) involve a feasible steady state and it is a saddle point, then the original system consisting of (4.45), (4.46), and (4.47) satisfies local determinacy. In contrast, if the steady state of (4.51) and (4.52) is asymptotically stable, then (4.45), (4.46), and (4.47) exhibit local indeterminacy.

More precisely, upon inspection of the eigenvalue values of the coefficient matrix of (4.51) and (4.52) linearized around the steady state, we find that signs of the trace and the determinant of the coefficient matrix of the linearized system fulfill the following:

$$\begin{aligned}&\text{sign (trace)}\\&= \text{sign}\left\{\left(1-\beta_2-\frac{\beta_2(\alpha+\varepsilon-1)}{\alpha+\varepsilon}\right)l^*+\frac{\beta_2(\alpha+\varepsilon-1)}{\alpha+\varepsilon}+\frac{\rho+(1-\alpha)\delta}{\alpha}\right\},\\&\text{sign (det)} = \text{sign}\left\{\beta_2-\alpha+\frac{\alpha\gamma\beta_2}{\rho+(1-\alpha)\delta}(2l^*-1)\right\}.\end{aligned}$$

Therefore, the coefficient matrix has two stable eigenvalues if and only if the following conditions hold:

$$\left(1-\beta_2-\frac{\beta_2(\alpha+\varepsilon-1)}{\alpha+\varepsilon}\right)l^*+\frac{\beta_2(\alpha+\varepsilon-1)}{\alpha+\varepsilon}+\frac{\rho+(1-\alpha)\delta}{\alpha}<0, \tag{4.56}$$

$$\beta_2-\alpha+\frac{\alpha\gamma\beta_2}{\rho+(1-\alpha)\delta}(2l^*-1)>0. \tag{4.57}$$

On the other hand, if

$$\beta_2-\alpha+\frac{\alpha\gamma\beta_2}{\rho+(1-\alpha)\delta}(2l^*-1)<0, \tag{4.58}$$

then the coefficient matrix involves one positive and one negative eigenvalues. As a consequence, we have obtained the following outcomes:

Proposition 4.2 *Suppose that $\sigma = \alpha$ and $\theta = 1$. Then, the balanced-growth equilibrium is locally determinate if and only if* (4.58) *is satisfied, while it is locally indeterminate if and only if* (4.56) *and* (4.57) *hold.*

Using the same examples shown in Sect. 3.3, when $\alpha = \sigma = 0.3$, $\beta_2 = 0.7$, $\rho = 0.03$, $\delta = 0.04$, and $\gamma = 0.2$, in the unique balanced-growth equilibrium, we find that (4.56) and (4.57) hold. Thus, the balanced-growth path is locally indeterminate. In the presence of dual balanced-growth equilibria that hold when $\alpha = \sigma = 0.3$, $\beta_2 = 0.6$, $\rho = 0.03, \delta = 0.04$, and $\gamma = 0.15$, it is shown that the balanced-growth path with a lower l satisfies (4.58), while that with a higher l fulfils (4.56) and (4.57). Hence, the steady state with a higher growth rate is locally determinate, but the other steady state with a lower growth rate exhibits local indeterminacy

4.3.6 Global Dynamics

Since interesting global dynamics can be shown in the case of dual balanced-growth equilibria, in what follows, we assume that the dynamic system consisting of (4.51) and (4.52) has two steady states.[5] In the presence of dual steady states, we find he following:

Proposition 4.3 *If the system has dual steady states, it holds that (i) the steady state with a higher growth rate is locally determinate and (ii) the steady state with a lower growth rate is locally intermediate if* (4.56) *and* (4.57) *are satisfied, while it is totally unstable if* (4.57) *holds but* (4.56) *does not.*

It is easy to confirm the above proposition by depicting the phase diagrams of (4.51) and (4.52). Figure 4.8a, b display typical phase diagrams when there are dual steady state equilibria. First, we should confirm that in these figures, the stationary point with a lower l and higher q (point E_1 in the figures) attains higher growth rate. To see this, first note that from (4.55) the steady state level of k increases with l. On the other hand (4.49) presents

$$v^* = \frac{x^*}{k^*} = \lambda^{\frac{1}{\alpha+\varepsilon}} \left(\frac{\alpha + (1-\alpha)\,\delta}{\alpha} \right)^{-\frac{1}{\alpha+\varepsilon}} k^* q^{*\frac{1}{\alpha+\varepsilon}-1}.$$

Since $0 < \alpha + \varepsilon < 1$, the above means that a lower l^* and a higher q^* yield a lower v^*. As a result, the balanced-growth rate, $g = \gamma\,(1 - l^* - v^*) - \delta$, attained at equilibrium E_1 is higher than that at E_2 which associates with a higher l and lower q. We see that (4.58) holds at E_1 and that (4.57) is satisfied at E_2. In addition, E_2 is a sink under (4.56) and is a source if (4.56) does not hold.

In Fig. 4.8a, the steady state with a lower growth rate is a sink, so that there is a continuum of equilibrium paths converging to E_2. On the other hand, since E_1 is a saddle point, there are two converging paths toward E_1. Given the initial level of capital ratio, k_0, the economy's initial position is on the dotted line that expresses equation (4.50). Hence, the initial levels of l and q are uniquely determined on the converging saddle path (point A in the figure). If the economy starts from point A, it converges monotonically toward E_1. During the transition, l decreases and q increases monotonically. However, this is only a sample of possible equilibrium paths in this economy. In fact, since E_2 is a sink,any path stating between Point A and B can converges to E_2. Moreover, it is seen that any path stating within the shaded area will coverage either to point E_1 or to point E_2. Therefore, this system holds global indeterminacy.

Figure 4.8b illustrates the case in which the low-growth steady state is a source, so that the steady state E_2 is locally determinate: unless the initial position is E_2 itself, any trajectory around E_2 will diverge. We should note that any path

[5] Xie (1994) also conducted transitional analysis of the Lucas model with multiple equilibria. Since his model involves a unique steady state, the patterns of dynamics are simpler than in our model.

Fig. 4.8 (**a**) Pattern of dynamics (I). (**b**) Pattern of dynamics (II)

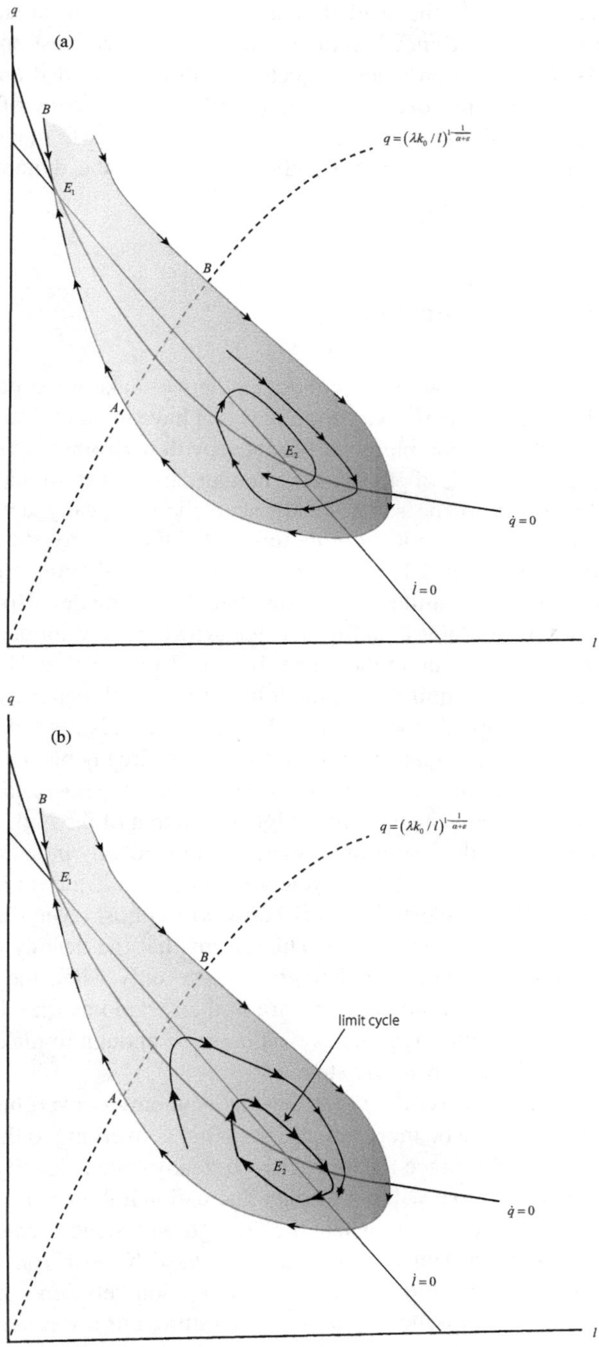

starting inside the shaded area will remain in this area. Consequently, in view of the Poincaré-Bendixson theorem, there exists at least one stable limit cycle around E_2. In other words, any trajectory within the shaded area eventually converges to the stable limit cycle. This indicates that the destiny of the economy is either the balanced-growth equilibrium with a higher growth rate or the cyclical growth path around the low-growth steady state. Again, the dynamic system displays global indeterminacy.

4.3.7 Implications

The graphical analyses conducted above make three points. First, when there are dual steady states, two economies that have the identical technology and preference may display completely different growth performances even though they start with the same levels of physical and human capital. Additionally, even when the economy converges to the same steady state that is locally determinate, the convergence trajectory may not be monotonic. If the economy starts from a position such as Point A in Fig. 4.1, the economy monotonically converges to the balanced-growth equilibrium, similar to the standard Lucas model. However, when the economy starts from Point C in Fig. 4.1, the growth rate of human capital first decreases and then increases up to the higher balanced-growth rate. Hence, when we focus on the determinate equilibrium, the long-term growth pattern would depend on the initial level of capital stocks. It is to be noted that this type of non-monotonic converging behavior of human capital formation has already been pointed out by Xie (1994).

Second, in the case of dual steady states, the possibility of realization of the low-growth steady state is much higher than that of the high-growth steady state. This is because, if the low-growth steady state is locally indeterminate (or locally unstable but there exists a stable cycle around it) and if the initial position of the economy is randomly selected, the economy will almost always converge to the steady state with a lower growth rate. This means that the destiny of the economy can be the steady state with a higher growth rate only when the economic agents share an optimistic view about the future of their economy. In other words, the conventional growth-promoting policies would not be enough to make the economy converge to the high-growth steady state.

Third, our result shows that the economy converging to the low-growth steady state tends to be more volatile than that converging to the steady state with a higher growth rate. Since the high-growth steady state is locally determinate, the economy converging to it will not display fluctuation if there is no fundamental, technological shock. In contrast, when the low-growth steady state is locally indeterminate, we may find sunspot fluctuations caused by extrinsic uncertainty that affects the agents' expectations. Although the relation between volatility and growth is still a controversial issue in empirical literature, our discussion suggests that the relation between growth and volatility would not be examined properly if the researchers presume that fundamental shocks are the only sources of economic fluctuations.

In his well cited paper on the growth miracle of East Asian countries, Lucas (1993) stated that the multiplicity of equilibrium may present a useful insight as to why countries with similar economic conditions display diverse growth performances in the long run. As a typical example, he referred to the comparative growth performances of South Korea and the Philippines. In the early 1960s, per capita income of both these countries was about the same. In addition, they shared many common features such as population size, degree of urbanization, rates of school enrollment, and the like. After three decades, per capita income of South Korea became more than three times as large as that of the Philippines. If we stick to the idea that the economies with the same economic conditions must follow the same growth process, we should seek more fundamental differences between South Korea and the Philippines that the economic theory usually dismisses, that is, the differences in political stability, religion, climate, social atmosphere, and so on. In contrast, if we consider the possibility of multiple equilibria, we may explain the reason for income divergence without considering these non-economic conditions. Obviously, we cannot claim that divergence of per capita income between South Korea and the Philippines has been generated by multiplicity of equilibrium alone. However, from the viewpoint of economic theory, it is insightful to use the growth models with multiple steady states and equilibrium indeterminacy when we explore the reasons why some East Asian countries have achieved excellent growth performances but counties in South East Asia with similar economic fundamentals have shown relatively poor growth performances.

4.4 References and Related Studies

Section 4.1 is based on Krugman (1991). Fukao and Benabou (1993) point out that Krugman's phase diagram analysis is not precise and that the region where expectations matter is smaller than that shown in the original article. Figure 4.2 follows Fukao and Benabou (1993). Matsuyama (1991) also studies a two-sector model similar to Krugman (1991). He presents a mathematically sophisticated analysis. Herrendorf and Walldman (2000) introduce agent heterogeneity into Matsuyama's (1991) model, and reveal that sufficient level of heterogeneity may exclude equilibrium indeterminacy. Frankel and Pauzner (2000) also re-examine the Matsuyama model. They show that introducing exogenous shocks to the model may pin down a unique equilibrium.

The concept of threshold externalities is introduced by Azariadis and Drazen. These authors study an overlapping generations model of endogenous growth where threshold external effects are associated with human capital formation. The neoclassical growth model with threshold externalities in Sect. 4.2 follows Futagami and Mino (1993). Futagami and Mino (1995) examine an endogenous growth model in which public capital gives rise to threshold externalities. They investigate global dynamics of the model economy in detail.

The two-sector endogenous growth model in Sect. 4.3 is based on Mino (2008). Greiner and Semmler (1995, 1996), Mattana et al. (2009), and Bella and Mattana (2014) also conduct global analysis of a Lucas-type two sector endogenous growth model in which the presence of externalities in the education sector yields multiple balanced-growth paths.

Chapter 5
Stabilization Effects of Policy Rules

The stabilization effects of fiscal and monetary policy in the context of dynamic macroeconomic models with rational expectations differ from the effects in traditional Keynesian models. In the rational expectations setting, if a policy rule eliminates multiplicity of equilibrium, that policy stabilizes the economy in the sense that it excludes sunspot-driven business fluctuations. Conversely, if a policy rule gives rise to equilibrium indeterminacy, that policy destabilizes the economy. Roughly speaking, if a policy rule stabilizes a Keynesian model with backward-looking expectations, the same policy often generates indeterminacy in the equilibrium models with rational expectations.

This chapter explores when and why fiscal and monetary policy rules generate equilibrium indeterminacy. We first consider fiscal rules in the real business cycle (RBC) model. We then introduce a monetary policy rule into the base model and examine the interactions of fiscal and monetary actions of the government. In addition, we consider the stabilization effects of fiscal and monetary policy rules in the context of endogenous growth models.

5.1 Fiscal Policy Rules in Real Business Cycle Models

In this section we focus on the two fiscal policy rules that have been frequently discussed in the literature on fiscal rules and equilibrium indeterminacy.

5.1.1 Balanced Budget Rule

Schmitt-Grohé and Uribe (1997) point out that distortionary taxation combined with the balanced-budget rule of the government may generate indeterminacy

K. Mino, *Growth and Business Cycles with Equilibrium Indeterminacy*,
Advances in Japanese Business and Economics 13,
DOI 10.1007/978-4-431-55609-1_5

in the standard RBC model. We first summarize their discussion. As usual, the representative household solves

$$\max \int_0^\infty e^{-\rho t} \left(\log C - B \frac{N^{1+\gamma}}{1+\gamma} \right) dt, \quad \rho > 0, \quad \gamma > 0, \quad B > 0$$

subject to

$$\dot{K} = rK + (1 - \tau) wN - C - \delta K,$$

under a given level of initial capital holding K_0. In the above, τ denotes the rate of tax on wage income. Note that tax is levied on the wage income alone. In the baseline model, (Schmitt-Grohé and Uribe 1997) assume the case of indivisible labor ($\gamma = 0$). Thus, the the optimization selection of the household gives the following conditions:

$$CB = (1 - \tau) w, \tag{5.1}$$

$$\dot{C} = C (r - \rho - \delta), \tag{5.2}$$

together with the transversality condition: $\lim_{t \to \infty} e^{-\rho t} K_t / C_t = 0$.

The production function is given by a Cobb-Douglas function that exhibits constant returns to scale as follows:

$$Y = AK^a N^{1-a}, \quad 0 < a < 1. \tag{5.3}$$

Hence, the competitive rate of return to capital and real wage rate are respectively given by

$$r = aK^{a-1} N^{1-a} = \alpha \frac{Y}{K}, \tag{5.4}$$

$$w = (1 - a) K^a N^{-a} = (1 - \alpha) \frac{Y}{N}. \tag{5.5}$$

5.1.1.1 A Fixed Government Expenditure

The government consumes a fixed amount of output, G, by financing tax revenue. The flow budget constraint is thus given by

$$G = \tau wN = \tau (1 - a) Y. \tag{5.6}$$

Finally, the market equilibrium condition for final goods is

$$Y = C + \dot{K} + \delta K + G. \tag{5.7}$$

Using (5.3), (5.4), and (5.5), we obtain dynamic equations of K and C as follows:

$$\dot{K} = [1 - (1 - \alpha)\,\tau]\,AK^{\alpha}N^{1-\alpha} - C - \delta K, \tag{5.8}$$

$$\dot{C} = C\left(\alpha AK^{\alpha-1}N^{1-\alpha} - \rho - \delta\right). \tag{5.9}$$

Here, the equilibrium level of hours worked is determined by

$$CB = (1 - \tau)(1 - \alpha)\,AK^{\alpha}N^{-\alpha}. \tag{5.10}$$

In addition, from the government budget (5.6), the rate of tax on wage income satisfies

$$\tau = \frac{G}{(1 - \alpha)\,AK^{\alpha}N^{1-\alpha}}. \tag{5.11}$$

In the steady state, K and C stay constant over time. From (5.8), (5.9), and (5.10), we find that the steady state conditions are given by the following:

$$\frac{C}{K} = [1 - (1 - \alpha)\,\tau]\,A\left(\frac{K}{N}\right)^{\alpha-1} - \delta,$$

$$\alpha A\left(\frac{K}{N}\right)^{\alpha-1} = \delta + \rho,$$

$$\frac{C}{K} = \frac{(1 - \tau)(1 - \alpha)}{B}A\left(\frac{K}{N}\right)^{\alpha}\frac{1}{K}.$$

Combining the above equations leads to

$$\frac{(1 - \tau)(1 - \alpha)}{B}A\left(\frac{\rho + \delta}{\alpha A}\right)^{\alpha}\frac{1}{K} = [1 - (1 - \alpha)\,\tau]\,A\left(\frac{\rho + \delta}{\alpha A}\right)^{\alpha-1} - \delta. \tag{5.12}$$

Equation (5.12) means that the steady state level of capital is expressed as $K^* = K(\tau)$ with $K'(\tau) < 0$. Therefore, the relation between the government's tax revenue in the steady state is expressed as

$$\tau wN = (1 - \alpha)\,\frac{\rho + \delta}{\alpha}\tau K(\tau).$$

Obviously, the tax revenue is zero if either $\tau = 0$ or $\tau = 1$. It is also confirmed that $\tau K(\tau)$ attains its maximum for $\tau \in [0, 1]$. Thus, the steady state relation between G and τ exhibits a Laffer curve.

In their dynamic analysis, Schmitt-Grohé and Uribe (1997) assume that the government fixes G and adjusts τ to balance its flow budget out of the steady state. Hence, τ is adjusted according to

$$\hat{G} = \left(\frac{1}{\alpha} - 1\right)(\rho + \delta)\,\tau K(\tau),$$

where $\hat{G}$ is a fixed level of the government's spending. Then, (5.10) becomes

$$CB = (1-\alpha)\left(AK^{\alpha}N^{-\alpha} - \frac{\hat{G}}{N}\right). \tag{5.13}$$

As usual, the left hand side of (5.13) represents the Frisch labor supply curve and the right hand side is the labor demand schedule. Under a sufficiently large level of $\hat{G}$, the labor demand curve may have a positive slope. This means that the fiscal rule adopted here plays the same role the external increasing returns play in the Benhabib-Farmer model.

As shown above, the government's tax revenue is an inversely U-shaped function of τ. Therefore, under a given level of G, there are two levels of τ $(= \tau_1,\ \tau_2)$ in the steady state that establish the following condition:

$$\hat{G} = (1-\alpha)\frac{\rho+\delta}{\alpha}\tau_1 K(\tau_1) = (1-\alpha)\frac{\rho+\delta}{\alpha}\tau_2 K(\tau_2).$$

If $\tau_2 > \tau_1$, then it holds that $0 < \tau_1 < \tau_{\max} < \tau_2 < 1$, where $\tau_{\max}$ is the tax rate that attaints the maximum level of the government's revenue.

Consolidation (5.13) states that the equilibrium level of hours worked is expressed as

$$N = N\left(K, C; \hat{G}\right),$$

As a result, a complete dynamic system under a fixed government spending is given by the following:

$$\dot{K} = [1 - (1-\alpha)\,\tau]\,AK^{\alpha}N\left(K, C; \hat{G}\right)^{1-\alpha} - C - \delta K,$$

$$\dot{C} = C\left[\alpha AK^{\alpha-1}N\left(K, C; \hat{G}\right)^{1-\alpha} - \rho - \delta\right].$$

Schmitt-Grohé and Uribe (1997) analyze log-linearized system of the above evaluated at each steady state. In this base line model the main conclusion is as follows. In the steady state with $\tau = \tau_1$, local indeterminacy holds if $\alpha < \tau_1 < \tau_{\max}$, In contrast, if the steady state tax rate is $\tau_2 \in [\tau_{\max}, 1]$, then the steady state is locally determinate. In a calibrated version of the model with $\alpha = 0.35$, it turns out that

$\tau_{\max} > 0.5$. Moreover, the average rate of labor income tax in the United States and other European countries ranges from 0.25 to 0.45. Consequently, there is relatively high possibility that the model economy with plausible values of parameters and tax rates tends to display indeterminacy under the balanced-budget rule.

The intuition behind this finding is rather obvious. Remember that the government revenue is positively related to the rate of tax when τ is close to τ_1 and it is negatively related to the tax rate when τ is close to τ_2. Now, suppose that the economy stays at the steady state and a positive sunspot shock hits the economy, which makes the household anticipate that their future income will increase. Then, if the labor demand curve in (5.13) slopes upward, a rise in consumption due to the income effect raises hours worked so that the current income rises. If the steady state is realized under $\tau = \tau_1$, then the economy stays on the positive side of the Laffer curve, meaning that a higher output reduces the tax rate to finance a given $\hat{G}$. This accelerates capital accumulation, and, hence, the initial expectation will be self-fulfilled. On the other hand, if the steady state is realized under $\tau = \tau_2$, the economy stays on the negative side of the Laffer curve. Therefore, a rise in income caused by the positive sunspot shock increases the tax rate to keep $G = \hat{G}$. This reduces the future income of households, so that their initial expectations are not self-fulfilled. Hence, equilibrium indeterminacy never arises.

5.1.1.2 A Fixed Tax Rate

It is to be noted that in the baseline model, in addition to the balanced-budget rule, fixing the government expenditure is a source of indeterminacy. To confirm this, according to Guo and Harrison (2004), suppose that the government fixes $\tau = \tau_0$ and adjusts G to fulfill (5.11) during the transition. Then, the dynamic system becomes

$$\dot{K} = [1 - \tau(1-\alpha)] AK^{\alpha}N^{1-\alpha} - C - \delta K,$$
$$\dot{C} = C\left[\alpha AK^{\alpha-1}N^{1-\alpha} - \rho - \delta\right].$$

where N satisfies

$$N = \left[\frac{(1-\alpha)(1-\tau)}{B}\right]^{-\alpha} K.$$

Since the technology exhibits constant returns to scale, this system will not generate indeterminacy under a given rate of τ. Therefore, the indeterminacy outcome under the balanced-budget rule hinges on the rule of the adjustment of the policy variable as well.

5.1.1.3 Generalized Rules

In the generalized model wherein distortionary taxes are levied on both capital income and wage income, the flow budget constraint for the household becomes

$$\dot{K} = (1 - \tau_k)(r - \delta) K + (1 - \tau_w) wN - C,$$

where τ_k denotes the rate of tax on capital income. The government's budget is replaced by

$$G = \tau_k (r - \delta) K + \tau_w wN.$$

In this formulation, we have four alternative policy schemes:

(i) τ_k and τ_w are fixed, while G is endogenously determined.
(ii) τ_k is endogenous, while G and τ_w are fixed.
(iii) τ_w is endogenous, while G and τ_k are fixed.
(iv) τ_k and τ_w are endogenous, while G depends on Y : for example, $G = \theta Y \ (0 < \theta < 1)$.

It is obvious that case (i) will not yield indeterminacy. Schmitt-Grohé and Uribe (1997) explore the indeterminacy conditions for cases (ii), (iii), and (iv). They found that regardless of the policy regime, the balanced-budget rule may generate indeterminacy rather easily under the specified parameter values that are plausible for the US economy. Ever since Schmitt-Grohé and Uribe's contribution, many authors have studied the role of balanced budget rules under alternative settings. We briefly mention those investigations in the last section of this chapter.

5.1.1.4 Consumption Tax

Based on Giannitsarou (2007), we now assume that the government expenditure is financed by consumption tax alone. The flow budget constraints for the representative household and the government are respectively replaced with

$$\dot{K} = (r - \delta)K + wN - (1 + \tau_c) C,$$
$$G = \tau_c C, \tag{5.14}$$

where τ_c stands for the rate of consumption tax. In this policy regime, the household's optimal choice condition (5.1) is expressed as

$$CN^{\gamma} = \frac{(1 - \alpha)}{1 + \tau_c} AK^{a} N^{-a}. \tag{5.15}$$

Since taxation does not distort the modified golden-rule condition, the steady state level of the capital-labor ratio is determined by

$$\rho + \delta = r = aA \left(\frac{K}{N} \right)^{a-1}. \tag{5.16}$$

Therefore, from (5.15) and (5.16) the steady state level of consumption is

$$C = \frac{1-a}{a(1+\tau_c)(\rho+\delta)},$$

implying that the government's flow budget (5.14) yields

$$G = \frac{\tau_c (1-a)}{a(1+\tau_c)(\rho+\delta)}.$$

Since the right hand side of the above monotonically increases with τ_c, the steady state level of τ_c is uniquely determined under a given level of G. Thus, as opposed to the case of labor income taxation, the steady state equilibrium under consumption tax is uniquely given. In addition, it is easy to confirm that the unique steady state satisfies local saddle stability, so that indeterminacy will not arise if a fixed government spending is fully financed by consumption tax.[1]

5.1.2 *Nonlinear Taxation*

5.1.2.1 The Guo and Lansing Formulation

Guo and Lansing (1998) introduce a nonlinear tax schedule into the standard one-sector RBC model. The production function is given by (5.3). The optimization problem for the representative household is

$$\max \int_0^\infty e^{-\rho t} \left(\log C - \frac{N^{1+\gamma}}{1+\gamma} \right) dt$$

[1]Giannitsarou (2007) also analyzes an alternative policy rule under which the government consumption is finacced by consumption tax as well as by income tax, thereby, the government budget constraint is

$$G = \tau_c C + \tau_y Y.$$

Giannitsarou (2007) numerically shows that in this policy regime, indeterminacy may arise, but the parameter space generating indeterminacy is smaller than the case with labor-income taxation.

We should note that the above outcome depends on the assumption that the instantaneous utility function is additively separable between consumption and labor. Bambi and Venditti (2016) assume that the representative household has a general, non-separable utility function. They reveal that balancing the government budget by adjusting consumption tax may yield indeterminacy.

subject to

$$\dot{K} = (1 - \tau)(rK + wN) - C - \delta K,$$

where τ is the rate of income tax.

Guo and Lansing (1998) set the taxation rule in such a way that

$$\tau = 1 - \eta \left(\frac{Y^*}{Y} \right)^{\phi}, \quad 0 < \eta < 1, \quad \frac{\alpha - 1}{\alpha} < \phi, \tag{5.17}$$

where Y^* denotes the steady state level of aggregate income. This is an ingenious formulation, because in the steady state the rate of tax becomes a flat rate of $1 - \eta$, so that it is easy to evaluate the tax rate in the steady state equilibrium. Out of the steady state, the rate of tax increases with the actual income. Here, the marginal rate of tax is

$$\frac{d(\tau Y)}{dY} = \tau + \frac{d\tau}{dY} Y = \tau + \eta\phi \left(\frac{Y^*}{Y} \right)^{\phi}.$$

Remember that a tax schedule is progressive (regressive), if the marginal tax revenue is higher (lower) than the average tax revenue. In the above formulation, it holds that

$$\frac{d(\tau Y)}{dY} > (<) \frac{\tau Y}{Y} = \tau \Leftrightarrow \phi > 0 \ (\phi < 0).$$

This means that the taxation is progressive (regressive) if $\phi > 0$ ($\phi < 0$).

Given the above tax schedule, the household's optimal selection of C and N yields

$$CN^{\gamma} = \eta (1 - \phi)(1 - \phi) \left(\frac{Y^*}{Y} \right)^{\phi} (1 - \alpha) \frac{Y}{N}.$$

From (5.3), this condition is rewritten as

$$CN^{\gamma} = \eta (1 - \phi)(1 - \alpha) Y^{*\phi} A K^{\alpha(1-\phi)} N^{(1-\alpha)(1-\phi)-1}. \tag{5.18}$$

Again, the left hand side of the above represents the Frisch labor supply curve, and the right hand side corresponds to the labor demand curve. Since the necessary condition for local indeterminacy in the one-sector RBC model is that the labor demand curve is positively sloped and steeper than the labor demand curve, the presence of equilibrium indeterminacy requires that

$$(1 - \alpha)(1 - \phi) > \gamma + 1.$$

Therefore, unless the taxation schedule is sufficiently regressive to hold $\phi < -\frac{1+\gamma}{1-\alpha}$, the necessary condition for indeterminacy is not fulfilled.

If the production technology is associated with external effects, so that the social production function is $Y = AK^{\alpha}N^{\beta},\ \ \alpha + \beta > 1$, then the necessary condition for indeterminacy is

$$\beta (1 - \phi) > \gamma + 1.$$

The above shows that even if β is sufficiently large, progressive taxation reduces the possibility of equilibrium indeterminacy. Therefore, as far as the one-sector model is concerned, progressive taxation acts as a built-in stabilizer in the sense that it may eliminate sunspot-driven business fluctuations.

5.1.2.2 Productive Government Spending

The model discussed above assumes that the government consumes its tax revenue. Chen and Guo (2013) modify the base model by assuming that the government conducts public investment that contributes to enhancing private production. In their formulation, the aggregate production function is given by

$$Y = AK^{\alpha}N^{1-a}G^{\theta},\ \ 0 < \theta < 1. \tag{5.19}$$

Here, private firms take the government spending, G, as an external effect, and the social production function exhibits increasing returns to scale with respect to the capital, labor, and public spending. Since the government budget constraint is $G = \tau Y$, the reduced form of production function is written as

$$Y = A^{\frac{1}{1-\theta}} K^{\frac{\alpha}{1-\theta}} N^{\frac{1-\alpha}{1-\theta}} \tau^{\frac{\theta}{1-\theta}}. \tag{5.20}$$

Since the taxation rule follows (5.17), the government budget constraint is

$$G = \left[1 - \eta \left(\frac{Y^*}{Y}\right)^{\phi}\right] Y.$$

Thus, (5.18) is rewritten as

$$CN^{\gamma} = \eta (1 - \phi) \left(\frac{Y^*}{Y}\right)^{\phi} w = \eta(1 - \phi)(1 - \alpha) Y^{*\phi} Y^{1-\phi} \frac{1}{N}.$$

Substituting (5.20) into the right hand side of the above, we obtain

$$CN^{\gamma} = \eta(1 - \phi)(1 - \alpha) A^{\frac{1-\phi}{1-\theta}} K^{\frac{\alpha(1-g)}{1-\theta}} N^{\frac{(1-\alpha)(1-\phi)}{1-\theta} - 1} \tau^{\frac{\theta(1-\phi)}{1-\theta}}. \tag{5.21}$$

Equation (5.21) shows that if $(1-\alpha)(1-\phi)/(1-\theta) > 1$, the labor demand represented by the right hand side of (5.21) slopes upward with respect to N under a given tax rate, τ. Although a rise in N raises τ due to an increase in the aggregate income, its impact is relatively small if $\theta(1-\phi)/(1-\theta)$ is small. Hence, if the government spending enhances the aggregate productivity of private technology, equilibrium indeterminacy may hold even under the progressive taxation.

5.1.2.3 Utility Generating Government Spending

Alternatively, we may assume that public service increases the felicity of the representative household. Chen and Guo (2014) assumed that the objective function of the household is

$$U = \int_0^{\infty} e^{-\rho t} \left[\frac{\left(C^{\theta} G^{\theta_2}\right)^{1-\sigma}}{1-\sigma} - \frac{N^{1+\gamma}}{1+\gamma} \right] dt, \quad \theta_1, \theta_2 > 0.$$

Again, the household maximizes U subject to the flow budget constraint and a given sequence of $\{G_t\}_{t=0}^{\infty}$. For simplicity, we ignore the productive government spending and thus the production function is (5.3).

In this model, the household's optimization conditions yield

$$\theta C^{1-\theta_1(1-\sigma)} G^{\theta_2(\sigma-1)} N^{\gamma} = \eta (1-\phi) \left(\frac{Y^*}{Y}\right)^{\phi} w,$$

which leads to

$$\theta C^{1-\theta(1-\sigma)} \left[Y - \eta Y^{*\phi} Y^{1-\phi} \right]^{\theta_2(1-\sigma)} N^{\gamma} = \eta (1-\phi) \left(\frac{Y^*}{Y}\right)^{\phi} \alpha \frac{Y}{N}. \tag{5.22}$$

Equation (5.22) demonstrates that the Frisch labor supply curve represented by the left hand side may slope downward if private consumption and public services are Edgeworth complement, that is, $\sigma < 1$. In this case, a rise in Y caused by an increase in N reduces G. If this effect is large enough to offset a rise in the private marginal disutility of labor, N^{γ}, then the Frisch labor supply curve has a negative slope. Hence, the situation becomes similar to the model in Sect. 2.4.2 of Chap. 2, so that equilibrium may emerge. In contrast, it is easy to see that if private consumption and public services are Edgeworth substitutes ($\sigma > 1$), the negative effect of a decrease in G will not hold, so that equilibrium indeterminacy cannot emerge.

5.2 Interaction Between Fiscal and Monetary Policies

Along with fiscal policy rules, the stabilization effect of the monetary policy rule has been discussed extensively. In Sect. 1.3 of Chap. 1, we refer to a simple model of monetary economy with an interest control rule and show that the policy scheme may play a critical role in establishing determinacy of equilibrium. Our discussion has suggested that if fiscal and monetary policy rules are appropriately selected, the economy can be free from sunspot-driven business fluctuations. However, since the mainstream literature investigates the stabilization effects of fiscal and monetary policy rules separately, it is rather unclear whether or not these rules strengthen their stabilizing effects with one another if the fiscal authority and central bank adopt specific actions simultaneously.

In this section, we introduce the taxation schedule discussed in the previous section into a monetary business cycle model in which the monetary authority follows an interest-rate control rule. Our main concern in this section is to examine how the interaction between monetary and fiscal policy rules may generate equilibrium indeterminacy.

5.2.1 Model

5.2.1.1 Households

We consider a monetary version of the baseline RBC model. There is a continuum of identical, infinitely lived households with a unit mass. The flow budget constraint for the household is

$$\dot{M} = (1 - \tau)\, py + pT - pc - pv,$$

where M is the nominal stocks of money, p is the price level, y is the real income per capita, c is the real consumption, v is the gross investment for capital, τ is the rate of factor income tax, and T is the real transfer from the government (or lump-sum tax if it has a negative value). Since we have normalized the number of household to unity, M, y, T. c and v represent their aggregate values as well. The real income consists of rent from capital and wage revenue as follows:

$$y = rk + wN,$$

where r is the real rate of return to capital, w is the real wage rate and N is the labor supply. Denoting real money balances as $m \equiv M/p$ and the rate if inflation as $\pi \equiv \dot{p}/p$, we rewrite the household's flow budget constraint as

$$\dot{m} = (1 - \tau)\,(rk + wN) + T - c - v - \pi m. \tag{5.23}$$

The stock of capital changes according to

$$\dot{k} = v - \delta k, \tag{5.24}$$

where $\delta \in (0, 1)$ denotes the rate of capital depreciation. In addition, a cash-in-advance constraint applies to consumption spending, so that $pc \leq M$ or

$$c \leq m \tag{5.25}$$

at each moment of time. In this model we assume that investment spending is not subject to the cash-in-advance constraint.

The instantaneous utility of the representative family depends on consumption and labor supply. Following the standard specification, we assume that the objective function of the household is

$$U = \int_0^\infty e^{-\rho t} \left(\log c - B \frac{N^{1+\gamma}}{1+\gamma} \right) dt, \quad \gamma > 0, \ \rho > 0, \ B > 0.$$

Given the initial holdings of k_0 and m_0, the household maximizes U subject to (5.23), (5.24), and (5.25) under given sequences of $\{r_t, w_t, \tau_t, T_t\}_{t=0}^{\infty}$.

To derive the optimization conditions for the household, we set up the current-value Hamiltonian function in the following manner:

$$\begin{aligned}\mathcal{H} = &\log c - B \frac{l^{1+\gamma}}{1+\gamma} + \lambda \left[(1-\tau)(rk + wN) + T - c - v - \pi m \right] \\ &+ \mu (v - \delta k) + \zeta (m - c),\end{aligned}$$

where λ and μ respectively denote the costate variables of m and k, and ζ is a Lagrange multiplier corresponding to the cash-in-advance constraint on consumption spending. In what follows, we assume that the rate of tax, τ, depends on the level of individual income. The rate of income tax is thus given by

$$\tau = \tau(y) = \tau(rk + wN).$$

Considering such a taxation rule, we find that the necessary conditions for an optimum involve the following:

$$\partial \mathcal{H} / \partial c = 1/c - (\lambda + \zeta) = 0, \tag{5.26a}$$

$$\partial \mathcal{H} / \partial l = -BN^{\gamma} + \lambda \left[1 - \tau(y) - \tau'(y) y \right] w = 0, \tag{5.26b}$$

$$\partial \mathcal{H} / \partial v = -\lambda + \mu = 0, \tag{5.26c}$$

$$\zeta (m - c) = 0, \quad m - c \geq 0, \quad \zeta \geq 0, \tag{5.26d}$$

$$\dot{\lambda} = \lambda (\rho + \pi) - \zeta, \tag{5.26e}$$

$$\dot{\mu} = (\rho + \delta) \mu - \lambda \left[1 - \tau(y) - \tau'(y) y) \right] r, \tag{5.26f}$$

together with the transversality conditions, $\lim_{t\to\infty} b_t\lambda_t e^{-\rho t} = 0$ and $\lim_{t\to\infty} m_t\mu_t e^{-\rho t} = 0$, as well as the initial conditions on m and k. In conditions (5.26b) and (5.26f), $\tau(y) + \tau'(y)y$ represents the marginal tax rate perceived by the household. As in Guo and Lansing (1998), we assume that each household takes the proportional tax rule into account when deciding its optimal consumption plan.

In what follows, we focus on the situation in which the cash-in-advance constraint is always effective, so that $c = m$ holds for all $t \geq 0$. First, (5.26c) means that $\mu = \lambda$, so that from (5.26e) and (5.26f) we obtain

$$\zeta = \lambda\left\{\left[1 - \tau(y) - \tau'(y)y\right]r + \pi\right\}. \tag{5.27}$$

Thus (5.26a) is written as

$$\frac{1}{c} = \lambda\left\{1 + \left[1 - \tau(y) - \tau'(y)y\right]r + \pi - \delta\right\}. \tag{5.28}$$

Then, (5.26b) and (5.28) yield:

$$cl^{\gamma}B = \frac{\left[1 - \tau(y) - \tau'(y)y\right]w}{1 + \left[1 - \tau(y) - \tau'(y)y\right]r + \pi}. \tag{5.29}$$

The left hand side of the above is the marginal rate of substitution between consumption and the labor, and the right hand side expresses the effective, after-tax rate of real wage rate. Since we assume that the cash-in-advance constraint always binds, an additional consumption generates an additional opportunity cost of holding money, which is given by the after-tax, net rate of return to capital plus the rate of inflation. Thus the right hand side of (5.29) expresses the real wage rate in terms of the effective price including the cost of money holding.

5.2.1.2 Firms

The production side of the model economy follows the standard formulation. There are identical, infinite number of firms, and the total number of firms is normalized to one. The production function of an individual firms is given by

$$y = Ak^{\alpha}N^{1-\alpha}, \quad 0 < \alpha < 1, \quad A > 0. \tag{5.30}$$

In a competitive economy, α represents the income share of capital. We focus on the case where α has an empirically plausible value, so that in what follows, we assume that α is less than 0.5. The commodity market is assumed to be competitive and thus the rate of return to capital and the real wage equal the marginal products of capital and labor, respectively:

$$r = \alpha Akf^{\alpha-1}N^{1-\alpha} = \alpha\frac{y}{k}, \tag{5.31}$$

$$w = (1-\alpha)\,Ak^{\alpha}N^{-\alpha} = (1-\alpha)\,\frac{y}{N}. \tag{5.32}$$

5.2.1.3 Policy Rules

The fiscal and monetary authorities respectively control the rate of income tax, τ, and the nominal interest rate, R, according to their own policy rules. As assumed by Schmitt-Grohé and Uribe (1997) and Guo and Lansing (1998), the fiscal authority follows the balanced-budget discipline. To emphasize this assumption, we assume away government debt. The flow budget constraint for the government is thus given by

$$\tau y + \dot{m} + \pi m = g + T,$$

where g denotes the government's consumption spending. Here, we assume that under the balanced-budget rule the fiscal authority cannot use seigniorage income to finance the government consumption.[2] This means that

$$g = \tau y \tag{5.33}$$

holds in each moment. As a consequence, the real seigniorage income, $\dot{M}/p$, is transferred back to the households, so that $\dot{m} + \pi m = T$.

Given the general principle mentioned above, the monetary authority is assumed to follow an interest-rate control rule such that

$$R(\pi) = \pi + r^{*}\left(\frac{\pi}{\pi^{*}}\right)^{\mu}, \quad r^{*} > 0, \ \ \pi^{*} \geq 0, \tag{5.34}$$

where $r^{*} > 0$ is the steady state level of net rate of return to capital and π^{*} expresses the target rate of inflation. We assume that the target rate of inflation is positive so that π^{*} is a positive constant set by the monetary authority. Under given r^{*} and π^{*}, we see that $R'(\pi) > 1$ ($R'(\pi) < 1$) according to $\mu > 0$ ($\mu < 0$). Hence, if $\mu > 0$, then the monetary authority adopts an active control rule under which it adjusts the nominal interest rate more than one-for-one with inflation. Conversely, when $\mu < 0$, the interest rate control is passive in the sense that the monetary authority changes the nominal interest rate less than one-for-one with inflation. When $\mu = 0$, the monetary authority controls the nominal interest rate to keep the real interest rate at

[2] Hence, fiscal policy is "passive" in the sense of Leeper (1991).

r^*. Notice that the Fisher equation gives the relation between the nominal and real interest in such a way that

$$R = r + \pi. \tag{5.35}$$

Therefore, (5.34) and (5.35) yield

$$\pi = \left(\frac{r}{r^*}\right)^{\frac{1}{\mu}} \pi^*, \tag{5.36}$$

which gives the relation between the equilibrium rate of inflation and the real rate of return to capital. This means that in our setting the nominal interest rate control is to adjust the rate of inflation tax according to a specified rule.

As for the fiscal rule under balanced-budget, we follow Guo and Lansing (1998), so that taxation schedule is given by

$$\tau(y) = 1 - \eta \left(\frac{y^*}{y}\right)^{\phi}, \quad -\frac{1-\alpha}{\alpha} < \phi < 1, \ 0 < \eta < 1, \tag{5.37}$$

where y^* denotes the steady state level of per capita income.[3]

5.2.1.4 Capital Accumulation

Combining the flow budget constraints for the household and the government yields the commodity-market equilibrium condition: $y = \dot{k} + \delta k + c + g$. Under the first fiscal rule, the government consumption is endogenously determined, and thereby the market equilibrium is written as

$$\dot{k} = (1 - \tau) y - c - \delta k. \tag{5.38}$$

5.2.2 *Policy Rules and Macroeconomic Stability*

In this section, we assume that the fiscal authority uses the taxation rule given by (5.37). We first derive the dynamic system that describes the equilibrium dynamics of the model economy and explore the stability condition around the steady state equilibrium.

[3]As shown in Sect. 3.2, the restriction $\phi > -(1-\alpha)/\alpha$ ensures that the steady state level of consumption has a positive value.

5.2.2.1 Dynamic System

In order to derive a complete dynamic system that summarizes the model displayed above, we focus on the behaviors of capita stock, k, and the shadow value of real money balances, λ. First observe that (5.37) gives

$$1 - \tau(y) - \tau'(y)\, y = \eta(1 - \phi\left(\frac{y^*}{y}\right)^{\phi}.$$

Using the above equation, together with (5.26b) and (5.32), we express the equilibrium level of employment in the following way:

$$N = \left[\frac{\eta(1-\phi)(1-\alpha)}{B}\right]^{\frac{1}{1+\gamma}} y^{*\frac{\phi}{1+\gamma}} y^{\frac{1-\phi}{1+\gamma}} \lambda^{\frac{1}{1+\gamma}}.$$

Inserting the above into the production function (5.30) and solving it with respect to y, we obtain

$$y = \hat{A} k^{\frac{\alpha(1+\gamma)}{\Delta}} \lambda^{\frac{1-\alpha}{\Delta}} \equiv y(k, \lambda), \tag{5.39}$$

where

$$\Delta = \alpha + \gamma + \phi(1-\alpha),$$

$$\hat{A} = A^{\frac{1+\gamma}{\Delta}} \left[\frac{\eta(1-\phi)(1-\alpha)}{B}\right]^{\frac{1-\alpha}{\Delta}} y^{*\frac{\phi(1-\alpha)}{\Delta}\phi}.$$

Equation (5.39) represents the short-run production function under a given level of y^*. Similarly, the real interest rate is expressed as

$$r = \alpha\frac{y}{k} = \alpha\hat{A} k^{-\frac{(1-\alpha)(\gamma+\phi)}{\Delta}} \lambda^{\frac{1-\alpha}{\Delta}},$$

implying that the after-tax marginal rate of return to capital is

$$\begin{aligned}\left(1 - \tau - \tau' y\right) r &= \alpha\eta(1-\phi)\, y^{*\phi} \hat{A}^{1-\phi} k^{\frac{\alpha\gamma(1-\phi)-(\gamma+\phi)}{\Delta}} \lambda^{\frac{(1-\phi)(1-\alpha)}{\Delta}} \\ &\equiv \hat{r}(k, \lambda).\end{aligned}$$

For determining the equilibrium rate of inflation, in view of (5.31), (5.36), and (5.39), we can express π as a function of k and λ in such a way that

$$\pi = \pi^* \left(\frac{\alpha\hat{A}}{r^*}\right)^{\frac{1}{\eta}} k^{-\frac{(1-\alpha)(\gamma+\phi)}{\eta\Delta}} \lambda^{\frac{1-\alpha}{\eta\Delta}} \equiv \pi(k, \lambda). \tag{5.40}$$

Hence, using (5.40), we see that the optimal consumption depends on k and λ in the following manner:

$$c = \frac{1}{\lambda[1 + \hat{r}(k,\lambda) + \pi(k,\lambda) - \delta]} \equiv c(k,\lambda). \tag{5.41}$$

Summing up the above manipulation, we find that the dynamic equation of capital stock is expressed as

$$\dot{k} = (1-\tau_0)y^{*\phi}y(k,\lambda)^{1-\phi} - c(k,\lambda) - \delta k, \tag{5.42}$$

and the shadow value of capital changes according to

$$\dot{\lambda} = \lambda[\rho + \delta - \hat{r}(k,\lambda)]. \tag{5.43}$$

A pair of differential equations, (6.28) and (5.43), constitute a complete dynamic system under the interest-rate control and the taxation rule with endogenous government expenditure. Note that $y(k,\lambda)$ and $\hat{r}(k,\lambda)$ satisfy

$$\hat{r}(k,\lambda) = \alpha\eta(1-\phi)\frac{y(k,\lambda)}{k}, \tag{5.44}$$

$$\pi(k,\lambda) = \pi^*\left(\frac{r}{r^*}\right)^{\frac{1}{\mu}} = \pi^* r^{*-\frac{1}{\eta}}\left(\frac{y(k,\lambda)}{k}\right)^{\frac{1}{\mu}}. \tag{5.45}$$

5.2.2.2 Steady State Equilibrium

In the steady state where k and λ stay constant over time, it should hold that $\pi = \pi^*$, $r = r^*$ and $y = y^*$. It is to be noted that in the steady state, we obtain

$$1 - \tau(y^*) - \tau'(y^*)y^* = \eta(1-\phi).$$

We should also note that from (5.39), the production function in the steady state is given by

$$y^* = \hat{A}^{\frac{\Delta}{\alpha+\gamma}} k^{*\frac{\alpha(1+\gamma)}{\alpha+\gamma}} \lambda^{*\frac{1-\alpha}{\alpha+\gamma}}, \tag{5.46}$$

and the values of k, c and λ satisfy the following conditions:

$$\frac{y^*}{k^*} = \frac{\rho+\delta}{\alpha(1-\tau_0)(1-\phi)}, \tag{5.47}$$

$$\frac{c^*}{k^*} = (1-\tau_0)\frac{y^*}{k^*} - \delta = \frac{\rho + \delta[1-\alpha(1-\phi)]}{\alpha(1-\phi)}, \tag{5.48}$$

$$\lambda^* k^* = \frac{k^*}{c^*(1+\rho+\pi^*)}. \tag{5.49}$$

In the above, k^*, c^* and λ^* denote their steady state values. Equation (5.47) is the modified golden-rule condition corresponding to $\dot{\lambda} = 0$, while (5.48) comes from the long-rum market equilibrium condition: $\dot{k} = 0$. The modified golden-rule condition (5.12) determines the income-capital ratio, y^*/k^*, which gives the consumption-capital ratio, c^*/k^* by (5.48). Then, the steady state implicit value of capital, $k^*\lambda^*$, is given by (5.49). The last condition (5.49) yields

$$\lambda^* = \frac{\alpha\,(1-\phi)}{(1+\rho+\pi^*)\,[\rho+\delta(1-\alpha\,(1-\phi))]\,k^*} = \frac{\beta}{k^*},$$

where β denotes the coefficient of $1/k^*$. Using the above relation, together (5.46) and (5.47), we find that the steady state level of capital is uniquely determined in such a way that

$$k^* = A^{\frac{1}{1-\alpha}} \left[\frac{\alpha\eta\,(1-\phi)}{\rho+\delta}\right]^{\frac{(1-\alpha)(1+\gamma)}{\alpha+\gamma}} \left[\frac{(1-\alpha)\,\eta\,(1-\phi)}{B}\right]^{\frac{1}{1-\alpha}} \beta^{\frac{1}{1+\gamma}}. \tag{5.50}$$

Therefore, the steady state values of k and λ are uniquely expressed by all the parameters involved in the model. Once k^* and λ^* are given, the steady state levels of $c\ (= m)$ and l are determined uniquely as well.

The steady state value of capital given by (5.50) demonstrates that policy parameters, η_0, ϕ, μ and π^* affect the long-run levels of capital, income, employment and consumption in a complex manner. However, it is rather easy to obtain intuitive implications of the effects of a change in policy parameters. First, observe that the degree of activeness of interest-rate control, η, fails to affect the steady state levels of capital, employment and income. Second, regardless of the taxation scheme (i.e., the sign of ϕ), the steady state capital decreases with τ_0, ϕ, and π^*. Third, (5.47) and (5.48) show that a change in π^* will not affect y^*/k^* and c^*/k^*, so that it alters k^*, y^*, and c^* proportionally. Additionally, (5.48) also shows that a rise in ϕ increases c^*/k^*, while τ_0 does not affect c^*/k^*.

Finally, by use of (5.29), (5.31), (5.32), (5.47), and (5.48), the steady state rete of employment satisfies the following relation:

$$N^{*\gamma+1} = \frac{(1-\alpha)\,(\rho+\delta)\,(1-\phi)}{(1+\rho+\pi^*)\,\{\rho+\delta\,[1-\alpha\,(1-\phi)]\}},$$

which shows that N^* decreases with ϕ and π^*, while τ_0 does not affect N^*.

5.2.2.3 Equilibrium (In)determinacy

In order to examine the equilibrium dynamics near the steady state, let us conduct linear approximation of (5.42) and (5.43) at the steady state equilibrium. The coefficient matrix of the approximated system is given by

$$J = \begin{bmatrix} (1-\tau_0)(1-\phi)\, y_k(k^*,\lambda^*) - c_k(k^*,\lambda^*) - \delta, & (1-\tau_0)(1-\phi)\, y_\lambda(k^*,\lambda^*) - c_\lambda(k^*,\lambda^*) \\ -\lambda^* \hat{r}_k(k^*,\lambda^*), & -\lambda^* \hat{r}_\lambda(k^*,\lambda^*) \end{bmatrix}.$$

Since the shadow value of capital, λ, is a jump variable, if J has one stable root, the converging path under perfect foresight is at least locally unique. Thus, determinacy of equilibrium is established when the determinant of J has a negative value. In contrast, when $\det J > 0$ and the trace of J is negative, there exists a continuum of equilibria around the steady state. Using the steady state conditions, we find that the partial derivatives appearing in J can be expressed by the given parameter values. The trace and determinant of J are respectively written as:

$$\text{trace}\, J = \rho - \frac{1}{(1+\pi^*+\rho)\Delta}\frac{\rho+\delta[1-\alpha(1-\phi)]}{\alpha(1-\phi)} \times \left\{ [\phi(\alpha\gamma+1)+\gamma(1-\alpha)](\rho+\delta) + (1-\alpha)(\gamma+\phi)\frac{\pi^*}{\eta} \right\}, \tag{5.51}$$

$$\det J = -\frac{\rho+\delta[1-\alpha(1-\phi)]}{\alpha(1-\phi)}\frac{\rho+\delta}{\Delta}\left[(\gamma+1)(1-\alpha(1-\phi)) + \frac{\phi(1-\alpha)\pi^*}{\eta(1+\pi^*+\rho)}\right]. \tag{5.52}$$

where $\Delta = \alpha + \gamma + \phi(1-\alpha)$.

First of all, it is easy to see that if (i) the target rate of inflation, π^*, is positive, (ii) income taxation is progressive ($\phi > 0$) and (iii) the interest rate control is active ($\eta > 0$), then $\det J$ has a negative value, so that the steady state equilibrium is locally determinate. Similarly, if $-\frac{\alpha+\gamma}{1-\alpha} < \phi < 0$ (so that $\Delta > 0$) and $\eta < 0$, then $\det J < 0$. Hence, in this case, indeterminacy of equilibrium will not emerge either. In addition, if $\phi = 0$ and the rate of tax is fixed at τ_0, then

$$\det J = -\frac{\rho+\delta(1-\alpha)}{\alpha^2}(\rho+\delta)(\gamma+1)(1-\alpha) < 0,$$

implying that regardless of the monetary policy rules, the dynamic system exhibits equilibrium determinacy. To sum up, a set of sufficient conditions for equilibrium determinacy are the following:

Proposition 5.1 *(i) Given a positive rate of target inflation, either if income taxation is progressive and interest-rate control is active or if income taxation is regressive to satisfy* $-\frac{\alpha+\gamma}{1-\alpha} < \phi < 0$ *and interest rate control is passive, then the steady state equilibrium is locally determinate. (ii) If income tax is flat* ($\phi = 0$)*, local determinacy holds regardless of the monetary policy rule.*

To focus on the other possibilities of equilibrium (in)determinacy as clear as possible, let us assume that the elasticity of labor supply is zero: $\gamma = 0$. This case corresponds to the RBC model with indivisible labor analyzed by Hansen (1985). Given this assumption, we obtain

$$\text{trace}\, J = \rho - \frac{\rho + \delta\left[1 - \alpha(1-\phi)\right]}{\alpha(1-\phi)(1+\pi^* + \rho)}\left[\rho + \delta + (1-\alpha)\frac{\pi^*}{\mu}\right]\frac{\phi}{\Delta}, \tag{5.53}$$

$$\det J = -\frac{\{\rho + \delta\left[1 - \alpha\left(1-\phi\right)\right]\}\left(\rho+\delta\right)}{\alpha\left(1-\phi\right)}\left[1 - \alpha\left(1-\phi\right) + \frac{\phi(1-\alpha)\pi^*}{\mu(1+\pi^*+\rho)}\right]\frac{1}{\Delta}, \tag{5.54}$$

where

$$\Delta \equiv \alpha + \phi\left(1-\alpha\right).$$

First, assume that income taxation is progressive ($\phi > 0$). In this case, $\Delta > 0$ and, hence, the necessary and sufficient condition for determinacy is

$$1 - \alpha\left(1-\phi\right) + \frac{\phi(1-\alpha)\pi^*}{\mu(1+\pi^*+\rho)} > 0.$$

The above condition implies that if $\pi^* \geq 0$, equilibrium determinacy is established under the following conditions:

$$\mu > 0 \ \text{ or } \ \mu < -\frac{(1-\alpha)\pi^*\phi}{\left[1-\alpha\left(1-\phi\right)\right]\left(1+\rho+\pi^*\right)}. \tag{5.55}$$

If η satisfies

$$-\frac{(1-\alpha)\pi^*\phi}{\left[1-\alpha\left(1-\phi\right)\right]\left(1+\rho+\pi^*\right)} < \mu < 0, \tag{5.56}$$

then we see that $\det J > 0$. It is easy to see that in this case, we obtain $\rho + \delta + (1-\alpha)\frac{\pi^*}{\mu} < 0$, and, hence, from (5.53), the trace of J has a positive value. Therefore, if μ satisfies (5.56), the steady state is a source and there is no converging path around it.

To sum up, denoting

$$\hat{\mu} = -\frac{(1-\alpha)\pi^*\phi}{\left[1-\alpha\left(1-\phi\right)\right]\left(1+\rho+\pi^*\right)},$$

we find that in the progressive taxation regime ($\phi > 0$), the steady state is a saddle point for either $\mu > 0$ or $\mu < \hat{\mu}$, while it is either a sink or a source for $\hat{\mu} < \mu < 0$. It is to be pointed out that, as shown by numerical examples presented in Fujisaki and Mino (2008), when $0 < \phi < 1$, condition (5.56) may not be satisfied for plausible parameter values. Therefore, the steady state is mostly unstable for the case of $-\hat{\eta} < \eta < 0$.

To sum up, in the case of progressive taxation we obtain the following:

Proposition 5.2 *If income taxation is progressive and the target rate of inflation is non-negative, the perfect-foresight competitive equilibrium is locally determinate, either if the interest-rate control is active or if it is sufficiently passive. Equilibrium indeterminacy may not emerge in this regime.*

Next, consider the case of regressive taxation ($\phi < 0$). In this case, the necessary and sufficient condition for local determinacy is

$$(1-\phi) + \frac{(1-\alpha)\pi^*\phi}{\mu(1+\pi^*+\rho)}\frac{1}{\Delta} > 0. \tag{5.57}$$

This condition is fulfilled either if

$$-\frac{\alpha}{1-\alpha} < \phi < 0 \ (\Longleftrightarrow \Delta > 0) \text{ and } \mu > -\frac{(1-\alpha)\pi^*\phi}{[1-\alpha(1-\phi)](1+\rho+\pi^*)} \equiv \hat{\mu}(>0)$$

or if

$$\phi < -\frac{\alpha}{1-\alpha} \ (\Longleftrightarrow \Delta < 0) \text{ and } 0 < \mu < -\frac{(1-\alpha)\pi^*\phi}{[1-\alpha(1-\phi)](1+\rho+\pi^*)} \equiv \hat{\mu}\ (>0).$$

In words, a relatively low degree of regressive taxation, coupled with a high degree of passive interest-rate control, may produce indeterminacy.

In contrast, the necessary conditions for equilibrium indeterminacy are the following:

$$\left[1-\alpha(1-\phi) + \frac{(1-\alpha)\pi^*\phi}{\mu(1+\pi^*+\rho)}\right]\frac{1}{\Delta} < 0, \tag{5.58}$$

$$\left[\rho+\delta+(1-\alpha)\frac{\pi^*}{\mu}\right]\frac{\phi}{\Delta} > 0. \tag{5.59}$$

If $-\alpha/(1-\alpha) < \phi < 0$ (so $\Delta > 0$), then both (5.58) and (5.59) are satisfied if and only if

$$-\frac{(1-\alpha)\,\pi^*}{\rho+\delta} < \mu < -\frac{(1-\alpha)\,\pi^*\phi}{1+\pi^*+\rho}.$$

Note that the above condition is necessary but not sufficient for establishing equilibrium indeterminacy: if trace $J > 0$ in (5.53), the steady state is a source (unstable). In contrast, if $-\frac{1-\alpha}{\alpha} < \phi < -\frac{\alpha}{1-\alpha}$ (so $\Delta < 0$), we find that indeterminacy may emerge more easily. Table 5.1 gives a classification of dynamic patterns in the case of regressive taxation.

Table 5.1 Stability properties under regressive taxation $\hat{\eta} \equiv -\frac{(1-\alpha)\pi^{*}\phi}{[1-\alpha(1-\phi)](1+\rho+\pi^{*})}$ (>0), $\bar{\eta} = -\frac{(1-\alpha)\pi^{*}}{\rho+\delta}$ (<0)

	$-\frac{\alpha}{1-\alpha} < \phi < 0$	$-\frac{1-\alpha}{\alpha} < \phi < -\frac{\alpha}{1-\alpha}$
$-\hat{\mu} < \mu$	Saddle point	Sink or source
$0 < \mu < -\hat{\mu}$	Sink or source	Saddle point
$\bar{\mu} < \mu < 0$	Saddle point	Sink or source
$\mu < \bar{\mu}$	Saddle point	Sink

The following proposition summarizes our finding.

Proposition 5.3 *(i) Suppose that income taxation is mildly regressive and the target rate of inflation is positive. Then the steady state is locally determinate either if interest-rate control is sufficiently active or if it is passive. (ii) Suppose that income taxation is sufficiently regressive and the target rate of inflation is positive. Then, the steady state holds equilibrium determinacy only when interest-rate control is mildly active.*

5.2.3 Discussion

To obtain the intuitive implication of determinacy/indeterminacy conditions displayed in Propositions 5.1, 5.2, and 5.3, let us inspect the optimization condition (5.29) in detail. Using $w = \alpha y/l$, this condition is rewritten as

$$cN^{\gamma}B = \frac{(1-\tau_0)(1-\phi)(1-\alpha)\, y^{*\phi} A^{1-\phi} k^{\alpha(1-\phi)} N^{(1-\alpha)(1-\phi)-1}}{1+\hat{r}+\pi}. \tag{5.60}$$

Under a given level of consumption, c, the left hand side of (5.60) represents the Frisch labor supply curve, and the right hand side is considered the labor demand curve. Given c, $\hat{r}$, and π. If we assume that $\gamma = 0$ for expositional simplicity, the labor supply curve becomes a horizontal line. Hence, if $(1-\phi)(1-\alpha)-1 = -\Delta < 0$, the labor demand curve has a negative slope, and thus less steeper than the labor supply curve. In contrast, if $\Delta < 0$, then the labor demand has a positive slope, and steeper than the labor supply curve.

Now suppose that the economy initially stays at the steady state equilibrium. Suppose further that a sunspot-driven shock makes agents optimistic and households anticipate that the output and employment will expand. This raises consumption demand and the labor supply curve shifts upward and, hence, the equilibrium employment decreases as long as the labor demand curve does not shift. Remember that the after-tax rate of return, $\hat{r}$, and the rate of inflation, π, are respectively expressed in the following manner:

$$\hat{r} = \alpha(1-\eta)(1-\phi)\, y^{*\phi} A^{1-\phi} k^{\alpha(1-\phi)-1} N^{(1-\alpha)(1-\phi)},$$

$$\pi = r^{*-\frac{1}{\eta}} \pi^{*} y^{*\phi} A^{\frac{1}{\eta}} k^{\frac{\alpha}{\eta}-1} N^{\frac{1-\alpha}{\eta}}.$$

These expressions show that an expected increase in l raises $\hat{r}$. It also increases inflation, if $\eta > 0$. As a result, the anticipated increase in employment shifts the labor demand curve downwards. Then, the equilibrium employment decreases further, implying that the initial, optimistic expectation will not be self-fulfilled because the aggregate output will contract rather than expand. Consequently, such expectation-driven fluctuations cannot be realized so that equilibrium is determinate.

Note that if η is negative and its absolute value is small, a rise in employment yields a sufficiently large decrease in inflation. This may reduce the after-tax nominal interest rate, $\hat{r} + \pi$, and, therefore, the labor demand curve may shift up. If such a shift large enough to enhance the equilibrium level of employment, the initial optimistic expectations can be self-fulfilled. Hence, as Table 5.1 shows, if the interest-rate control is mildly passive, there may exist multiple converging paths. In contrast, if the interest0rate control is strongly passive so that the absolute value of η is large enough, a decrease in the after-tax nominal interest rate, $\hat{r} + \pi$, is small. As a result, an upward shift of the labor demand curve cannot cancel a reduction in employment due to an upward shift of labor supply curve. Consequently, if η is small enough to fulfill $\eta < -\hat{\eta}\phi$, the possibility of equilibrium indeterminacy is eliminated.

Next, assume that $\Delta < 0$ so that the labor demand curve has a positive slope. If the after-tax nominal interest rate, $\hat{r} + \pi$, is constant, then the initial shift of labor supply curve due to an increase in consumption raises the equilibrium level of employment. If we consider the effective real wage, the labor demand curve may have a negative slope even if $\Delta < 0$. In particular, when η has a small positive value, a rise in N yields a large increase in π so that the labor demand curve may have a negative slope. In this case, the initial expectation cannot be self-fulfilled. At the same time, if $\eta > 0$, both $\hat{r}$ and π are increased by an expansion of employment, which yields a downward shift of the labor demand curve. Since the labor demand curve is steeper than the labor supply curve, this shift produces a further enhancement of the employment level. As a consequence, the initial expectation can be self-fulfilled and equilibrium indeterminacy emerges. In contrast, if $\eta < 0$ and η is close to zero, a higher employment may lower the after-tax nominal interest rate, implying that the labor demand curve shifts upward. If this is the case, the equilibrium level of employment may not increase, which means that the initial expected change in the economic condition cannot be realized. Consequently, indeterminacy may not emerge in this situation.

5.3 Policy Rules in Endogenous Growth Models

In this section, we re-examine the stabilization effects of the tax schedule and interest-rate control rule in the context of endogenous growth models. Our main emphasis in this section is on showing that the stabilization effects of fiscal and monetary policy rules are sometimes quite different from each other in the exogenous and endogenous growth settings.

5.3.1 Nonlinear Taxation Under Endogenous Growth

As pointed out in Sect. 5.1.2, the progressive tax rule may act as a built-in stabilizer in the one-sector RBC model in the sense that it may reduce the possibility of indeterminacy even in the presence of strong external increasing returns. Chen and Guo (2015) find that such a conclusion would not hold in endogenous growth models. We first summarize their finding in the context of a simple model of endogenous growth.

5.3.1.1 Setup

For expositional convenience, in this subsection we add a time subscript to each endogenous variable. Consider an *AK* growth model in which the aggregate production function is given by

$$Y_t = AK_t^{\alpha}\bar{K}_t^{1-\alpha}, \quad A > 0, \ \ 0 < \alpha < 1,$$

where Y_t is the total output, K_t denotes the private capital, and $\bar{K}_t$ represents external effects associated with the social average capital. In the representative agent setting, $\bar{K}_t = K_t$ holds in equilibrium, implying that the social production function is $Y_t = AK_t$, and the private rate of return on capital is given by $r_t = \alpha A$. The representative household maximizes a discounted sum of utilities

$$U = \int_0^{\infty} e^{-\rho t} \log C_t dt, \quad \rho > 0$$

subject to

$$\dot{K}_t = (1-\tau_t)\, Y_t - C_t - \delta K_t, \ \ K_0 = \text{given},$$

where C_t is consumption of the household and τ_t denotes the rate of income tax.[4]

Following Guo and Lansing (1998), we assume that the fiscal authority adjusts the rate of income tax according to the following rule:

$$\tau_t = 1 - \eta\left(\frac{Y_t^*}{Y_t}\right)^{\phi}, \quad 0 < \eta < 1, \ \phi_0 < \phi < 1, \tag{5.61}$$

where Y_t^* denotes a reference level of income on the balanced-growth path. Note that, unlike the model in Sect. 5.1.2, the reference income Y_t^* is not fixed even in the

[4]No substantial change arises, if we use a more general CES utility function such that $u(C_t) = C_t^{1-\sigma}/(1-\sigma), \ \sigma > 0.$

long-run equilibrium. In (5.61) ϕ_0 is given by

$$\phi_0 = \max\left\{\frac{\eta - 1}{\eta}, \frac{\alpha - 1}{\alpha}\right\}. \tag{5.62}$$

The restriction on η means that when $Y_t = Y_t^*$ holds, the rate of average tax is between 0 and 1. The condition on ϕ ensures that if $Y_{t'} = Y_t^*$, the after-tax income of the representative household increases with Y_t and that the after-tax rate of return on the private capital decreases with K_t.[5] Under this policy rule, the marginal tax revenue given by

$$\frac{d}{dY_t}(\tau_t Y_t) = 1 - (1-\phi)\,\eta\left(\frac{Y_t^*}{Y_t}\right)^{\phi}.$$

is higher (lower) than the average tax revenue, τ_t, if $0 < \phi < 1$ $(-\phi_0 < \phi < 0)$. Thus, taxation is progressive (regressive) if $0 < \phi < 1$ $(\phi_0 < \phi < 0)$.

We assume that when solving the optimization problem, the representative household takes sequences of the reference income and external effects of capital, $\{Y_t^*, \bar{K}_t\}_{t=0}^{\infty}$, as given. The optimization conditions yield the Euler equation such that

$$\frac{\dot{C}_t}{C_t} = (1-\phi)\,\eta\left(\frac{Y_t^*}{Y_t}\right)^{\phi}\alpha A - \rho - \delta.$$

The transversality condition is given by $\lim_{t\to\infty} e^{-\rho t}(K_t/C_t) = 0$. Denoting the government consumption as G_t, the flow budget constraint for the government is

$$G_t = \tau_t Y_t = \left[1 - \eta\left(\frac{Y_t^*}{Y_t}\right)^{\phi}\right] Y_t.$$

Here, the government simply consumes its tax revenue and the level of G_t directly affects neither production activities nor households' felicity. The equilibrium condition for the final goods gives

$$\dot{K}_t = (1-\tau_t)\,Y_t - C_t - \delta K_t.$$

5.3.1.2 Taxation Rules and Indeterminacy

On the balanced-growth path, it holds that

$$\frac{\dot{C}_t}{C_t} = \frac{\dot{K}_t}{K_t} = \frac{\dot{Y}_t}{Y_t} = \frac{\dot{Y}_t^*}{Y_t^*} \equiv g,$$

[5]Note that the after-tax income is $(1-\tau_t)\,Y_t = Y_t - \eta Y_t^{1-\phi} Y_t^{*\phi}$ and the after tax rate of return on private capital is given by $(1-\tau_t)\,\alpha Y_t/K_t = \eta Y_t^{*\phi} A^{1-\phi} K_t^{\alpha(1-\phi)-1} \bar{K}_t^{(1-\alpha)(1-\phi:)}$.

where g denotes a common balanced growth rate that is endogenously determined. We define $z_t = C_t/K_t$, and $x_t = Y_t^*/Y_t$. Then, the growth rates of capital and consumption are respectively given by

$$\frac{\dot{K}_t}{K_t} = \eta A x_t^{\phi} - z_t - \delta,$$

$$\frac{\dot{C}_t}{C_t} = (1-\phi)\,\eta\alpha A x_t^{\phi} - \rho - \delta.$$

Since $\dot{Y}_t^*/Y_t^* = g$, a complete dynamic system is as follows:

$$\frac{\dot{x}_t}{x_t} = g - \eta A x_t^{\phi} + z_t + \delta, \tag{5.63a}$$

$$\frac{\dot{z}_t}{z_t} = -\phi\eta\alpha A x_t^{\phi} + z_t - \rho. \tag{5.63b}$$

In the steady state where $\dot{z}_t = \dot{x}_t = 0$, the following conditions are fulfilled:

$$g - \eta A x^{\phi} + z + \delta = 0, \tag{5.64a}$$

$$-\phi\eta\alpha A x^{\phi} + z - \rho = 0. \tag{5.64b}$$

In the above, x and z respectively denote the steady state values of x_t and z_t. Since these two equations involve three endogenous variables, x, z, and g, we need to have an additional condition to determine the steady state. A natural condition is that $Y_t = Y_t^*$ holds on the balanced growth path, so that the steady state level of $x = 1$. Then, the steady state value of z is

$$z = \phi\eta A + \rho,$$

and the balanced-growth rate is given by

$$g = (1-\phi)\,\eta\alpha A - \rho - \delta.$$

The coefficient matrix of the above dynamic system linearized at $x = 1$ and z is

$$J_0 = \begin{bmatrix} 1 & 0 \\ 0 & z \end{bmatrix} \begin{bmatrix} -\phi\eta A & 1 \\ -\phi^2\eta\alpha A & 1 \end{bmatrix}.$$

We see that

$$\det J_0 = zA\eta\phi\,(\alpha\phi - 1)\,, \quad \operatorname{trace} J_0 = z - \eta\phi A.$$

As a result, if $0 < \phi < 1$, then $\det J < 0$, so that J has one negative eigenvalue. If $\phi < 0$, then $\det J_0 > 0$ trace $J_0 > 0$, meaning that both eigenvalues of J have positive real parts. Since the initial level of the reference income, Y_0^*, is not predetermined even though its growth rate is fixed at g, both x_t and z_t are jump variables.

If J has no stable root, then $x_t = x = 1$ and $z_t = z$ for all $t \geq 0$. In this case, the initial levels of Y_t^* and C_t are respectively given by

$$Y_0^* = AK_0, \quad C_0 = (\phi\eta A + \rho)K_0.$$

In contrast, when J has one stable root, there is a unique converging path in (x_t, z_t) space. It is easy to confirm that this stable path has a positive slope and, hence, the relation between the equilibrium levels of x_t and z_t around the steady state is expressed as $x_t = \Phi z_t$, where Φ is a positive constant. This means that the initial levels of Y_t and C_t satisfy

$$Y_0^* = \Phi A C_0. \tag{5.65}$$

Since the initial level of C_0 can take any value if the equilibrium is realized on the stable saddle path, the initial level of Y_0^* is not historically specified either. Consequently, in contrast with the neoclassical (exogenous) growth model where Y_t^* is fixed at the steady state level of output, progressive taxation generates sunspot-driven fluctuations, while regressive taxation establishes determinacy of equilibrium. Such a conclusion is completely opposite to the result obtained in the standard, one-sector RBC model.[6]

To give an intuitive implication of the above result, suppose that the tax scheme is progressive ($0 < \phi < 1$) and that a positive sunspot shock raises the future income anticipated by the households. Hence, due to the income effect, the households increase their current consumption. Equation (5.65) means that such a rise in consumption increases the reference level of income Y^*, which depresses the rate of income tax under our taxation rule. A lower tax rate accelerates capital accumulation so that income will increase. Therefore, the initial anticipated rise in future income can be self-fulfilled. If the tax rule is regressive ($\phi < 0$), the economy always stays on the balanced-growth path. Hence, the economy will not respond to an extrinsic sunspot shock. Figure 5.1 depicts the above intuition. In this figure, the economy is assumed to stay on the balanced growth path denoted by Path A until time $\bar{t}\,(> 0)$. Now suppose that a positive sunspot shock hits at $t = \bar{t}$. If taxation

[6] When the model economy does not allow endogenous growth, the reference level of income Y^* is the steady state level of Y_t, which is fixed. As a result, the rate of income tax $\tau_t = 1 - \eta\left(\frac{Y^*}{Y_t}\right)^{\phi}$ increases (decreases) if $\phi > 0$ ($\phi < 0$). Hence, an expansion of income caused by an optimistic sunspot shock raises the rate of income tax, under which the expectations generated by the sunspot shock will not be self-fulfilled, This stabilization effect of progressive tax may not hold in an endogenous growth environment where Y_t^* is also affected by sunspots.

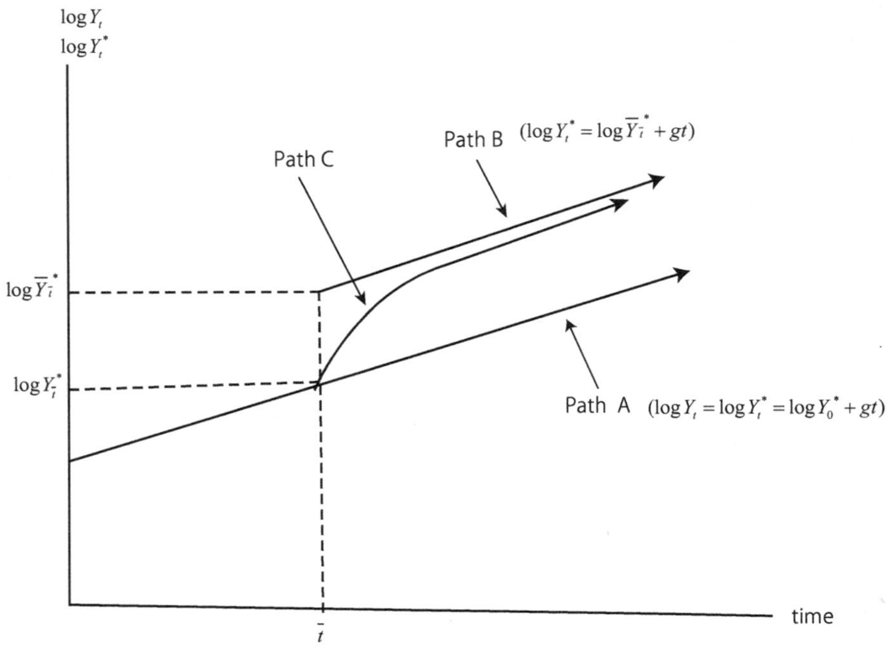

Fig. 5.1 The effects of a sunspot shock

is regressive, such an extrinsic shock fails to affect the equilibrium path of the economy and, hence, the economy continues staying on Path A. However, if taxation is progressive, a positive sunspot shock raises $Y_{\bar{t}}^*$ up to $\bar{Y}_{\bar{t}}^* \left(> Y_{\bar{t}}^*\right)$. As a result, the reference income Y_t^* starts following Path B if further shocks will not hit the economy afterwards. In this situation, the actual income Y_t follows Path C that converges to Path B.

5.3.2 Interest-Rate Control Rules Under Endogenous Growth

Many authors have explored whether the interest-rate control rule based on Taylor's (1993) proposal contributes to reducing equilibrium indeterminacy which generates expectations-driven economic fluctuations. In this literature, it has been well known that an economy following the interest-rate control may easily produce multiple equilibria, if the model economy does not consider capital accumulation. For example, Benhabib et al. (2001a) confirm that an active interest-rate control under which the nominal interest rate is adjusted more than one-for-one with the rate of inflation, the competitive equilibrium is determinate. Conversely, under a passive interest-rate feedback rule, which controls the nominal interest rate less than one-for-one with inflation, the competitive equilibrium tends to be indeterminate. At the same time, Benhabib et al. (2001b) demonstrate that those results would be reversed if the production function contains the stock of real money balances as an input.

In contrast to the models without capital, Meng and Yip (2004) show that the possibility of equilibrium indeterminacy under the interest-rate control rule is significantly reduced, if the economy allows capital accumulation.[7] Technically speaking, introducing capital adds a non-jump state variable to the model, which often contributes to eliminating multiple converging paths. Meng and Yip (2004) also reveal that such a conclusion still holds if the monetary authority changes the nominal interest rate by observing the level of real income as well as inflation.[8]

The following discussion reconsiders the issue of equilibrium determinacy under interest-rate control rules in the context of a simple growth model. We use a standard money-in-the-utility function model with an *Ak* technology and exogenous labor supply. In this setting, regardless of interest-rate control rules, money is superneutral on the balanced-growth path, and the long-term growth rate of income is uniquely determined by the technology and preference parameters alone. In addition, if the monetary authority adjusts the nominal interest rate by observing the rate of inflation alone, such a monetary policy only affects the steady state rate of inflation, and thus the behaviors of consumption and capital do not respond to the monetary authority's behavior. However, if the monetary authority adopts Taylor's (1993) original suggestion, so that it controls nominal interest in response to not only inflation but also the growth rate of income, then the balanced-growth path may exhibit indeterminacy: there is a continuum of equilibrium paths converging to the balanced-growth equilibrium. In this case, although the balanced-growth path satisfies superneutrality of money, the transition process is affected by the monetary policy. We reveal that, in addition to the activeness of interest-rate control, the intertemporal substitutability in felicity also has a key effect on the presence of equilibrium indeterminacy.[9]

[7]Meng and Yip (2004) used a neoclassical monetary growth model based on the money-in-the-utility function formulation. Yip and Li (2004), on the other hand, showed that if a cash-in-advance constraint applies to both investment and consumption so that money is not superneutral in the steady state, the interest-rate control rule may generate indeterminacy. See also Dupor (2001).

[8]Indeterminacy may emerge if the model introduces labor-leisure choice. As pointed out by Meng and Yip (2004), this possibility, however, requires that the labor supply curve has a positive slope.

[9]When the nominal interest rate responds to inflation alone in an *Ak* growth model, intermediacy would emerge either if labor supply is endogenous or if a cash-in-advance constraint applies to investment as well; see Itaya and Mino (2004, 2007) and Suen and Yip (2005). In these cases, money is not superneutral on the balanced-growth path, which is different from our present formulation in which monetary policy cannot affect long-term economic growth.

5.3.2.1 Setup

We employ a standard money-in-the-utility-function model with an Ak technology. The representative household maximizes a discounted sum of utilities

$$U = \int_0^{\infty} e^{-\rho t} u(c, m)\, dt, \quad \rho > 0$$

subject to the flow budget and wealth constraints:

$$\dot{a} = ra - c - Rm,$$

$$a = k + m,$$

where c is the consumption, m is the real money balances, k is the capital stock, a is the total wealth, r is the real interest rate, and R denotes the nominal interest rate. The initial holding of a is exogenously given. Here, we specify the instantaneous utility function in the following manner:

$$u(c, m) = \frac{\left(c^{\gamma} m^{1-\gamma}\right)^{1-\sigma}}{1-\sigma}, \quad 0 < \gamma < 1, \quad \sigma > 0, \quad \sigma \neq 1.$$

Denoting the shadow value of a as q, we find that the optimization conditions include the following:

$$\frac{(1-\gamma)\, c}{\gamma m} = R, \tag{5.66a}$$

$$\gamma c^{\gamma(1-\sigma)-1} m^{(1-\sigma)(1-\gamma)} = q, \tag{5.66b}$$

$$\dot{q} = q(\rho - A), \tag{5.66c}$$

together with the transversality condition: $\lim_{t\to\infty} e^{-\rho t} aq = 0$. Equation (5.66a) means that the marginal rate of substitution between consumption and real money balances equals the nominal interest rate.

We assume that the production function is specified as

$$y = Ak, \tag{5.67}$$

where y denotes the aggregate output. The commodity market is assumed to be competitive so that the real interest rate is determined by

$$r = A. \tag{5.68}$$

We ignore capital depreciation, and thus the equilibrium condition for the commodity market is $y = \dot{k} + c$, which yields

$$\frac{\dot{k}}{k} = A - z, \tag{5.69}$$

where $z = c/k$.

Following Taylor (1993), we assume that the monetary authority adjusts the nominal interest rate by observing the level of real income as well as the rate of inflation. Since we deal with a growing economy in which real income continues expanding, we consider that the monetary authority changes the nominal interest rate in response not to the level of income but to the growth rate of income.[10] The monetary policy rule is thus specified as

$$R = \phi(\pi) + \eta(g). \quad \phi' > 0, \quad \eta' > 0, \tag{5.70}$$

where g denotes the growth rate of income. From (5.67) and (5.69), g is given by

$$g = \frac{\dot{y}}{y} = \frac{\dot{k}}{k} = A - z.$$

In view of the Fisher condition, the relation between nominal and real interest rates is described by

$$r + \pi = R. \tag{5.71}$$

From (5.68), (5.70), and $g = A - z$, we obtain

$$A + \pi = \phi(\pi) + \eta(A - z), \tag{5.72}$$

which yields

$$\frac{d\pi}{dz} = \frac{\eta'(A - z)}{\phi'(\pi) - 1}.$$

As a result, the relation between π and z is expressed as

$$\pi = \pi(z), \tag{5.73}$$

[10]In our notation, Taylor's principle is expressed as $R = 1.5(\pi - \pi^*) + 0.5y$ (or $R = 1.5(\pi - \pi^*) + 1.0y$), where π^* denotes the target rate of inflation.

where

$$\text{sign } \pi'(z) = \text{sign } \left[\phi'(\pi) - 1\right].$$

Namely, the equilibrium rate of inflation is positively (negatively) related to the consumption-capital ratio, z, if the monetary authority actively (passively) responds to a change in the rate of inflation.

5.3.2.2 Dynamic System

To derive a complete dynamic system, first note that from (5.66a), (5.68), and (5.71) we obtain

$$\frac{c}{m} = \frac{\gamma}{1-\gamma}[A + \pi(z)].$$

Taking the time derivatives of the both sides of the above, we obtain

$$\frac{\dot{c}}{c} - \frac{\dot{m}}{m} = \frac{\pi'(z)\dot{z}}{A + \pi(z)}. \tag{5.74}$$

Equations (5.66b) and (5.66c) lead to

$$[\gamma(1-\sigma) - 1]\frac{\dot{c}}{c} + (1-\sigma)(1-\gamma)\frac{\dot{m}}{m} = \rho - A. \tag{5.75}$$

Eliminating $\dot{m}/m$ from (5.74) and (5.75) yields

$$\frac{\dot{c}}{c} = \frac{1}{\sigma}(A-\rho) - \left(\frac{1}{\sigma} - 1\right)(1-\gamma)\frac{\pi'(z)\dot{z}}{A + \pi(z)}. \tag{5.76}$$

Since it holds that $\dot{z}/z = \dot{c}/c - \dot{k}/k$, equations (5.69) and (5.76) present the following:

$$\frac{\dot{z}}{z} = \frac{1}{\sigma}(A-\rho) - \left(\frac{1}{\sigma} - 1\right)(1-\gamma)\frac{\pi'(z)\dot{z}}{A + \pi(z)} - A + z.$$

The above is rewritten as

$$\frac{\dot{z}}{z} = \frac{\frac{1}{\sigma}(A-\rho) - A + z}{\Gamma(z)}, \tag{5.77}$$

where

$$\Gamma(z) = 1 + \left(\frac{1}{\sigma} - 1\right)(1-\gamma)\frac{\pi'(z)\, z}{A + \pi(z)}.$$

Equation (5.77) gives a complete dynamic equation that summarizes the dynamic behavior of our economy.

5.3.2.3 Policy Rules and Aggregate Stability

It is easy to see that either if $0 < \sigma < 1$ and $\pi'(z) > 0$ or if $\sigma > 1$ and $\pi'(z) < 0$, then

$$\Gamma(z) > 0,$$

so that a unique balanced-growth path in which z is determined by

$$\frac{1}{\sigma}(A - \rho) - A + z^* = 0 \tag{5.78}$$

is unstable. This means that the economy always stays on the balanced-growth path, which means that the economy exhibits global determinacy. Note that both active control ($\phi' > 1$ so that $\pi'(z)$ is positive) and passive control ($\phi' < 1$ so that $\pi'(z)$ is negative) may yield determinacy depending on the magnitude of σ.

In contrast, either if $\sigma > 1$ and $\pi'(z) > 0$ or if $\sigma < 1$ and $\pi'(z) < 0$, then it is possible to hold $\Gamma(z) < 0$, and thus $d(\dot{z}/z)/dz < 0$ on the balanced-growth path. In this case, we see that the balanced-growth path is stable and it exhibits local indeterminacy.

To sum up, we have shown the following:

Proposition 5.4 *Suppose that the interest-rate control rule is given by (5.70). Then, either if $\phi'(\pi) > 0$ and $0 < \sigma < 1$ or if $\phi'(\pi) < 1$ and $\sigma > 1$, the balanced-growth path satisfies global determinacy.*

Proposition 5.5 *The necessary and sufficient condition for global indeterminacy is*

$$1 + \left(\frac{1}{\sigma} - 1\right)\frac{\eta'(A-z)(1-\gamma)z}{[\phi'(\pi) - 1][A + \pi(z)]} < 0, \tag{5.79}$$

where z^* and π^* are their steady state values.[11]

[11] Global indeterminacy emerges if (5.79) is satisfied for all $z \in (0, A)$, which imposes further restrictions on the $\phi(\pi)$ and $\eta(g)$ functions.

The intuitive implication of the above results is as follows. Suppose that the economy is initially in the balanced-growth equilibrium in which capital, consumption, and real money balances grow at a common rate of $g^* = (1/\sigma)(A - \rho)$. Suppose further that due to a sunspot-driven expectations change, households anticipate a rise in the rate of capital accumulation and that the consumption-capital ratio, z, declines. Then, for example, if $0 < \sigma < 1$ and $\phi' > 1$, equation (5.76) indicates that the growth rate of consumption will decrease.[12] This means that consumption growth is insufficient to meet the output expansion caused by the expected acceleration of capital formation. Hence, the initial expectations are not self-fulfilled, implying that the balanced-growth path itself is a unique competitive equilibrium and the economy has no transition process. Conversely, if (5.79) is satisfied, (5.76) indicates that consumption growth is enhanced. Therefore, there would be enough consumption demand for the expected increase in production, so that the initial expectations are self-fulfilled. If this is the case, there exists an infinite number of converting trajectories at least around the balanced-growth equilibrium: the economy can be out of the balanced-growth equilibrium, and monetary disturbances can affect the dynamic behavior of the economy.

To be more concrete, let us specify the policy-rule function in such a way that

$$R = \pi^* \left(\frac{\pi}{\pi^*}\right)^{\phi} + A\left(\frac{g}{g^*}\right)^{\eta}, \quad \phi > 0, \quad \eta > 0, \tag{5.80}$$

where π^* is the target rate of inflation and g^* denotes the balanced-growth rate determined by $g^* = (1/\sigma)(A - \rho)$. In this specification, the target rate of inflation is set by the monetary authority, and (5.71) is satisfied on the balanced-growth path where $g = g^*$ and $\pi = \pi^*$. Given this specification, equation (5.71) becomes

$$A + \pi = \pi^* \left(\frac{\pi}{\pi^*}\right)^{\phi} + A\left(\frac{A - z}{A - z^*}\right)^{\eta},$$

which yields

$$\frac{d\pi}{dz} = \frac{\frac{A\eta}{A - z^*}\left(\frac{A - z}{A - z^*}\right)^{\eta - 1}}{\phi\left(\frac{\pi}{\pi^*}\right)^{\phi - 1} - 1}.$$

[12] In this situation, the substitution effect of a change in the nominal interest rate dominates the income effect, which depresses the growth of consumption demand.

When we evaluate the above on the balanced-growth path on which $z = z^*$ and $\pi = \pi^*$, in view of (11), we obtain

$$\left.\frac{d\pi}{dz}\right|_{z=z^*} \equiv \pi'\left(z^*\right) = \frac{1}{\phi - 1}\left[\frac{\sigma A \eta}{A - \rho}\right].$$

Using the above, we find that

$$\begin{aligned}\Gamma\left(z^*\right) &= 1 + \left(\frac{1}{\sigma} - 1\right)(1-\gamma)\frac{\pi'\left(z^*\right) z^*}{A + \pi\left(z^*\right)} \\ &= 1 + \frac{(1-\sigma)(1-\gamma) A\eta}{\sigma (A + \pi^*)(\phi - 1)(A - \rho)}\left[A - \frac{1}{\sigma}(A - \rho)\right]. \qquad (5.81)\end{aligned}$$

Therefore, $\Gamma\left(z^*\right)$ is strictly negative if and only if

$$\frac{\eta(1-\sigma)}{\phi - 1} < -\frac{\sigma(A + \pi^*)(A - \rho)}{A(1-\gamma)\left[A - \frac{1}{\sigma}(A - \rho)\right]} (< 0). \qquad (5.82)$$

The necessary conditions to hold this inequality are $\sigma < 1$ and $\phi < 1$ or $\sigma > 1$ and $\phi > 1$. If one of these conditions are met, the possibility of indeterminacy increases as η has a larger value; that is, the monetary authority is more sensitive to a divergence between the actual growth rate and the long-run target rate of income expansion.

As an numerical example, let us set

$$A = 0.07, \quad \rho = 0.04, \quad \gamma = 0.7, \quad \pi^* = 0.02.$$

Then, the relation between ϕ, σ, and η that satisfies $\Gamma\left(z^*\right) = 0$ in (5.81) is given by

$$\phi = 1 + \frac{7.77(\sigma - 1)\left[0.07(\sigma - 1) + 0.04\right]}{\sigma^2}\eta. \qquad (5.83)$$

Figure 5.2a, b depict the graphs between ϕ and η under given levels of σ. Figure 5.2 assumes that $\sigma = 2.0$ so that the balanced-growth rate is $g^* = (1/\sigma)(A - \rho) = 0.015$, while Fig. 5.2a sets $\sigma = 0.5$, and thus $g^* = 0.06$. As these figures demonstrate, in both cases the region of the value of ϕ under which indeterminacy emerges is enhanced as η increases. Figure 5.2b shows the graph of (5.83) with a given η. Since in this figure, z^* has a negative value for $0 < \sigma < 0.428$, we focus on the region where $\sigma > 0.428$. Again, the graph means that an increase in η enhances the region of indeterminacy in the (ϕ, σ) space.

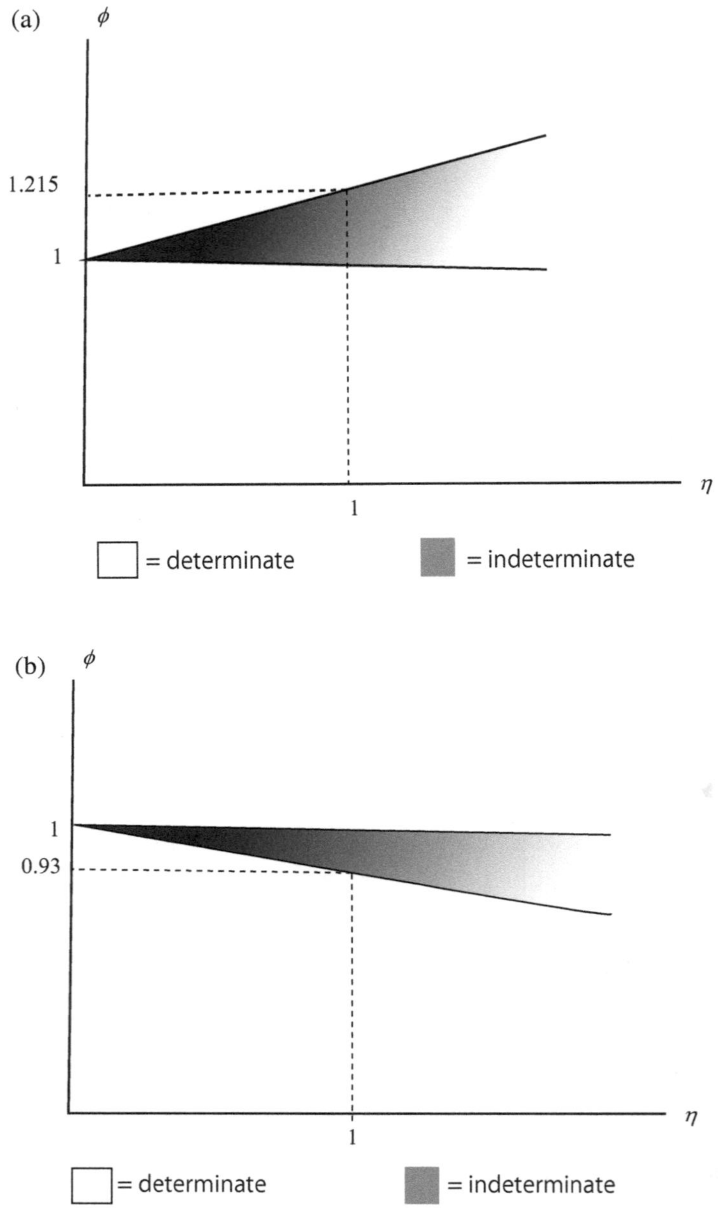

Fig. 5.2 (**a**) $\sigma = 2.0$, (**b**) $\sigma = 0.5$

5.4 References and Related Studies

Several authors conduct investigations on the relation between fiscal discipline and equilibrium indeterminacy discussed in Sect. 5.1.1. Ghilardi and Rossi (2014) reconsider Schmitt-Grohé and Uribe's (1997) finding under a more general CES production function and show that empirical plausibility of the indeterminacy outcome can be enhanced. Linnemann (2007) analyzes a model in which the utility function is non-separable between consumption and labor, while Meng (2015) examines the role of balanced-budget rule in small open economies. Instead of assuming a continuing balanced budget, Futagami et al. (2008) and Nishimura et al. (2015) introduce government debt under a given fiscal rule. These studies assume that the government adjusts its spending to realize a target level of debt-GDP ratio. They find that this type fiscal discipline may give rise to equilibrium indeterminacy. Futagami et al. (2008) and Hori and Maebayashi (2016) explore the same issue in the context of small open economies.

As mentioned in Sect. 5.1.2, Guo and Lansing (1998) formulation of the non-linear taxation rule has been used widely in the literature. For example, Guo and Harrison (2001b, 2004) analyze the stabilization effect taxation rule in two-sector real business cycle models with sector specific externalities. Chen and Guo (2014) examine the relation between indeterminacy and progressive taxation in a model with productive government spending, while they discussed the same issue in a model with utility-enhancing government spending (Chen and Guo 2015). On the other hand, Bond et al. (1996), Amano et al. (2008), and Amano and Itaya (2013) explore the relation between flat-rate taxation and indeterminacy in two-sector endogenous growth models. Chen (2006), Palivos et al. (2003), and Park and Philippoulos (2004) study indeterminacy in endogenous growth models in which public capital sustains continuing growth.

Stabilization effects of interest-rate control rule has been extensively dicussed. In addition to the literature in in prvious sections, we refere to Yip and Li (2004), Huang and Meng (2007), and Weder (2006a,b, 2008). The model of interaction between the fiscal and monetary policy rule in Sect. 5.2 is based on Fujisaki and Mino (2008). There is extensive literature on the stabilization effect of monetary policy rules in the context of New Keynesian models. Although the model in Sect. 5.2 assumes price flexibility, it is closely related to the studies by Leeper (1991), Dupor (2001), and Carlstrom and Fuerst (2005). For further discussion on the relation between equilibrium indeterminacy and fiscal-monetary policy combination, see Lubik (2003), Benhabib and Eusepi (2005), Edge and Rudd (2007), Kurozumi (2006), Kurozumi and Van Zandweghe (2008), Kurozumi and Zandweghe (2011), and Linnemann (2006).

As for the stabilization effect of taxation rule in endogenous growth model mentioned in Sect. 5.3.1, Chen and Guo (2016) confirm that their main findings still hold when the model allows labor-leisure choice of households. Chen et al. (2016) reconsider Chen and Guo's (2015) findings in the context of small-open economy. They show that stabilization effect critically depends on how the small open economy is closed in the sense of Schmitt-Grohé and Uribe (2003).

The monetary endogenous growth examined in Sect. 5.3.2 is based on Fujisaki and Mino (2007), Mino and Shibata (1995), and Itaya and Mino (2003, 2004, 2007) discuss related issues. Under the assumption of constant money growth rule, Meng and Yip (2004), Suen and Yip (2005), and Itaya and Mino (2003, 2007) explore indeterminacy in monetary endogenous growth models.

Chapter 6
Indeterminacy in Open Economies

In the previous chapters, we restrict our attention to closed-economy models. This chapter examines equilibrium indeterminacy in open economies. The central concern of this chapter is to explore how international transactions affect the dynamic behaviors of macroeconomies. In particular, we focus on the difference in the indeterminacy conditions between open economies and their closed economy counterparts. We first discuss small open economies and then explore the world economy consisting of two large countries.

6.1 A One-Sector Model of Small Open Economy

6.1.1 Baseline Model

We start with a small open economy version of the Benhabib and Farmer (1994) model. The basic setup is the same as the original, closed economy model, but we impose the following additional assumptions that are standard in open-macroeconomics literature. First, households in the home country can freely lend to or borrow from foreign households. Second, the home country and the rest of the world produce homogeneous goods, implying that international trade means intertemporal trade rather than intratemporal trade.

6.1.1.1 Setup

The production side of the economy is the same as that in Benhabib and Farmer (1994). The production function of the home country is

$$Y = AK^{a}N^{1-a}\bar{K}^{\alpha-a}\bar{N}^{\beta-(1-a)}, \quad 0 < a < 1, \quad 1 > \alpha > a, \;\; \beta > 1-a,$$

K. Mino, *Growth and Business Cycles with Equilibrium Indeterminacy*,
Advances in Japanese Business and Economics 13,
DOI 10.1007/978-4-431-55609-1_6

where $\bar{K}$and $\bar{N}$ represent the country-specific external effects in production activities. We assume that there is no international spillover effect of the production technology. As before, the social production function is

$$Y = AK^{\alpha}N^{\beta},$$

and the factor prices are given by

$$r = a\frac{Y}{K}, \quad w = (1-a)\frac{Y}{N}. \tag{6.1}$$

The representative household in a small-open economy solves the following problem:

$$\max \int_0^{\infty} e^{-\rho t}\left(\log C - \frac{N^{1+\gamma}}{1+\gamma}\right) dt$$

subject to

$$\dot{B} = RB + rK + wH - C - I - \phi\left(\frac{I}{K}\right)K,$$

$$\dot{K} = I - \delta K,$$

where B denotes the stock of international bonds (international IOUs) and R is the real interest rate on B which is assumed to be given for the home country. The term $\phi(I/K)K$ stands for the investment adjustment costs. We assume that function $\phi(.)$ is monotonically increasing and strictly convex in I/K. In the following discussion, we specify

$$\phi\left(\frac{I}{K}\right) = \frac{\theta}{2}\left(\frac{I}{K}\right)^2, \quad \theta > 0.$$

Additionally, we impose the non-Ponzi game condition such that

$$\lim_{t\to\infty} \exp\left(-\int_0^t Rds\right)B_t \geq 0.$$

The Hamiltonian function for the households' optimization problem is set as

$$\mathcal{H} = \log C - \frac{N^{1+\gamma}}{1+\gamma} + \lambda\left[RB + rK + wN - C - I - \frac{\theta}{2}\left(\frac{I}{K}\right)^2 K\right]$$
$$+q(I - \delta K),$$

where λ and q respectively denote the utility values of bond and capital. The optimization conditions are:

$$1/C = \lambda, \tag{6.2a}$$

$$N^{\gamma} = \lambda w, \tag{6.2b}$$

$$\lambda\left(1+\theta\frac{I}{K}\right) = q, \tag{6.2c}$$

$$\dot{\lambda} = \lambda\left(\rho - R\right), \tag{6.2d}$$

$$\dot{q} = q\left(\rho+\delta\right) - \lambda\left[r + \frac{\theta}{2}\left(\frac{I}{K}\right)^2\right], \tag{6.2e}$$

together with the transversality conditions:

$$\lim_{t\to\infty} e^{-\rho t}\lambda B = 0, \quad \lim_{t\to\infty} e^{-\rho t} qK = 0. \tag{6.2f}$$

In view of (6.2d), we should assume

$$\rho = R. \tag{6.3}$$

Otherwise, either the non-Ponzi game or the transversality condition will be violated. This condition means that λ and C stay constant over time even out of the steady state.

From (6.2a) and (6.2b) we obtain

$$CN^{\gamma} = w = (1-a)AK^{\alpha}N^{\beta-1}, \tag{6.4}$$

which yields

$$N = \left[\frac{1}{\bar{C}}(1-a)AK^{\alpha}\right]^{\frac{1}{1+\gamma-\beta}}. \tag{6.5}$$

Condition (6.2c) presents

$$\frac{I}{K} = \frac{1}{\theta}\frac{q}{\lambda} - 1. \tag{6.6}$$

As a result, the capital stock changes according to

$$\dot{K} = I - \delta K = K\left(\frac{1}{\theta}\frac{q}{\lambda} - 1 - \delta\right). \tag{6.7}$$

Using (6.2e), (6.5), and (6.6), we obtain

$$\dot{q} = q(\rho+\delta) - \lambda \left\{ aAK^{\alpha-1} \left[\frac{1}{C}(1-a)AK^{\alpha} \right]^{\frac{\beta}{1+\gamma-\beta}} + \frac{\theta}{2}\left(\frac{1}{\theta}\frac{q}{\lambda} - 1 \right)^2 \right\}. \tag{6.8}$$

The dynamic system consisting of (6.7) and (6.8) has a unique steady state. Keeping in mind that λ and C stay constant, we see that the coefficient matrix of the linearized system around the steady state is given by

$$J_1 = \begin{bmatrix} 0 & \frac{K^*}{\theta\lambda} \\ \frac{\partial \dot{q}}{\partial K} & \rho \end{bmatrix}.$$

Here, it is shown that

$$\text{sign} \frac{\partial \dot{q}}{\partial K} = \text{sign} \frac{\beta - (1-\alpha)(1+\gamma)}{1+\gamma-\beta}.$$

Thus, the following holds:

$$\text{trace } J_1 = \rho > 0, \ \ \text{sign } \det J_{12} = \text{sign} \frac{\beta - (1-\alpha)(1+\gamma)}{\beta - (1+\gamma)}. \tag{6.9}$$

Considering that q is a jump variable, the facts in (6.9) show that the steady state of the small open economy is a saddle point if and only if

$$(1-\alpha)(1+\gamma) < \beta < 1+\gamma. \tag{6.10}$$

Otherwise, the steady state is a source so that the economy is totally unstable. Since $\beta > 1+\gamma$ is the necessary condition for indeterminacy in the closed economy model, we see that the same condition completely destabilizes the economy in the standard small open economy setting.

Using the non-Ponzi game scheme and the transversality conditions, we find that the household's intertemporal budget constraint is written as

$$B_0 + \int_0^{\infty} e^{-Rt} w_t N_t dt = \int_0^{\infty} e^{-Rt} \left\{ C_t + \left[\frac{I_t}{K_t} + \frac{\theta}{2}\left(\frac{I_t}{K_t} \right)^2 \right] K_t \right\} dt.$$

Since $C_t = C_0$ and $\lambda_t = 1/C_0$ for all $t \geq 0$, from (6.1), (6.2a) and (6.6) , the above is expressed as

$$B_0 + \int_0^{\infty} e^{-Rt} (1-\alpha) AK_t^{\alpha} \left[\frac{1}{C_0}(1-a)AK_t^{\alpha} \right]^{\frac{\beta}{1+\gamma-\beta}} dt$$
$$= \int_0^{\infty} e^{-Rt} \left\{ C_0 + \left[\frac{1}{\theta} C_0 q_t - 1 + \frac{\theta}{2}\left(\frac{1}{\theta} C_0 q_t - 1 \right)^2 \right] K_t \right\} dt. \tag{6.11}$$

Under (6.10), a unique stable saddle path exists and it is expressed as $q_t = \chi(K_t)$. We see that the left hand side of (6.11) decreases with C_0 under (6.10), while the right hand side increases with C_0. Therefore, given a sequence of $\{K_t\}_{t=0}^{\infty}$, there generally exists a unique level of C_0 $(= 1/\lambda_0)$ that satisfies the intertemporal budget constraint of the household. As a consequence, the steady state level of financial asset holding of the household is uniquely determined by

$$B^* = \frac{1}{R}\left[Y^* - C_0 - \delta K^* - \frac{\theta}{2}\delta^2 K^*\right],$$

where B^* and K^* respectively denote the steady state levels of foreign bond and capital. On the other hand, if $\beta > 1 + \gamma$, the presence of strong external increasing returns means that the social rate of return to capital increases as the aggregate capital expands. Equation (6.8) shows that $\dot{q}/q$ becomes negative so that the utility price of capital rises. At the same time, from (6.7) a higher q yields a further increase in K, which makes the dynamic system totally unstable.

The above results suggest that a small open economy tends to be more stable than the corresponding closed economy because sunspot-driven fluctuations are difficult to obtain. However, this conclusion can be applied to the one-sector, exogenous growth model alone. We will see that indeterminacy may emerge easily in small open economy versions of endogenous growth models or two-sector exogenous growth models. In the following, we briefly examine an endogenous growth version of the above model. We then analyze a two-sector model in the next section.

6.1.2 Endogenous Growth

As shown in Sect. 3.1 of Chap. 3, if we set $\alpha = 1$ in the Benhabib-Farmer model, we obtain an endogenous growth version of the baseline real business cycle (RBC) model with external increasing returns. Similarly, the small open economy discussed above can sustain continuing growth if $\alpha = 1$. Chin et al. (2012) analyze this case. When continuing growth in the long-run equilibrium is allowed, consumption grows at a constant rate in the balanced-growth equilibrium. In this case, the balanced-growth rate is exogenously determined by

$$\frac{\dot{C}}{C} = R - \rho = -\frac{\dot{\lambda}}{\lambda}.$$

Therefore, as long as $R > \rho$, the home country can grow at a positive constant rate, implying that we do not need to assume $\rho = R$ to obtain a feasible equilibrium. Given the restriction $\alpha = 1$, the utility price of capital changes according to

$$\frac{\dot{q}}{q} = \rho + \delta - \frac{\lambda}{q}\left\{aA\left[\frac{K}{C}(1-a)A\right]^{\frac{\beta}{1+\gamma-\beta}} + \frac{\theta}{2}\left(\frac{1}{\theta}\frac{q}{\lambda} - 1\right)^2\right\}.$$

Consequently, denoting $q/\lambda = x$ and $C/K = z$, we obtain a complete dynamic system of a small open economy with endogenous growth as follows:

$$\frac{\dot{x}}{x} = \rho + \delta - \frac{1}{x}\left\{aA\left[(1-a)A\frac{1}{z}\right]^{\frac{\beta}{1+\gamma-\beta}} + \frac{\theta}{2}\left(\frac{1}{\theta}x - 1\right)^2\right\}, \quad (6.12)$$

$$\frac{\dot{z}}{z} = R - \rho - \frac{x}{\theta} + 1 + \delta. \quad (6.13)$$

In the balanced growth equilibrium where x and z stay constant over time, the following conditions hold:

$$\rho + \delta - \frac{1}{x}\left\{aA\left[(1-a)A\frac{1}{z}\right]^{\frac{\beta}{1+\gamma-\beta}} + \frac{\theta}{2}\left(\frac{1}{\theta}x - 1\right)^2\right\} = 0,$$

$$R - \rho - \frac{x}{\theta} + 1 + \delta = 0.$$

Inspecting the above equations, it is easy to confirm that the balanced growth path is uniquely given. The coefficient matrix of the dynamic system evaluated at the steady state is

$$J_1 = \begin{bmatrix} \frac{1}{\theta}x^* - 1 & \alpha(1-\alpha)A^2\frac{\beta}{1+\gamma-\beta}\frac{1}{z^*} \\ -\frac{z^*}{\theta} & 0 \end{bmatrix}.$$

Hence, we see that

$$\operatorname{sign} J_1 = \operatorname{sign}\ (1+\gamma-\beta).$$

Since both x and z are jump variables, the above means that the steady state is a saddle point (a source) if $\beta > 1+\gamma$ $(\beta < 1+\gamma)$. Therefore, the balanced-growth equilibrium is locally indeterminate (determinate) if $\beta > 1+\gamma$ $(\beta < 1+\gamma)$.

In this model, two outcomes stand out. First, unlike the exogenous growth case discussed previously, if continuing growth is allowed in the small open economy, indeterminacy emerges under $\beta > 1+\gamma$. Second, departing from the closed economy model of endogenous growth in Sect. 2.1 of Chap. 2, the small open economy model has a unique balanced-growth path even under $\beta > 1+\gamma$. Comparing the models in this section to those discussed in Sect. 2.2 of Chap. 2 as well and in Sect. 3.1 of Chap. 3, we see that determinacy/indeterminacy conditions critically depend on openness of the economy as well as on whether or not the economy allows continuing growth in the long-run equilibrium.

6.2 A Two-Sector Model of Small Open Economy

It must be pointed out that if we consider two-sector models, the small open economy may hold indeterminacy even though the model economy does not allow endogenous growth. In what follows, we examine a simple two-sector model in which the first sector produces investment goods, while the second sector produces pure consumption goods. Following Weder (2001) and Meng and Velasco (2003, 2004), we assume that investment goods are not traded, while consumption goods are tradable.

6.2.1 Production

The production structure is similar to that used in Sect. 3.4 in Chap. 3. The production technology of each sector is associated with sector-specific external effects and exhibits social constant returns. The production function of each sector is given by

$$Y_i = A_i K_i^{a_i} N_i^{b_i} \bar{K}_i^{\alpha_i - a_i} \bar{N}_i^{1-\alpha_i - b_i}, \quad i = 1, 2,$$

where Y_i, K_i and N_i are the i-th sector's output, capital, and labor input, respectively. Here, $\bar{K}_i$ and $\bar{N}_i$ denote the sector-specific production externalities generated by the total capital and labor employed by sector i. We assume

$$a_i < \alpha_i < 1, \;\; 0 < b_i < 1, \;\; \alpha_i + b_i < 1, \quad i = 1, 2.$$

Normalizing the number of producers to one, it holds that $\bar{K}_i = K_i$ and $\bar{N}_i = N_i \;\; (i = 1, 2)$ in equilibrium. This means that the i-th sector's social production technology that internalizes the external effects is

$$Y_i = A_i K_i^{\alpha_i} N_i^{1-\alpha_i}, \quad i = 1, 2.$$

Hence, the social technology satisfies constant returns to scale, while the private technology exhibits decreasing returns to scale.[1]

The factor and product markets are competitive, so that the private marginal product of each production factor equals its real factor price. These conditions are given by the following:

$$r = p a_1 \frac{Y_1}{K_1} = a_2 \frac{Y_2}{K_2}, \tag{6.14a}$$

[1]This specification of production technology is first introduced by Benhabib and Nishimura (1998) who demonstrate that equilibrium intermediacy may hold even in the absence of social increasing returns. Benhabib et al. (2000), Meng (2003), Meng and Velasco (2003, 2004), Mino (2001), and Nishimura and Shimomura (2002a,b) use the same production functions.

$$w = pb_1\frac{Y_1}{N_1} = b_2\frac{Y_2}{N_2}, \tag{6.14b}$$

where w is the real wage rate, r is the rental rate of capital, and p denotes the price of the investment good in terms of the consumption good.

Considering that $\bar{K}_i = K_i$ and $\bar{N}_i = N_i$, we find that (6.14a) and (6.14b) yield the following:

$$r = pa_1A_1k_1^{\alpha_1-1} = a_2A_2k_2^{\alpha_2-1}, \tag{6.15a}$$

$$w = pb_1A_1k_1^{\alpha_1} = b_2A_2k_2^{\alpha_2}, \tag{6.15b}$$

where $k_i = K_i/N_i \ (i = 1,2)$. By use of (6.15a) and (6.15b), we can express the optimal factor intensity in each production sector as a function of relative price:

$$k_1 = \left(\frac{A_1}{A_2}\right)^{\frac{1}{\alpha_2-\alpha_1}}\left(\frac{a_1}{a_2}\right)^{\frac{\alpha_2}{\alpha_2-\alpha_1}}\left(\frac{b_1}{b_2}\right)^{\frac{\alpha_2-1}{\alpha_1-\alpha_2}} p^{\frac{1}{\alpha_2-\alpha_1}} \equiv k_1(p),$$

$$k_2 = \left(\frac{A_1}{A_2}\right)^{\frac{1}{\alpha_2-\alpha_1}}\left(\frac{a_1}{a_2}\right)^{\frac{\alpha_1}{\alpha_2-\alpha_1}}\left(\frac{b_1}{b_2}\right)^{\frac{\alpha_1-1}{\alpha_1-\alpha_2}} p^{\frac{1}{\alpha_2-\alpha_1}} \equiv k_2(p).$$

These expressions show that

$$\text{sign}\,[k_1(p) - k_2(p)] = \text{sign}\left(\frac{a_1}{b_1} - \frac{a_2}{b_2}\right), \tag{6.17}$$

$$\text{sign}\,k_i'(p) = \text{sign}\,(\alpha_2 - \alpha_1), \quad i = 1,2. \tag{6.18}$$

In the above, the sign of $a_1/b_1 - a_2/b_2$ represents the factor intensity ranking from the private perspective, while the sign of $(\alpha_1 - \alpha_2)$ expresses the factor intensity ranking from the social perspective.

We assume that production factors can shift freely between the sectors, but they cannot cross the border. Thus, the full employment conditions for capital and labor in the home country are respectively given by

$$K_1 + K_2 = K, \quad N_1 + N_2 = 1,$$

where K denotes the aggregate capital in the home country. The labor supply is assumed to be constant and normalized to one. These full-employment conditions are summarized as

$$k_1(p)N_1 + (1 - N_1)k_2(p) = K. \tag{6.19}$$

In the following, we restrict our attention to the interior equilibrium in which the home country produces both consumption and investment goods.[2] Hence, we focus on the situation in which the labor allocation to the first sector given by (6.19) satisfies the following:

$$N_1 = \frac{K - k_2(p)}{k_1(p) - k_2(p)} \in (0, 1). \tag{6.20}$$

The supply functions of investment and consumption goods are respectively given by

$$y^1(K,p) \equiv N_1 A_1 k_1(p)^{\alpha_1} = \frac{K - k_2(p)}{k_1(p) - k_2(p)} A_1 k_1(p)^{\alpha_1}, \tag{6.21a}$$

$$y^2(K,p) = (1 - N_1) A_2 k_2(p)^{\alpha_2} \equiv \frac{k_1(p) - K}{k_1(p) - k_2(p)} A_2 k_2(p)^{\alpha_2}. \tag{6.21b}$$

It is easy to see that these supply functions satisfy

$$\left.\begin{aligned} \operatorname{sign} y_K^1(K,p) &= \operatorname{sign}\left(\frac{a_1}{b_1} - \frac{a_2}{b_2}\right), \\ \operatorname{sign} y_p^1(K,p) &= \operatorname{sign}\left(\frac{a_1}{b_1} - \frac{a_2}{b_2}\right)(\alpha_1 - \alpha_2), \\ \operatorname{sign} y_K^2(K,p) &= -\operatorname{sign}\left(\frac{a_1}{b_1} - \frac{a_2}{b2}\right), \\ \operatorname{sign} y_p^2(K,p) &= -\operatorname{sign}\left(\frac{a_1}{b_1} - \frac{a_2}{b_2}\right)(\alpha_1 - \alpha_2). \end{aligned}\right\} \tag{6.22a}$$

Note that if the private and social factor intensity rankings have opposite signs, that is, $\left(\frac{a_1}{b_1} - \frac{a_2}{b_2}\right)(\alpha_1 - \alpha_2) < 0$, then the duality between the Rybczynski and Stolper–Samuelson effects fails to hold.

6.2.2 *Households*

There is a continuum of identical households with a unit mass. Each household supplies one unit of labor in each moment. The objective function of the representative household is given by

$$U = \int_0^{\infty} \frac{C^{1-\sigma} - 1}{1 - \sigma} e^{-\rho t} dt, \quad \sigma > 0, \quad \rho > 0,$$

[2]See Footnote 11 on this restriction.

where C is consumption and ρ denotes a given time discount rate. When $\sigma = 1$, then the instantaneous felicity function is $\log C$. When households in the home country can lend to or borrow from foreign households, then their flow budget constraint is given by

$$\dot{\Omega} = R\Omega + w + \pi_1 + \pi_2 - C, \tag{6.23}$$
$$\Omega = B + pK,$$

where B is the stock of bonds (IOUs) and Ω denotes the total wealth; both are expressed in terms of the consumption good. Note that since the private technology exhibits decreasing returns to scale, there are excess profits in both production sectors. These are represented by π_1 and π_2 in (6.23), both of which are assumed to be distributed back to the representative household. We assume that bond and capital are perfect substitutes, and, hence, the non-arbitrage condition between the two assets requires that the rate of return to bond equal the net rate return to capital plus capital gain:

$$R = \frac{r}{p} - \delta + \frac{\dot{p}}{p}. \tag{6.24}$$

Using (6.24) and $\dot{\Omega} = \dot{B} + p\dot{K} + \dot{p}K$, the flow budget constraint (6.23) is rewritten as

$$\dot{B} = RB + rK + w + \pi_1 + \pi_2 - C - pI, \tag{6.25}$$

where I denotes gross investment, which leads to

$$\dot{K} = I - \delta K. \tag{6.26}$$

The representative household maximizes U subject (6.25), (6.26), and the non-Ponzi-game scheme given by

$$\lim_{t \to \infty} \exp\left(-\int_0^t R_s ds\right) B_t \geq 0.$$

We set up the Hamiltonian function for the optimization problem in the following manner:

$$\mathcal{H} = \frac{C^{1-\sigma} - 1}{1 - \sigma} + \lambda \left[RB + rK + w + \pi_1 + \pi_2 - C - pI\right] + q\left(I - \delta K\right),$$

where λ and q respectively denote the implicit prices of bonds and domestic capital. Focusing on an interior solution, we see that the necessary conditions for an optimum are

$$C^{-\sigma} = \lambda, \tag{6.27a}$$

$$p\lambda = q, \tag{6.27b}$$

$$\dot{\lambda} = \lambda\,(\rho - R)\,, \tag{6.27c}$$

$$\dot{q} = q\,(\rho + \delta) - \lambda r = q\left(\rho + \delta - \frac{r}{p}\right). \tag{6.27d}$$

The optimization conditions also involve the transversality conditions on holding bond and capital: $\lim_{t\to\infty}\lambda e^{-\rho t}B = 0$ and $\lim_{t\to\infty} q e^{-\rho t}K = 0$.

6.2.3 Equilibrium (In)determinacy

Since we have assumed that investment goods are not internationally traded, the market equilibrium condition for investment goods in the home country is $Y_1 = I$. Hence, capital formation is described by

$$\dot{K} = y^1\,(K,p) - \delta K. \tag{6.28}$$

Equation (6.27b) means that the price of investment goods equals the relative utility price between capital and bond, q/λ. Thus, using (6.15a), (6.27b), and (6.27d), we obtain the dynamic equation of p in such a way that

$$\dot{p} = p\left[R + \delta - a_1 A_1 k_1\,(p)^{\alpha_1 - 1}\right]. \tag{6.29}$$

Then, we have a complete dynamic system consisting of (6.28) and (6.29), which depicts behaviors of K and p.

The steady-state conditions are given by

$$\frac{K - k_2\,(p)}{k_1\,(p) - k_2\,(p)} A_1 k_1\,(p)^{\alpha_1} = \delta K,$$
$$a_1 A_1 k_1\,(p)^{\alpha_1 - 1} = \rho + \delta.$$

The second condition of the above determines a unique steady state value of p. The steady state level of per capita capital, K, is given by the first condition, which yields a unique level of K under a given steady state level of p.

The coefficient matrix of the dynamic system approximated at the steady state is

$$J_2 = \begin{bmatrix} y^1_K\,(K^*,p^*) - \delta & y^1_p\,(K^*,p^*) \\ 0 & p^*\,(1-\alpha)\,A_1 k_1'\,(p^*)\,k_1\,(p^*)^{\alpha - 2} \end{bmatrix},$$

where K^* and p^* are the steady state values of K and p, respectively. This matrix yields

$$\det J_2 = \left[y_K^1\left(K^*, p^*\right) - \delta\right]\left[p^*\left(1-\alpha\right)A_1 k_1'\left(p^*\right)k_1\left(p^*\right)^{\alpha-2}\right],$$

$$\text{Trace } J_2 = y_K^1\left(K^*, p^*\right) - \delta + p^*\left(\alpha-1\right)A_1 k_1'\left(p^*\right)k_1\left(p^*\right)^{\alpha-2}.$$

Here, we see that

$$y_K^1\left(K^*, p^*\right) - \delta = \frac{1}{k_1\left(p^*\right) - k_2\left(p^*\right)}A_1 k_1\left(p\right)^{\alpha_1} - \delta,$$

which has a negative sign if $k_2 > k_1$. Note that the steady state condition gives

$$\frac{1}{k_1\left(p^*\right) - k_2\left(p^*\right)}A_1 k_1\left(p\right)^{\alpha_1} = \delta + \frac{k_2\left(p^*\right)/K^*}{k_1\left(p^*\right) - k_2\left(p^*\right)},$$

implying that $y_K^1\left(.\right) > \delta$, if $k_1 > k_2$.

First, suppose that the factor intensity ranking from the private perspective is the same as that from the social perspective. In this case, it holds that

$$\left(\frac{a_1}{b_1} - \frac{a_2}{b_2}\right)\left(\alpha_1 - \alpha_2\right) > 0,$$

which leads to

$$\text{sign }\left[k_1\left(p\right) - k_2\left(p\right)\right] = \text{sign } y_K^1\left(K, p\right) = -\text{sign } k_1'\left(p\right).$$

Here, we confirm that $\det J_2 < 0$, so that local determinacy holds around the steady state.

If the social factor intensity ranking diverges from the private one, we obtain

$$\left(\frac{a_1}{b_1} - \frac{a_2}{b_2}\right)\left(\alpha_1 - \alpha_2\right) < 0.$$

This means that

$$\text{sign }\left[k_1\left(p\right) - k_2\left(p\right)\right] = \text{sign } y_K^1\left(K, p\right) = \text{sign } k_1'\left(p\right).$$

Therefore, if $k_1 > k_2$ and $\alpha_1 < \alpha_2$, we find that $\det J_2 > 0$ and trace $J_2 > 0$. On the other hand, if $k_2 > k_1$ but $\alpha_1 > a_2$, then it holds that $\det J_2 > 0$ and trace $J_2 < 0$. Consequently, if the investment good sector uses more capital-intensive technology from the private perspective but it uses more labor-intensive technology from the social perspective than the consumption good sector, then the steady state of the small country is totally unstable. In contrast, if the investment good sector's technology is more labor-intensive from the private perspective but it is more capital-intensive from the social perspective, then the steady state exhibits local indeterminacy.

To sum up, according to Meng and Velasco (2004), the main outcome of this model is the following:

Proposition 6.1 *If the social factor intensity ranking between the consumption and investment sector is the same as the private factor intensity ranking, then the equilibrium path of the two-sector small-open economy is determinate. If the investment good sector uses more labor (capital) intensive technology from the private perspective but it uses more capital (labor) intensive technology from the social perspective, then the equilibrium path is indeterminate (unstable).*

6.2.4 Remarks

The indeterminacy condition derived above is exactly the same as that for the closed economy, two-sector model of endogenous growth examined in Sect. 3.4 of Chap. 3. Furthermore, the condition is also same as that for the two-sector exogenous growth model of a closed economy with a linear utility function; see Benhabib and Nishimura (1998). In fact, these three models have the same mathematical structure. In the linear utility function model explored by Benhabib and Nishimura (1998), the household's problem in the form of the pseudo-planning problem is

$$\max \int_0^\infty e^{-\rho t} C dt$$

subject to

$$\dot{K} = Y_i = A_1 K_1^{a_1} N_i^{b_1} \bar{K}_1^{\alpha_1 - a_1} \bar{N}_1^{1-\alpha_1-b_1} - \delta K,$$
$$C = A_2 (K - K_1)^{a2} (1 - N_1)^{b_2} \bar{K}_2^{\alpha 2 - a_2} \bar{N}_2^{1-\alpha_2-b_2}.$$

In the above, the planner takes the sequences of $\{K_{i,t}, N_{i,t}\}_{t=0}^\infty$ $(i = 1, 2)$ as given. The Hamiltonian function of this planning problem can be set as

$$\mathcal{H} = C + q\left(A_1 K_1^{a1} N_1^{b_1} \bar{K}_1^{\alpha_1 - a_1} \bar{N}_1^{1-\alpha_1-b_1} - \delta K\right)$$
$$+\lambda \left(A_2 (K - K_1)^{a_2} (1 - N_1)^{b_2} \left(\bar{K} - \bar{K}_1\right)^{\alpha_2 - a_2} \left(1 - \bar{N}_1\right)^{1-\alpha_2-b_2} - C\right).$$

Maximization with respect to C gives $\lambda = 1$, Thus, the optimal choice conditions for K_1 and N_1 evaluated at $\bar{K} = K$, $\bar{K}_1 = K_1$ and $\bar{N}_1 = N_1$ are written as:

$$q a_1 \frac{Y_1}{K_1} = a_2 \frac{Y_2}{K_2}, \quad q b_1 \frac{Y_1}{N_1} = b_2 \frac{Y_2}{N_2}.$$

This means that as before, the rate of return to capital held in the market economy counterpart can be expressed as $r(q)$. Since the marginal utility is one, the utility price of capital exactly corresponds to the market price of the investment good in terms of the consumption good. Hence, in view of (6.14a), the dynamic equation of q given by (6.27d) is re-expressed as

$$\dot{p} = p\left[\rho + \delta - a_1 k_1 (p)^{\alpha_1 - 1}\right].$$

Consequently, a complete dynamic system consists of (6.28) and (6.29), which is identical to the dynamic system of a two-sector small open economy model discussed so far.

Intuitively, households in an open economy with free trade of consumption goods and financial assets can make their consumption perfectly smooth. Similarly, if the utility function is linear in consumption, the elasticity of intertemporal substitution as to the consumption is infinite, which means that the optimal consumption follows the same behavior as that in the small open economy with free trade of consumption goods and financial assets. Given this fact, together with the production structure that satisfies social constant returns, the dynamic behavior of the closed economy model with a linear utility function becomes identical to the dynamics of the small open economy with free trade of consumption goods and financial assets.

6.3 A Two-Country Model with Free Trade of Commodities

In this and the next sections, we examine the two-sector model analyzed above in the context of the global economy. We set up a global economy model with two large countries in which the specification of production structure in each country is the same as in the model in the previous section. The primary purpose of the following two sections is to elucidate how the trade structure affects equilibrium (in)determinacy of the world economy. To see this in a clear manner, we first consider a two-country model with financial autarky. In this model we assume that the home and foreign countries have the same production technology and identical preference structure. Additionally, the social production functions satisfy constant returns to scale, and the utility function is homothetic.

6.3.1 Baseline Setting

Consider a world economy consisting of two countries; home and foreign. Both countries have the same production technologies. In each country there a continuum of identical household with a unit mass. Households in both countries have an identical time discount rate and the same form of instantaneous felicity function. The only difference between the two countries is the initial stock of capital held by the households in each country. Hence, the objective function of the foreign household is

$$U^* = \int_0^\infty e^{-\rho t} \frac{C^{*1-\sigma}}{1-\sigma} dt$$

and the production functions are given by

$$Y_i^* = A_i K_i^{*a_i} N_i^{*b_i} \bar{K}_i^{*\alpha_i - a_i} \bar{N}_i^{*1-\alpha_i - b_i}, \quad i = 1, 2.$$

In the above, an asterisk attached to each variable represents the foreign country.

Given our assumptions, the supply function of each sector in the foreign country has the same form of the home country's counterparts; that is, we have

$$y^1 \left(K^*, p^*\right) = \frac{K^* - k_2\left(p^*\right)}{k_1\left(p\right) - k_2\left(p\right)} A_1 k_1 \left(p^*\right)^{\alpha_1}, \tag{6.30a}$$

$$y^2 \left(K^*, p^*\right) = \frac{k_1\left(p^*\right) - K^*}{k_1\left(p^*\right) - k_2\left(p^*\right)} A_2 k_2 \left(p^*\right)^{\alpha_2}, \tag{6.30b}$$

where p^* denotes the price of the investment good in terms of the consumption good held in the foreign country.

Finally, according to the standard setting of the Heckscher-Ohlin model, we assume that capital and labor cannot cross the border. Additionally, it is assumed that the external effects associated with capital and labor do not diffuse internationally.

We first assume that there is only intratemporal trade: both investment and consumption goods are freely traded but households in each country neither lend to nor borrow from the foreign households. This is the traditional Heckscher-Ohlin setting employed by Nishimura and Shimomura (2002b). This section summarizes the main results of their contribution in order to clarify the effects of introducing nontraded goods and financial transactions into the base model.

In what follows, we restrict our attention to the case in which neither home nor foreign countries specialize. Hence, the free trade of both the investment and consumption goods between two countries establishes $p = p^*$, so that both factor intensity in both countries are the same, that is $k_i\left(p\right) = k_i^*\left(p\right)$. As a consequence, the factor prices, r and w, are also the same in both countries. The representative household in the home country maximizes U subject to

$$\dot{K} = \left(\frac{r}{p} - \delta\right) K + \frac{1}{p}\left(w + \pi_1 + \pi_2 - C\right),$$

Similarly, the foreign household maximizes U^* under the constraint of

$$\dot{K}^* = \left(\frac{r}{p} - \delta\right) K^* + \frac{1}{p}\left(w + \pi_1^* + \pi_2^* - C^*\right).$$

Let us denote the utility prices of K and K^* by q and q^*, respectively. Then, the optimization conditions of the home and foreign households' problems present $C^{-\sigma} = p/q$ and $C^{*-\sigma} = p/q^*$. Hence, we obtain

$$\frac{C^*}{C} = \left(\frac{q^*}{q}\right)^{-1/\sigma}. \tag{6.31}$$

In addition, using $r/p = A_1 k_1 (p)^{\alpha-1}$, we obtain

$$\dot{q}/q = \dot{q}^*/q^* = \rho + \delta - A_1 k_1 (p)^{\alpha-1},$$

which shows that q^*/q stays constant over time. Hence, (6.31) means that C^* is related to C in such a way that

$$C^* = nC, \tag{6.32}$$

where n is a positive constant.

6.3.2 *Global Equilibrium Conditions*

The world market equilibrium conditions for investment and consumption goods are respectively given by

$$Y_1 + Y_1^* = \dot{K} + \dot{K}^* + \delta K + \delta K^*, \tag{6.33}$$

$$Y_2 + Y_2^* = C + C^*. \tag{6.34}$$

When both countries produce both goods, all the firms in the world economy face the common world price, p.[3] Since it holds that $k_i (p) = k_i^* (p)$ $(i = 1, 2)$, from (6.21a) and (6.33) the aggregate capital in the world market changes according to

$$\dot{K}_w = \frac{K_w - 2k_2 (p)}{k_1 (p) - k_2 (p)} A_1 k_1 (p)^{\alpha_1} - \delta K_w, \tag{6.35}$$

where $K_W = K + K^*$.

[3]Our discussion depends on this assumption. If at least one country completely specializes, the dynamic system of the world economy becomes different from that examined in this section. However, provided that both countries have identical taste and technology, the steady state equilibrium of the world economy is inside the diversification cone where both countries produce both goods. Therefore, our assumption is justified as long as we focus on the local dynamics of the world economy around the steady state equilibrium. To analyze the global behavior of the model, we need to treat the model out of the diversification cone. Atkeson and Kehoe (2000) explored the dynamic behavior of a small country that specializes in producing one of the two goods. Caliendo (2010) presents a detailed analysis of the dynamic behavior of a 2 × 2 × 2 model outside the diversification cone.

Using (6.32), the global consumption is

$$C_w = C + C^* = (1+n)\,C.$$

The market equilibrium condition for the consumption good is thus expressed as

$$\frac{2k_1(p) - K_w}{k_1(p) - k_2(p)} A_2 k_2(p)^{\alpha_2} = (1+n)\,C. \tag{6.36}$$

Note that the optimization conditions (6.27a) and (6.27b) yield $C = (q/p)^{-1/\sigma}$. Substituting this into (6.36), we can express the equilibrium level of p as a function of K_w, q and n:

$$p = p(K_w, q; n). \tag{6.37}$$

Consequently, a complete dynamic system of the world economy is given by the following pair of differential equations:

$$\dot{K}_w = \frac{K_w - 2k_2(p(K_w, q; n))}{k_1(p(K_w, q; n)) - k_2(p(K_w, q; n))} A_1 k_1(p(K_w, q; n))^{\alpha_1} - \delta K_w, \tag{6.38}$$

$$\dot{q} = q\left[\rho + \delta - f_1'(k_1(p(K_w, q; n)))\right]. \tag{6.39}$$

This system involves an undetermined constant, n. Otherwise, the system is identical to the closed economy model with social constant returns examined by Benhabib and Nishimura (1998).

6.3.3 Equilibrium Indeterminacy and Patterns of Trade

It is easy to see that the world economy has a unique steady state. First, the condition $\dot{q} = 0$ in (6.39) gives $\hat{r}(p) = \rho + \delta$, which determines a unique level of relative price in the steady state. Then $\dot{K}_w = 0$ in (6.38) yields a unique steady state value of K_w. The steady state level of q is thus given by (6.37). As to determinacy of the global steady state, Nishimura and Shimomura (2002b) found the following:

Proposition 6.2 *The steady state equilibrium of the world economy is locally indeterminate if* $\frac{a_1}{b_1} - \frac{a_2}{b_2} < 0$ *and* $\alpha_1 - \alpha_2 > 0$ *and (ii)* $1/\sigma > \max\{1,\ 1/\bar{\sigma}\}$, *where* $\bar{\sigma}$ *is a function of parameters involved in the model.*[4]

[4]The precise expression of $1/\bar{\sigma}$ is

$$\frac{1}{\bar{\sigma}} = \frac{(1-\alpha_1)a_2 b_1(\rho+\delta) + \alpha_1 a_1\left[\rho b_2 + \delta b_1 a_2 + (1-a_1)b_2\delta\right]}{(a_2 b_1 - a_1 b_2)(\alpha_1 - \alpha_2)\left[\rho + \delta(1-a_1)\right]}.$$

Since the dynamics of the global economy have the same structure as that of a closed, single-country model, the above conditions are essentially the same as the conditions given by Benhabib and Nishimura (1998) who analyze a two-sector closed economy model with social constant returns.

Observe that the steady state conditions of the world economy alone cannot determine the steady state levels of K and K^* held by each country. When the dynamic system has a saddle point property, the world economy has a unique converging path toward the steady state. If this is the case, it can be verified that the value of q/q^* (and the value of $\bar{n}$) is uniquely determined depending on the initial holding of capital in each country, K_0 and K_0^*. To understand this clearly, note that the intertemporal budget constraint for the household in each county is respectively given by

$$\int_0^\infty \exp\left(-\int_0^t r_s ds\right) C_t dt = \int_0^\infty \exp\left(-\int_0^t r_s ds\right) y^2\left(K_t, p_t\right) dt + K_0,$$
$$\int_0^\infty \exp\left(-\int_0^t r_s ds\right) C_t^* dt = \int_0^\infty \exp\left(-\int_0^t r_s ds\right) y^2\left(K_t^*, p_t\right) dt + K_0^*.$$

Using $C_t^* = nC_t$, from these two equations, we derive

$$1 + n = \frac{\int_0^\infty \exp\left(-\int_0^t r_s ds\right) y^2\left(K_t, p_t\right) dt + K_0}{\int_0^\infty \exp\left(-\int_0^t r_s ds\right) y^2\left(K_t^*, p_t\right) dt + K_0^*}. \tag{6.40}$$

If the equilibrium path under given levels of K_0 and K_0^* is determinate, then the right hand side of the above is uniquely given, so that n is uniquely determined as well. Moreover, it depends on the distribution of initial capital stocks between the two countries. In this case the steady state levels of capital are also unique and they are given by

$$\hat{K} = \frac{1}{\delta}\left[y^1\left(\hat{K}, \hat{p}\right) + \frac{1}{\hat{p}} y^2\left(\hat{K}, \hat{p}\right) - \hat{C}\right],$$
$$\hat{K}^* = \frac{1}{\delta}\left[y^1\left(\hat{K}^*, \hat{p}\right) + \frac{1}{\hat{p}} y^2\left(\hat{K}^*, \hat{p}\right) - \hat{C}^*\right].$$

As Chen (1992) demonstrated, if the initial position of the world economy is not far from its steady state, the sign of $K_0 - K_0^*$ is the same as sign $\left(\hat{K} - \hat{K}^*\right)$. Hence, the initial comparative advantage determined by the initial distribution of capital still holds in the steady state. This outcome is a dynamic version of the Hechscher-Ohlin proposition.

However, if the equilibrium path is indeterminate, the value of the right hand side of (6.40) depends on which specific path is taken. This means that the steady state distribution of capital (and the long-run pattern of trade) would be affected by a change in the expectations of agents. In other words, sunspot shocks may affect

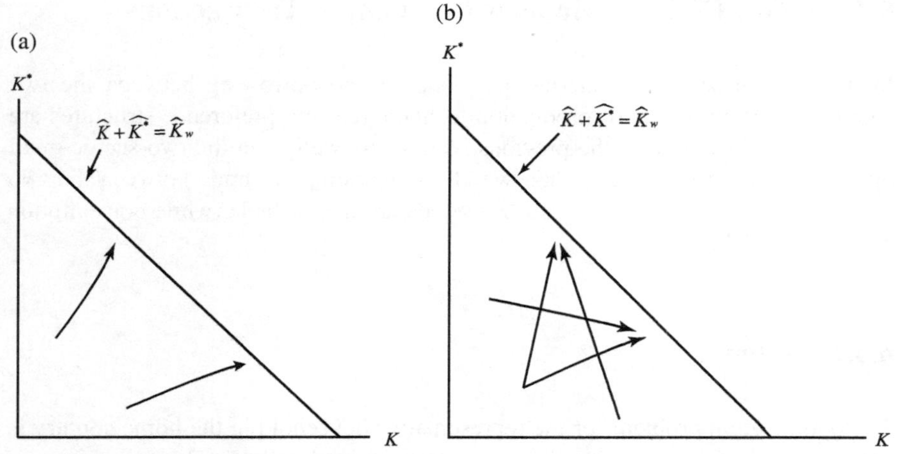

Fig. 6.1 (**a**) The case of determinacy (**b**) The case of indeterminacy

the long-run patterns of trade between the two countries and, hence, the dynamic Heckscher-Ohlin theorem fails to hold.

For example, suppose that the home country is initially more abundant in capital than the foreign country. Then, as long as both countries are always in the diversification cone during the transition, the home country can maintain the comparative advantage in producing capital intensive goods in the steady state equilibrium as well. In this sense, if the equilibrium path is determinate, the Heckscher-Ohlin theorem of determination of trade pattern still holds even though the capital stock in each country changes over time during the transition toward the steady state.[5] Figure 6.1 depicts the above discussion intuitively. Since the steady state level of $\hat{K}_w$ is uniquely given, the steady state levels of K and K^* satisfy $\hat{K} + \hat{K}^* = \hat{K}_w$. As Fig. 6.1a shows, if determinacy is established under a given set of $\left(K_0, K_0^*\right)$, there is a unique converging path to the steady state distribution of capital. If indeterminacy holds, then a path starting from the same initial position may reach a different stationary point, and which steady state is realized depends on expectations. In sum, sunspots do matter for determining the long-run patterns of trade between the two countries.

[5]This conclusion depends on the functional forms of production and utility functions we use as well as on the fact that we restrict our attention to the model behavior near the steady state. As for more general analyses on income and wealth distribution among the countries in the Heckscher-Ohlin setting, see Atkeson and Kehoe (2000) and Bajona and Kehoe (2010). Atkeson and Kehoe treated a small-country model, while Bajona and Kehoe (2010) explored a two-country model.

6.4 A Two-Country Model with Financial Transactions

In this section we allow international lending and borrowing between the two countries. Specifications of production technologies and preference structures are the same as these used in the previous section. As well as in the two-sector small open economy model in Sect. 6.2, we allow intertemporal trade between the two countries by assuming that investment goods are not tradable, while consumption goods are tradable.

6.4.1 Setup

The optimization problem for the representative household in the home country is the same as the two-sector small-open economy model in Sect. 6.2:

$$\max \int_0^\infty e^{-\rho t} \frac{C^{1-\sigma}-1}{1-\sigma} dt, \quad \sigma > 0, \quad \rho > 0$$

subject to

$$\dot{B} = RB + rK + w + \pi_1 + \pi_2 - C - pI, \tag{6.41}$$

$$\dot{K} = I - \delta K. \tag{6.42}$$

Note that unlike the small open economy model in Sect. 6.2, the interest rate on bond, R, is endogenously determined in the world financial market. The representative household maximizes U subject (6.41), (6.42), and the non-Ponzi-game scheme given by

$$\lim_{t\to\infty} \exp\left(-\int_0^t R_s ds\right) B_t \geq 0.$$

Since the optimization problem is the same as that in the corresponding small open economy model, the key optimization conditions for the representative household in the home country are (6.27a) through (6.27d), together with the transversality condition $\lim_{t\to\infty} e^{-\rho t} q_t K_t = 0$ and $\lim_{t\to\infty} e^{-\rho t} \lambda B = 0$.

Similarly, the foreign household solves

$$\max \int_0^\infty e^{-\rho t} \frac{C^{*1-\sigma}}{1-\sigma} dt$$

subject to

$$\dot{B}^* = RB^* + r^* K + w^* + \pi_1^* + \pi_2^* - C^* - p^* I^*,$$
$$\dot{K}^* = I^* - \delta K^*.$$

Hence, the optimization conditions for the foreign household include the following:

$$C^{*-\sigma} = \lambda^*, \tag{6.43a}$$

$$p^* \lambda^* = q^*, \tag{6.43b}$$

$$\dot{\lambda}^* = \lambda^* (\rho - R), \tag{6.43c}$$

$$\dot{q}^* = q^* (\rho + \delta) - \lambda^* r = q^* \left(\rho + \delta - \frac{r^*}{p^*} \right). \tag{6.43d}$$

We should note that since the investment goods are not internationally traded, the relative price of commodities and factor prices are not equalized between the two countries.

6.4.2 *Market Equilibrium Conditions and Aggregate Dynamics*

We now assume that consumption goods are internationally traded and financial capital mobility is allowed, but investment goods are non-tradables.[6] Although such an assumption is restrictive, it helps to elucidate the role of trade structure in a dynamic world economy. Since investment goods are traded in the domestic markets alone and consumption goods are traded internationally, the market equilibrium conditions for investment and consumption goods are respectively given by

$$Y_1 = \dot{K} + \delta K, \quad Y_1^* = \dot{K}^* + \delta K^*, \tag{6.44}$$

$$Y_2 + Y_2^* = C + C^*. \tag{6.45}$$

The equilibrium condition for the bond market is

$$B + B^* = 0, \tag{6.46}$$

[6] In the small-country setting, the trade structure assumed here is a type of dependent economy model discussed in open-economy macroeconomics literature. Turnovsky and Sen (1995) treated a small-open economy model with non-tradable capital and Turnovsky (1997, Chapter 7) studied a neoclassical two-country, two-sector model in which capital goods are not traded. Mino (2008) also examined a similar two-country model with external increasing returns. See also Chapter 5 for a brief literature review.

which means that $\Omega + \Omega^* = pK + p^*K^*$. Bonds are IOUs traded between the home and foreign households, and, hence, the aggregate value of bonds is zero in the world financial market at large.

Using (6.44), we find that the capital stock in each country changes according to

$$\dot{K} = \frac{K - k_2(p)}{k_1(p) - k_2(p)} A_1 k_1(p)^{\alpha_1} - \delta K, \tag{6.47a}$$

$$\dot{K}^* = \frac{K^* - k_2(p^*)}{k_1(p^*) - k_2(p^*)} A_2 k_1(p^*)^{\alpha_1} - \delta K^*. \tag{6.47b}$$

Dynamics of the shadow values of capital are

$$\dot{q} = q[\rho + \delta - \widetilde{r}(p)], \tag{6.48a}$$

$$\dot{q}^* = q^*\left[\rho + \delta - \widetilde{r}(p^*)\right], \tag{6.48b}$$

where $\widetilde{r}(p) \equiv r/p = a_1 A_1 k_1(p)^{\alpha_1 - 1}$ and $\widetilde{r}(p^*) \equiv r^*/p^* = a_1 A_1 k_1(p^*)^{\alpha_1 - 1}$. Here, p does not equal p^* during the transition. Therefore, unlike the model in the previous section, the relative shadow value of capital, q/q^*, does not stay constant out of the steady state. Dynamic equations (6.47a), (6.47b), (6.48a) and (6.48b) depict behaviors of capital stocks and their implicit prices in the home and foreign countries.

To obtain a complete dynamic system, we should relate p and p^* to the state variables, K, K^*, q, and q^*. Combining optimization conditions (6.27c) and (6.43c) yields $\dot{\lambda}/\lambda = \dot{\lambda}^*/\lambda^* = \rho - R$. This shows that in view of (6.27a)and (6.43a), both λ^*/λ and C^*/C stay constant over time. Let us denote $C^*/C = (\lambda^*/\lambda)^{-1/\sigma} = \bar{m}\,(> 0)$. Then, the world market equilibrium condition for consumption (6.45) is expressed as

$$(1 + \bar{m})\,\lambda^{-\frac{1}{\sigma}} = y^2(K, p) + y^2\left(K^*, p^*\right), \tag{6.49}$$

where $y^2(K, p)$ is defined by (6.21b) and $y^2(K^*, p^*)$ is given by

$$y^2\left(K^*, p^*\right) = \frac{k_1(p^*) - K^*}{k_1(p^*) - k_2(p^*)} A_2 k_2(p^*)^{\alpha_2}.$$

In view of (6.49), we see that λ is expressed as a function of capital stocks, prices and $\bar{m}$ in the following way:

$$\lambda = (1 + \bar{m})^{\sigma}\left[y^2(K, p) + y^2\left(K^*, p^*\right)\right]^{-\sigma} \equiv \lambda\left(K, K^*, p, p^*; \bar{m}\right). \tag{6.50}$$

Thus optimization conditions (6.27b) and $q^* = \lambda^* p^*$ give

$$p = \frac{q}{\lambda(K, K^*, p, p^*; \bar{m})}, \quad p^* = \frac{q^*}{\bar{m}^{-\sigma}\lambda(K, K^*, p, p^*; \bar{m})}.$$

Solving these equations with respect to p and p^* presents the following expressions:

$$p = \pi\left(K, K^*, q, q^*; \bar{m}\right), \quad p^* = \pi^*\left(K, K^*, q, q^*; \bar{m}\right). \tag{6.51}$$

Substituting (6.51) into (6.47a), (6.47b), (6.48a), and (6.48b), we obtain a dynamic system of K, K^*, q and q^* under a given level of $\bar{m}$.

Alternatively, we can obtain a dynamic system of K, K^*, p, and p^* in the following manner. Differentiate both sides of (6.50) logarithmically with respect to time, which yields

$$\frac{\dot{\lambda}}{\lambda} = -\sigma\left[\frac{Y_K^2 K}{Y^2}\frac{\dot{K}}{K} + \frac{Y_{K^*}^2 K^*}{Y^2}\frac{\dot{K}^*}{K^*} + \frac{Y_p^2 p}{Y^2}\frac{\dot{p}}{p} + \frac{Y^2 p^*}{Y^2}\frac{\dot{p}^*}{p^*}\right], \tag{6.52}$$

where $Y^2 \equiv y^2(K,p) + y^2(K^*,p^*)$ denotes the aggregate supply of consumption goods in the world market. Note that from (6.27b), (6.27c), and (6.27d) we obtain:

$$\frac{\dot{p}}{p} = \frac{\dot{q}}{q} - \frac{\dot{\lambda}}{\lambda} = R + \delta - \widetilde{r}(p), \tag{6.53a}$$

$$\frac{\dot{p}^*}{p^*} = \frac{\dot{q}^*}{q^*} - \frac{\dot{\lambda}^*}{\lambda^*} = R + \delta - \widetilde{r}(p^*). \tag{6.53b}$$

Substituting (6.47a), (6.47b), (6.53a), and (6.53b) into (6.52) yields the following:

$$\rho - R = -\sigma\left[\frac{Y_K^2 K}{Y^2}\left(\frac{y^1(K,p) - \delta K}{K}\right) + \frac{Y_{K^*}^2 K^*}{Y^2}\left(\frac{y^2(K^*,p) - \delta K^*}{K^*}\right)\right.$$
$$\left. + \frac{Y_p^2 p}{Y^2}\left(R + \delta - \widetilde{r}(p)\right) + \frac{Y_{p^*}^2 p^*}{Y^2}\left(R + \delta - \widetilde{r}(p^*)\right)\right].$$

Observe that each side of the above equation does not involve $\bar{m}$. Solving the above with respect to R, we find that the equilibrium level of the world interest rate can be expressed as a function of K, K^*, p and p^*:

$$R = R\left(K, K^*, p, p^*\right). \tag{6.54}$$

Consequently, by use of (6.47a), (6.47b), (6.53a), (6.53b), and (6.54), we obtain the dynamic system with respect to (K, K^*, p, p^*) in such a way that

$$\left.\begin{aligned} \dot{K} &= y^1(K,p) - \delta K, \\ \dot{K}^* &= y^1(K^*,p^*) - \delta K^*, \\ \dot{p} &= p\left[R(K,K^*,p,p^*) + \delta - \widetilde{r}(p)\right], \\ \dot{p}^* &= p^*\left[R(K,K^*,p,p^*) + \delta - \widetilde{r}(p^*)\right]. \end{aligned}\right\} \tag{6.55}$$

6.4.3 Steady State of the World Economy

We first characterize the stationary equilibrium of the world economy. In the steady state, all of K, K^*, p, p^*, B, B^*, q and q^* stay constant over time. Inspecting the steady state conditions, we obtain the following:

Proposition 6.3 *There is a unique, feasible steady state equilibrium in which the steady state levels of capital and relative price in each country satisfy* $K = K^*$ *and* $p = p^*$.

Proof See "Appendix 2: Proof of Proposition 6.2" to this chapter. ■

It is to be noted that while the steady state levels of $K\,(= K^*)$ and $p\,(= p^*)$ are uniquely determined by the parameters involved in the model, the steady state values of utility prices of capital, q and q^*, cannot be determined by the parameter values alone. We can confirm this fact in the following way. In view of Proposition 6.3 and the optimization condition (6.27b), in the steady state, it holds that

$$\hat{p} = \hat{\lambda}\hat{q}, \quad \hat{p} = \bar{m}^{\sigma}\hat{\lambda}\hat{q}^*,$$

where a variable with a 'hat' denotes the steady state value of the corresponding variable. From (6.50) in the steady state the implicit price of bond held in the home country, λ, is given by

$$\hat{\lambda} = (1 + \bar{m})^{\sigma}\,[2y^2\left(\hat{K}, \hat{p}\right)]^{-\sigma}.$$

Since $\hat{\lambda}$ depends on $\bar{m}$, we should know the value of $\bar{m}$ to determine $\hat{\lambda}$ as well as $\hat{q}$ and $\hat{q}^*$. To find the value of $\bar{m}$, consider the current account of each country. Considering the market equilibrium condition for the investment goods in (6.44) and the factor income distribution relation such that $pY_1 + Y_2 = rpK + w + \pi_1 + \pi_2$ and $p^*Y_1^* + Y_2^* = r^*p^*K^* + w^* + \pi_1^* + \pi_2^*$, we see that the dynamic equation of foreign bonds is expressed as

$$\dot{B} = RB + Y_2 - C, \quad \dot{B}^* = RB^* + Y_2^* - C^*.$$

These equations represent the current accounts of both countries. In view of the non-Ponzi game and the transversality conditions, the intertemporal constraint for the current account of each country is respectively given by the following:

$$\int_0^{\infty} \exp\left(-\int_0^t R_s ds\right) C_t dt = \int_0^{\infty} \exp\left(-\int_0^t R_s ds\right) y^2\left(K_t, p_t\right) dt + B_0,$$

$$\int_0^{\infty} \exp\left(-\int_0^t R_s ds\right) C_t^* dt = \int_0^{\infty} \exp\left(-\int_0^t R_s ds\right) y^2\left(K_t^*, p_t^*\right) dt + B_0^*.$$

Since it holds that $C_t^* = \bar{m}C_t$ for all $t \geq 0$, the above equations yield

$$\bar{m} = \frac{\int_0^\infty \exp\left(-\int_0^t R_s ds\right) y^2\left(K_t^*, p_t^*\right) dt + B_0^*}{\int_0^\infty \exp\left(-\int_0^t R_s ds\right) y^2\left(K_t, p_t\right) dt + B_0}. \tag{6.56}$$

Equation (6.56) demonstrates that $\bar{m}$ depends on the initial holdings of bonds, B_0 and B_0^*, as well as on the discounted present value of consumption goods produced in each country. As a consequence, although $\hat{p}$ depends only on the parameter values involved in the model, the steady state levels of $\hat{q}\left(= \hat{\lambda}\hat{p}\right)$ and $\hat{q}^*\left(= \bar{m}^{-\sigma}\hat{\lambda}p^*\right)$ cannot be determined without specifying the initial holdings of bonds and the discounted present value of consumption goods in each country.

6.4.4 Indeterminacy Conditions

We now examine the local dynamics of the world economy around the steady state. A set of sufficient conditions for equilibrium indeterminacy for the model with nontradable investment goods is as follows:

Proposition 6.4 *If the investment good sector is more capital intensive than the consumption good sector from the social perspective but less capital intensive from the private perspective, that is,* $\frac{a_2}{b_2} - \frac{a_1}{b_1} > 0$ *and* $\alpha_1 - \alpha_2 > 0$*, then the steady state of the world economy where investment goods are non-tradable exhibits local indeterminacy.*

Proof See "Appendix 2: Proof of Proposition 6.2" to this chapter. ■

Proposition 6.4 claims that in our model, equilibrium indeterminacy may emerge regardless of the magnitude of σ. This is in contrast to Proposition 6.3 for the indeterminacy conditions for the case of free trade of both consumption and investment goods. In the regime of free trade of both investment and consumption goods,in addition to the factor-intensity ranking conditions, the intertemporal elasticity in consumption $(1/\sigma)$ is sufficiently high to hold indeterminacy. Since the closed economy version of our model is the same as the integrated world economy model discussed by Nishimura and Shimomura (2002b), we need the same condition for holding indeterminacy if our model economy is closed. Hence, our result shows that the financially integrated world economy with non-tradable capital goods may produce indeterminacy under a wider range of parameter spaces than its closed economy counterpart. In this sense, our model indicates that financial globalization may enhance the possibility of belief-driven economic fluctuations.

6.4.5 Long-Run Wealth Distribution

In dynamic system (6.55), if the steady state is locally determinate (i.e., the linearized dynamic system has two stable roots), then the equilibrium paths of p_t and p_t^* are uniquely expressed as functions of K_t and K_t^* on the two-dimensional stable manifold. When we denote the relation between the relative prices and capital stocks on the stable saddle path as $p = \phi(K, K^*)$ and $p^* = \phi^*(K, K^*)$, the behaviors of capital stocks on the saddle path are expressed as

$$\dot{K} = y^1\left(K, \phi\left(K, K^*\right)\right) - \delta K,$$
$$\dot{K}^* = y^1\left(K^*, \phi^*\left(K, K^*\right)\right) - \delta K^*.$$

These differential equations show that once the initial capital stocks, K_0 and K_0^*, are specified, the paths of $\left\{K_t, K_t^*\right\}_{t=0}^{\infty}$ are uniquely determined. As a result, the paths of $\left\{p_t, p_t^*, R_t\right\}_{t=0}^{\infty}$ are also uniquely given under the specified levels of K_0 and K_0^*. This means that when equilibrium determinacy holds, the level of $\bar{m}$ given by (6.56) is also uniquely selected under the given initial levels of K_0, K_0^*, B_0, and B_0^*.

By contrast, if the converging path of (6.55) is indeterminate (that is, the linearly approximated dynamic system of (6.55) has three or four stable roots), then the given initial levels of K_0 and K_0^* alone cannot pin down the equilibrium paths of p_t and p_t^*. Therefore, the level of $\bar{m}$ determined by (6.56) becomes indeterminate as well. In this situation, an extrinsic shock that affects the expectations of agents in the world market may alter the equilibrium path, and, hence, it changes the level of $\bar{m}$.

Note that in the steady state, it holds that $\dot{B} = \dot{B}^* = 0$ and $R = \rho$. Thus, remembering that $C + C^* = 2y^2\left(\hat{K}, \hat{p}\right)$ and $C^* = \bar{m}C$, we find that the steady state level of bond holdings in the home and foreign countries are respectively given by

$$\hat{B} = \frac{y^2\left(\hat{K}, \hat{p}\right) - C}{\rho} = \frac{\bar{m} - 1}{\rho(1 + \bar{m})} y^2\left(\hat{K}, \hat{p}\right), \tag{6.57a}$$

$$\hat{B}^* = \frac{y^2\left(\hat{K}, \hat{p}\right) - C^*}{\rho} = \frac{1 - \bar{m}}{\rho(1 + \bar{m})} y^2\left(\hat{K}, \hat{p}\right). \tag{6.57b}$$

The above expressions show that when $\bar{m}$ is selected, the long-run asset position of each country is also determined. In the steady state, the asset holding in each country is

$$\hat{\Omega} = \hat{B} + \hat{p}\hat{K}, \quad \hat{\Omega}^* = \hat{B}^* + \hat{p}\hat{K}.$$

Therefore, the long-run wealth distribution between the two countries depends on $\hat{B}$ and $\hat{B}^*$. It is obvious that whether the home country becomes a creditor or a debtor in the long run depends solely on whether or not $\bar{m}$ exceeds one. As (6.56) demonstrates, if the equilibrium path is determinate and if the initial stocks of capital and bonds held by the home households are relatively large, then the home country tends to be a creditor in the long-run equilibrium. However, if there is a continuum of covering path around the steady state, the value of $\bar{m}$ is affected by the expectation formation of agents. This implies that in the presence of equilibrium indeterminacy, the initial holding of wealth in each country alone does not determine the asset position of each country in the long-run equilibrium.

To sum up, we have shown the following:

Proposition 6.5 *If the steady state equilibrium of the world economy is locally determinate (indeterminate), then the steady state level of asset position of each country is determinate (indeterminate).*

6.4.6 Non-tradable Consumption Goods

Now consider the opposite situation in which the consumption goods are not internationally traded, but the investment goods are tradable and financial capital mobility is possible. In this case the commodity market equilibrium conditions are given by

$$I + I^* = Y_1 + Y_1^*, \quad C = Y_2, \quad C^* = Y_2^*. \tag{6.58}$$

We take the tradable investment good as a numeraire. Then, the net wealth held by the domestic household (in terms of investment good) is $\Omega = B + K$, and the flow budget constraint is written as

$$\dot{B} = R\,(B + K) + w + \pi_1 + \pi_2 - \widetilde{p}C - I,$$

where $\widetilde{p}$ $(= 1/p)$ denotes the domestic price of consumption good in terms of tradable investment good. The Hamiltonian function for the households in the home country is given by

$$H = \frac{C^{1-\sigma} - 1}{1-\sigma} + \lambda\,[RB + rK + w + \pi_1 + \pi_2 - \widetilde{p}C - I] + q\,(I - \delta K)$$

and the key first-order conditions for an optimum are

$$C^{-\sigma} = \lambda\widetilde{p}, \tag{6.59a}$$

$$\lambda = q, \tag{6.59b}$$

$$\dot{\lambda} = \lambda\,(\rho - R)\,, \tag{6.59c}$$

$$\dot{q} = q\,(\rho + \delta - r)\,. \tag{6.59d}$$

Conditions (6.59b), (6.59c), and (6.59d) lead to $R = r - \delta$.

Since households in both country face the common interest rate, R, in the international bond market, the rate of return to capital in both countries satisfy

$$r^* = R + \delta = r. \tag{6.60}$$

Therefore, $r(1/\widetilde{p}) = r(1/\widetilde{p}^*)$ holds in each moment, implying that $\widetilde{p}$ always equals $\widetilde{p}^*$.[7] This means that firms in each country select the same capital intensity in each production sector, so that the world-market equilibrium condition of investment good yields the dynamic equation of the aggregate capital given by (6.33). In addition, from the equilibrium condition for consumption goods in each country in (6.58) we obtain

$$C^{-1/\sigma} = y^2(K, \widetilde{p}), \quad C^{*-1/\sigma} = y^2(K^*, \widetilde{p}),$$

where it holds that $C^* = \bar{m}C$. The above equilibrium conditions present (6.36). Therefore, the dynamic system of the world economy is the same as that of the Nishimura-Shimomura model.

Proposition 6.6 *If consumption goods are not traded and financial capital mobility is possible, the indeterminacy conditions are the same as these for the case in which both goods are traded without financial capital mobility.*

Consequently, in this case, opening up international trade does not enhance the possibility of belief-driven business cycles. An intuitive implication of this result is as follows. If only investment goods are tradable, holding of a unit of bond is equivalent to holding a claim to the future capital good. Since bonds and capital are assumed to be perfect substitutes, holding a unit of bond should yield the same rate of return a unit of capital. Hence, the interest rate of foreign bonds equals the net rate of return to capital. The interest rate in the integrated financial market is common for both countries, implying that the rate of return to capital in both countries is the same. Because of symmetric technology, this means that the relative price in each country is also the same, so that the integrated world economy behaves exactly in the same manner as the Heckscher-Ohlin environment.

When only consumption goods are internationally traded, one unit of bond is a claim to the future consumption good. Hence, the non-arbitrage condition between holding of bond and capital shows that the rate of return to capital diverges from the world interest rate as long as the relative price between consumption and investment changes. This means that the factor prices (and thus the relative price between the two goods) in each country are not identical during the transition. The failure of factor-price equalization makes the system with non-traded investment goods diverge from the baseline Heckscher-Ohlin setting.

---

[7] Since $\widetilde{p} = 1/p$, the precise expression of $\widetilde{r}(1/\widetilde{p})$ is $\widetilde{r}(1\widetilde{p}) = r/p = pa_1 A_1 k_1 \left(\frac{1}{\widetilde{p}}\right)^{\alpha_1 - 1}$.

6.4.7 *Implication of the Indeterminacy Conditions*

The intuition behind the difference in indeterminacy conditions between Propositions 6.2 and 6.4 is as follows:

6.4.7.1 Free Trade of Commodities

First, consider the case in which both consumption and investment goods are traded without international lending and borrowing. Suppose that a sunspot shock hits the world economy and all the households in the world expect that the rates of return to their capital will increase. This raises the marginal values of capital, q and q^*. If σ is so small that the intertemporal substitution effect dominates the income effect, households in both countries reduce consumption and invest more. This leads to higher level of worldwide capital, K_w. As we have assumed that the consumption good sector is more capital intensive from the private perspective, (6.36) shows that an increase in K_w raises the worldwide production level of consumption goods. This increases the price of investment good p, and the firms select a lower capital intensity because the social technology of the capital goods sector is more capital intensive than that of the consumption good sector (see (6.18)).[8] Consequently, the rate of return to capital in the world economy increases and the sunspot-driven expectations are self-fulfilled.

In contrast, if σ is large enough, the income effect dominates the intertemporal substitution effect and, hence, a sunspot-driven expected rise in the marginal value of capital may increase consumption. As a result, investment in the world decreases and the relative price of investment goods, p, declines. In view of (6.18), a lower p raises $k_1(p)$. This leads to a lower rate of return to capital, and, hence, the initial change in expectations is not self-fulfilled.

6.4.7.2 Non-tradable Investment Goods

Next, consider the case in which investment goods are not tradable and international lending and borrowing are allowed. Again, suppose that households in both countries expect that the rates of return to their capital will increase. Then, households intend to rise their investment. In the Heckscher-Ohlin environment, this requires that households reduce their current consumption, and thus the magnitude of σ plays an important role. However, in the presence of the international financial

---

[8] The Rybczynski effect of a change in factor endowment depends on the factor-intensity ranking from the private perspective, while the Stolper-Samuelson effect of a price change depends on the factor-intensity ranking from the social perspective. Therefore, if the private and social factor intensity rankings are the same, we obtain the standard results and, hence, equilibrium indeterminacy will not arise.

market, households may increase their real investment by borrowing from foreign households rather than decrease their current consumption. Hence, investment demand may increase even if σ is not small. A higher investment in each country raises both p and p^*. Given the factor intensity ranking conditions in Proposition 6.4, higher levels of p and p^* decrease capital intensities so that the rates of retune to capital, r and r^* increase. In other words, the presence of international lending and borrowing cuts off the direct link between the current consumption and real investment held in the baseline Heckscher-Ohlin model (as well as in the closed economy model).

The above intuition is confirmed more clearly in a two-sector, small open economy model discussed in Sect. 6.2. In that model, since the world interest rate is exogenously given, the dynamic behavior of the small-open economy is described by

$$\dot{K} = y^1(K, p) - \delta K,$$
$$\dot{p} = p\left[\bar{R} + \delta - \hat{r}(p)\right],$$

where $\bar{R}$ denotes a given world interest rate. Since the shadow value of capital follows $\dot{q} = q\left(\delta + \rho - \bar{R}\right)$, it is assumed that $\delta + \rho = \bar{R}$ to keep q at a finite level. As a result, the current level of consumption, which satisfies $C^{-\sigma} = q$, stays constant as well. In this extreme case, there is no direct link between the current levels of savings and consumption, so that the dynamic behavior of the economy is independent of the intertemporal substitutability in consumption. In the present model of the global economy, the world interest rate is an endogenous variable. This is why the factor-ranking conditions are sufficient but not necessary for indeterminacy in our model. Despite such a difference, since we have focused on the local behavior of the world economy around the symmetric steady state in which both countries hold the same level of capital, our indeterminacy conditions are closed to those for the small open economy with non-tradable investment goods.

6.4.8 Remarks

The world economy as a whole is a closed economy in which there are multiple countries. Therefore, its model structure is similar to that of a closed, single-economy model with heterogeneous agents. In particular, if consumption and saving decisions are made by the representative household in each country, the world economy model is closely connected to the closed economy model with heterogeneous households. There is, however, an important difference between the world economy models and the single country setting: when dealing with the world economy model, we should specify the trade structure between the countries. This section has revealed that the assumption on trade structure is critical for the presence of equilibrium indeterminacy even if there is no international heterogeneity in technologies and preferences.

Recently, several authors have explored how the presence of heterogeneous preferences and technologies alters the determinacy/indeterminacy conditions in the equilibrium business cycle models with market distortions. These studies showed that the heterogeneity in preferences and technologies often affects indeterminacy conditions in a critical manner.[9] In a similar vein, Sim and Ho (2007) found that introducing technological heterogeneity into the Nishimura-Shimomura's (2002b) model may produce a substantial change in equilibrium indeterminacy results. In addition, even if taste and technologies are identical in both countries, introducing financial frictions, policy distortions, and adjustment costs of investment also break the symmetry between the home and foreign countries at least during the transition process. It is worth extending the model of this section by considering further heterogeneity between the two countries.[10]

6.5 A Two-Country Model with Variable Labor Supply

The final section of this chapter considers a two country model with variable labor supply. In this section, we use a two-country version of the Benhabib-Farmer model. Thus, the behavior of the representative household in each country is similar to that used in the small open economy model in Sect. 6.1 of the present chapter. We first examine an exogenous growth model where capital stock of each country stays constant in the steady state of the world economy. We then analyze a two-country endogenous growth model in which each country has an AK technology with variable labor supply, so that continuing growth of the world economy is sustained.

6.5.1 *Model*

There are two countries, country 1 and 2. Each country produces a country-specific, single good. We assume that country 1 specializes in good x and country 2 specializes in good y. Each good can be either consumed or invested for physical capital accumulation. It is assumed that imported goods can be consumed, but they cannot be used as investment goods. In addition, agents in each country do not have access to direct ownership of the foreign capital stock. However, agents in both countries may access the perfect international bond market, so that they can freely lend to or borrow from each other. Since the international bond market is assumed

---

[9] See, for example, Ghiglino and Olszak-Duquenne (2005).

[10] In the existing literature, Antras and Caballero (2009) introduced financial frictions into the Heckscher-Ohlin mode. Ono and Shibata (2010) and Jin (2012) introduced adjustment costs of investment into $2\times2\times2$ models.

to be perfect, the uncovered interest parity ensures that the nominal interest rates in both countries are equalized in each moment.[11] Although our assumption that imported goods cannot be used for investment is restrictive, it is helpful to determine real investment in each country without introducing additional assumptions such as the presence of adjustment costs of investment.

6.5.1.1 Production

The production technology of each country is described by

$$Z_i = K_i^{\alpha_i} N_i^{1-a_i} \bar{K}_i^{\alpha_i - a_i} \bar{N}_i^{\beta_i + a_i - 1}, \quad 0 < a_i < 1, \ \alpha_i, \beta_i > 0, \ \alpha_i + \beta_i > 1, \ \ i = 1, 2.$$

Here, Z_i denotes the output of country i, and Z_1 and Z_2 respectively represent good x and good y. As usual, imposing $\bar{K}_i = K_i$ and $\bar{N}_i = N_i$, we obtain the social production function in each country in the following manner:

$$Z_i = K_i^{\alpha_i} N_i^{\beta_i}, \quad i = 1, 2.$$

In what follows, we assume that $0 < \alpha_i < 1$, so that capital externalities are not so large that unbounded growth is possible. The rate of return to capital and the real wage rate are respectively given by

$$r_i = a_i K_i^{\alpha_i - 1} N_i^{\beta_i} - \delta_i, \ \ i = 1, 2, \tag{6.61}$$

$$w_i = (1 - a_i) K_i^{\alpha_i} N_i^{\beta_i - 1}, \ \ i = 1, 2. \tag{6.62}$$

6.5.1.2 Households

The number of households in each country is normalized to one. The objective function of the representative household in country i is a discounted sum of utilities such that

$$U_i = \int_0^{\infty} e^{-\rho t} u^i (x_i, y_i, N_i) \, dt,$$

[11] The structure of the base model is close to the two-country model examined by Turnovsky (1997; Chapter 7). Since Turnovsky (1997) did not assume the presence of external increasing returns, indeterminacy of equilibrium is not the issue in his argument. Baxter and Crucini (1995) used a similar model in their study on international real business cycles.

where

$$u^i(x_i, y_i, N_i) = \begin{cases} \dfrac{\left(x_i^{\theta_i} y_i^{1-i}\right)^{1-\sigma i} - 1}{1-\sigma_i} - \dfrac{N_i^{1+\gamma_i}}{1+\gamma_i}, & 0 < \theta_i < 1,\ \gamma_i > 0,\ \sigma_i > 0, \\ \theta_i \ln x_i + (1-\theta_i) \ln y_i - \dfrac{N_i^{1+\gamma_i}}{1+\gamma_i}, & \text{for } \sigma_i = 1. \end{cases}$$

In the above, x_i and y_i denote consumption of goods x and y . By our assumption, y_1 is exported from country 2 to country 1, and x_2 is exported from country 1 to country 2. We assume that the households in both countries may have different utility functions, but their discount rate is the same rate of ρ.[12]

The flow-budget constraint for the households in each country is given by

$$\dot{\Omega}_i = r_i \Omega_i + w_i N_i - m_i, \quad i = 1, 2, \tag{6.63}$$

where Ω_i is the real asset holding and m_i is real consumption expenditure. For notational convenience, Ω_i, w_i, and m_i are expressed in terms of the good country i produces. Hence, if p denotes the price of good y in terms of good x, the consumption spending in both countries are respectively determined by

$$m_1 = x_1 + p y_1, \quad m_2 = \frac{x_2}{p} + y_2. \tag{6.64}$$

The asset consists of capital stock, k_i, and the foreign bond holding, b_i. Therefore, we define

$$\Omega_i = K_i + B_i, \quad i = 1, 2,$$

where b_1 and b_2 are evaluated in terms of good x and good y, respectively.

The household maximizes U_i subject to (6.63), (6.64), and the initial value of Ω_i by controlling consumption levels and labor supply. We impose the no-Ponzi-game condition, and hence the following intertemporal budget constraint holds as well:

$$\Omega_i(0) + \int_0^\infty \exp\left(-\int_0^t r_i(s)\, ds\right) w_i(t)\, l_i(t)\, dt$$
$$= \int_0^\infty \exp\left(-\int_0^t r_i(s)\, ds\right) m_i(t)\, dt, \quad i = 1, 2.$$

We first consider an instantaneous optimization problem for the household in the home country:

$$\max\ \theta_1 \log x_1 + (1-\theta_1) \log y_1$$

---

[12]This assumption is introduced only for notational simplicity.

subject to $x_1 + py_1 = m_1$. The resulting optimal choices of good x_1 and good y_1 are:

$$x_1 = \theta_1 m_1, \quad y_1 = \frac{(1-\theta_1)\, m_1}{p}. \tag{6.65}$$

Using (6.65), we drive the instantaneous indirect subutility in such a way that

$$\hat{u}^1(m_1, p) = \log m_1 - (1-\theta_1)\log p + \theta_1 \log \theta_1 + (1-\theta_1)\log(1-\theta_1).$$

Similarly, we find that the static demand functions of the country 2's households are:

$$x_2 = \theta_2 m_2 p, \quad y_2 = (1-\theta_2)\, m_2, \tag{6.66}$$

implying that the instantaneous indirect subutility of the representative households in country 2 is

$$\hat{u}^2(m_2, p) = \log m_2 + \theta_2 \log p + \theta_2 \log \theta_2 + (1-\theta_2)\log(1-\theta_2).$$

To derive the optimization conditions for the representative household in each country, we set up a Hamiltonian function in which m_i is the control variable:

$$\mathcal{H}_i = \hat{u}^i(m_i, p) - \frac{l_i^{1+\gamma}}{1+\gamma} + q_i(r_i\Omega_i + w_i N_i - m_i), \quad i = 1, 2.$$

The optimization conditions include the following:

$$1/m_i = q_i, \quad i = 1.2, \tag{6.67a}$$

$$N_i^{\gamma} = q_i w_i, \quad i = 1, 2, \tag{6.67b}$$

$$\dot{q}_i = q_i(\rho - r_i), \quad i = 1, 2, \tag{6.67c}$$

$$\lim_{t\to\infty} q_i e^{-\rho t}\Omega_i = 0, \quad i = 1, 2. \tag{6.67d}$$

Equations (6.62) and (6.67b) give

$$N_i = \left[(1-a)\, K_i^{\alpha_i} q_i\right]^{\frac{1}{\gamma_i+1-\beta_i}}, \quad i = 1, 2. \tag{6.68}$$

The aggregate output of country i is thus expressed as

$$Z_i = (1-\alpha_i)^{\frac{\beta_i}{\gamma+1-\beta}} K_i^{\frac{\alpha_i(1+\gamma_i)}{1+\gamma_i-\beta_i}} q_i^{\frac{\beta}{\gamma+1-\beta}}, \quad i = 1, 2, \tag{6.69}$$

and the rate of return to capital is

$$r_i = a_i(1-\alpha_i)^{\frac{\beta_i}{\gamma+1-\beta}} K_i^{\frac{\alpha_i(1+\gamma_i)}{1+\gamma_i-\beta_i}-1} q_i^{\frac{\beta}{\gamma+1-\beta}}, \quad i = 1, 2. \tag{6.70}$$

6.5.1.3 Market Equilibrium Conditions

Since physical capital stocks are not traded, the market equilibrium conditions for the commodity markets are

$$Z_1 = x_1 + x_2 + \dot{K}_1 + \delta_1 K_1, \tag{6.71a}$$

$$Z_2 = y_1 + y_2 + \dot{K}_2 + \delta_2 K_2. \tag{6.71b}$$

The world financial market is assumed to be perfect. This means that the uncovered interest parity holds, so that

$$r_1 = r_2 + \frac{\dot{p}}{p}. \tag{6.72}$$

The international borrowing and lending in the world economy should be balanced in each moment, and, therefore, the equilibrium condition for the bond market is

$$B_1 + pB_2 = 0. \tag{6.73}$$

Note that the homogeneity of production functions gives $Z_i = r_i K_i + w_i N_i$ $(i = 1, 2)$. Hence, in view of (6.633) and $\Omega_i = K_i + B_i$, the flow budget constraints for the home and foreign households present the dynamic equations of B_1 and B_2 as follows:

$$\dot{B}_1 = r_1 B_1 + x_2 - py_1, \tag{6.74a}$$

$$\dot{B}_2 = r_2 B_2 + y_1 - \frac{x_2}{p}. \tag{6.75a}$$

Equations (6.63) and (6.64) respectively express the behavior of current accounts of each country.

6.5.2 *Equilibrium Dynamics*

Using (6.65), (6.66), and (6.69), we find that the capital stock in each country changes in the following manner:

$$\dot{K}_1 = (1-\alpha_i)^{\frac{\beta_i}{\gamma+1-\beta}} K_i^{\frac{\alpha_i(1+\gamma_i)}{1+\gamma_i-\beta_i}} q_i^{\frac{\beta}{\gamma+1-\beta}} - \frac{\theta_1}{q_1} - \frac{\theta_2 p}{q_2},$$

$$\dot{K}_2 = (1-\alpha_2)^{\frac{\beta_2}{\gamma_2+1-\beta_2}} K_2^{\frac{\alpha_2(1+\gamma_2)}{1+\gamma_2-\beta_2}} q_2^{\frac{\beta_2}{\gamma_2+1-\beta_2}} - \frac{1-\theta_1}{pq_1} - \frac{1-\theta_2}{q_2}.$$

The utility prices of K_1 and K_2 follow:

$$\dot{q}_1 = q_1 \left[\rho + \delta - a_1 (1-\alpha_i)^{\frac{\beta_1}{\gamma_1+1-\beta}} K_1^{\frac{\alpha_1(\gamma_1+1)}{\gamma_1+1-\beta_1}-1} q_1^{\frac{\beta_1}{\gamma_1+1-\beta_1}} \right], \tag{6.76a}$$

$$\dot{q}_2 = q_2 \left[\rho + \delta - a_2 (1-\alpha_2)^{\frac{\beta_2}{\gamma_2+1-\beta_2}} K_2^{\frac{\alpha_2(\gamma_2+1)}{\gamma_2+1-\beta_2}-1} q_2^{\frac{\beta_2}{\gamma_2+1-\beta_2}} \right]. \tag{6.76b}$$

The relative price (terms of trade in this model) changes in such a way that

$$\frac{\dot{p}}{p} = r_1 - r_2 = \frac{\dot{q}_2}{q_2} - \frac{\dot{q}_1}{q_1}.$$

As a result, we obtain

$$p = \mu \frac{q_2}{q_1},$$

where μ is a positive constant. As a result, the capital accumulation equations are expressed as follows:

$$\dot{K}_1 = (1-\alpha_1)^{\frac{\beta_1}{\gamma_1+1-\beta_1}} K_i^{\frac{\alpha_1(1+\gamma_1)}{1+\gamma_1-\beta_1}} q_1^{\frac{\beta_1}{\gamma_1+1-\beta_1}} - (\theta_1 + \theta_2) \frac{1}{q_1}, \tag{6.77a}$$

$$\dot{K}_2 = (1-\alpha_2)^{\frac{\beta_2}{\gamma_2+1-\beta_2}} K_2^{\frac{\alpha_2(1+\gamma_2)}{1+\gamma_2-\beta_2}} q_2^{\frac{\beta_2}{\gamma_2+1-\beta_2}} - (2 - \theta_1 - \theta_2) \frac{1}{q_2}. \tag{6.77b}$$

As a consequence, a complete system consists of (6.76a), (6.76b), (6.77a), and (6.77b) with respect to (K_1, K_2, q_1, q_2).

Note that under the assumption of additive separable utility, the dynamic behaviors of the home and foreign countries are independent of each other. For example, consider the dynamic system for the home country that is given by (6.76a) and (6.77a). It is easy to see that the steady state is uniquely given. The coefficient matrix evaluated at the steady state is

$$J_h = \begin{bmatrix} -\left(\frac{\beta_1-(1-\alpha_1)(\gamma_1+1)}{\gamma_1+1-\beta_1}\right)\frac{\rho+\delta}{K_1^*} & -\left(\frac{\beta_1}{\gamma_1+1-\beta_1}\right)(\rho+\delta) \\ \frac{\alpha_1(1+\gamma_1)}{a_1(1+\gamma_1-\beta_1)}(\rho+\delta) & \frac{\beta_1}{\gamma_1+1-\beta_1}\frac{Z_1^*}{q_1^*} + \frac{\theta_1+\theta_2}{q_1^{*2}} \end{bmatrix}.$$

Hence, if $(1-\alpha_1)(\gamma_1+1) > \beta_1$, the determinant of J_h is negative, so that the equilibrium of the home country is determinate. In contrast, if $\beta_1 > 1 + \gamma_1$, then the trace of J_h is negative and $\det J_h$ may have a positive value. This means that the presence of strong increasing returns associated with aggregate labor would give rise to indeterminacy, which is basically the same result as that in the baseline Benhabib-

Farmer model. This outcome can apply to the foreign country as well: if $\beta_2 > 1+\gamma_2$, the steady state of the foreign country may establish local indeterminacy. To sum up, we have found:

Proposition 6.7 *If the utility function is additively separable between domestic and imported good and production technologies of both countries satisfy* $(1-\alpha_i)(1+\gamma_i) > \beta_i > 0$ $(i = 1,2)$, *then the steady state of the world economy is determinate. If* $\beta_i > 1+\gamma_i$ $(i = 1,2)$, *then the steady state of the world economy may exhibit indeterminacy.*

6.5.3 Remarks

6.5.3.1 Spillover of Sunspot Shocks

As shown above, when $\beta_i > 1+\gamma_i$, both countries may hold equilibrium indeterminacy, and thus sunspot-driven international business cycles may arise. If $(1-\alpha_1)(1+\gamma_1) > \beta_1$ but $\beta_2 > 1+\gamma_2$, then the home country establishes equilibrium determinacy, whereas the foreign country may hold indeterminacy. Notice that even in this environment, the home country is not free from sunspot-driven fluctuations. To see this, remember the flow budge constraint for the home country is given by

$$\dot{B}_1 = r_1 B_1 + x_2 - y_1 = \theta_2 m_2 p - (1-\theta_1) m_1.$$

Thus, using $m_i = 1/q_i$ and $p = \mu q_2/q_1$, we obtain the intertermporal budget constraint:

$$B_1(0) + \theta_2 \mu \int_0^\infty \exp\left(-\int_0^t r_1(s)\,ds\right) m_1(t)\,dt$$
$$= (1-\theta_1)\int_0^\infty \exp\left(-\int_0^t r_1(s)\,ds\right) m_1(t)\,dt.$$

Since the home country holds determinacy, the sequences of $\{r_i(t), m_1(t)\}_{t=0}^{\infty}$ are unique. Therefore, the above equation determines a unique value of μ. In addition, under a given level of μ, $q_1(t)$ is uniquely related to $K_1(t)$.

On the other hand, the foreign country holds indeterminacy, there is no unique relation between $q_2(t)$ and $K_2(t)$.As a result, the terms of trade is expressed as

$$p(t) = \mu \frac{q_2(t)}{\phi(K_1(t))},$$

where $q_1(t) = \phi(K_1(t))$ represents the relation between $q_1(t)$ and $K_1(t)$ on the stable saddle path of the home country. We see that $q_2(t)$ may fluctuate in response to changes in expectations, so that sunspot shocks hitting the foreign country fluctuates the terms of trade. Since the indirect utility of the household in each country is affected by the terms of trade, $p(t)$, sunspot fluctuations that arise in the foreign country directly affect the welfare of the domestic households.

6.5.3.2 Non-seprable Utility

The simple dynamic structure of the above model relies on our assumption of log-additive utility. If $\sigma_i \neq 1$ so that the utility functions are of CES forms in consumption. Under this specification of the utility function, we can show that the demand functions are given by the following:

$$x_i = \Delta_x^i q_1^{\frac{(1-\acute{\sigma}_i)(1-\theta_i)-1}{\sigma_i}} q_2^{-\frac{(1-\sigma_i)(1-\theta_i)}{\sigma_i}} \quad i = 1, 2, \tag{6.78}$$

$$y_i = \Delta_y^i q_1^{\frac{(1-\sigma_i)(1-\theta_i)-1}{\sigma_i}+1} q_2^{-\frac{(1-\sigma_i)(1-\theta_i)}{\sigma_i}-1} -, \quad i = 1, 2, \tag{6.79}$$

where

$$\Delta_x^i = \frac{1}{\mu\theta_i}\left(\frac{\theta_i}{1-\theta_i}\right)^{(1-\sigma_i)(1-\theta_i)} > 0,$$

$$\Delta_y^i = \frac{1}{\mu\theta_i}\left(\frac{\theta_i}{1-\theta_i}\right)^{(1-\sigma_i)(1-\theta_i)+1} > 0.$$

Here, we use $p = \mu q_2/q_1$. We see that the own price effect is always negative, while the effects of foreign price on consumption demand for the home good depend on the sign of $1-\sigma_i$. If $\sigma_i > 1$, the substitution effect dominates so that a rise in foreign price increases in the consumption demand for home goods. Conversely, if $\sigma_i < 1$, a higher foreign good price lowers demand for the home goods.

The dynamic equations in the case of non-separable utility between x_i and y_i are thus displayed by

$$\dot{K}_1 = A_1 K_1^{\frac{\alpha_1(\gamma_1+1)}{\gamma_1+1-\beta_1}} q_i^{\frac{\beta_1}{\gamma_1+1-\beta_1}} - \sum_{i=1,2} \Delta_x^i q_1^{\frac{(1-\acute{\sigma}_i)(1-\theta_i)-1}{\sigma_i}} q_2^{-\frac{(1-\sigma_i)(1-\theta_i)}{\sigma_i}} - \delta_1 K_1,$$

$$\dot{K}_2 = A_2 K_2^{\frac{\alpha_2(\gamma_2+1)}{\gamma_2+1-\beta_2}} q_2^{\frac{\beta_2}{\gamma_2+1-\beta_2}} - \sum_{i=1,2} \Delta_y^i q_1^{\frac{(1-\sigma_i)(1-\theta_i)-1}{\sigma_i}+1} q_2^{-\frac{(1-\sigma_i)(1-\theta_i)}{\sigma_i}-1} - \delta_2 K_2,$$

together with (6.76a) and (6.76b).

We do not present details of the dynamic analysis of this system. It can be shown that indeterminacy of the world economy may still hold if $\beta_i > +\gamma_i$ $(i = 1, 2)$ and if σ_1 and σ_2 are sufficiently small.

6.5.4 Endogenous Growth

So far, we have considered a model of exogenous growth in which the world economy will not display sustained growth in the steady state equilibrium. In the following, we consider an endogenously growing world economy by modifying the base model. We assume that both countries have AK technologies in the sense that their production functions are linearly homogenous with respect to the private and social levels of capital. Hence, we assume that $\alpha_1 = \alpha_2 = 1$, implying that the social production function in each country becomes

$$Z_i = K_i^{a_i} N_i^{1-a_i} \bar{K}_i^{1-\alpha_i} \bar{N}_i^{\beta_i + a_i - 1} = N_i^{\beta_i} K_i, \quad i = 1, 2. \tag{6.80}$$

Hence, the factor prices are given by

$$r_i = a_i N_i^{\beta_i} - \delta_i, \quad i = 1, 2, \tag{6.81}$$

$$w_i = (1 - a_i) N_i^{\beta_i - 1} K_i, \quad i = 1, 2. \tag{6.82}$$

In the following discussion, we restrict our attention to the case of separable utility. As is well known, if the utility function is additively separable between consumption and labor, the sub-utility generating from consumption should be logarithmic to hold balanced-growth equilibrium with a positive growth rate. Thus, in this section, we assume that $\sigma_i = 1$, so that

$$u^i (x_i, y_i, N_i) = \theta_i \ln x_i + (1 - \theta_i) \ln y_i - \frac{N_i^{1+\gamma_i}}{1 + \gamma_i}, \quad i = 1, 2.$$

Given this specification, (6.67b) and (6.82)yield

$$N_i^{\gamma_i + 1 - \beta_i} = (1 - a_i) q_i K_i, \quad i = 1, 2.$$

Let us denote $q_i k_i = v_i$. Then, the equilibrium level of employment in country i is

$$N_i = \eta_i v_i^{\frac{1}{\gamma_i + 1 - \beta_i}}, \quad i = 1, 2, \tag{6.83}$$

where $\eta_i = (1 - a_i)^{\frac{1}{\gamma_i + 1 - \beta_i}}$. The equilibrium employment level in each country increases (decreases) with the value of capital, if $\gamma_i + 1 > \beta_i.(\gamma_i + 1 < \beta_i)$. In this case, the demand functions for final goods are given by

$$x_i = \mu_i \theta_i / q_i, \quad y_i = \mu_i (1 - \theta_i) / q_i, \quad i = 1, 2. \tag{6.84}$$

By use of (6.71a) and (6.71b), we show that the growth rates of capital stocks in both countries are expressed as follows:

$$\frac{\dot{K}_1}{K_1} = \eta_1 v_1^{\frac{\beta_1}{\gamma_1+1-\beta_1}} - \frac{\mu_1\theta_1 + \mu_2\theta_2}{v_1} - \delta,$$

$$\frac{\dot{K}_2}{K_2} = \eta_2 v_2^{\frac{\beta_2}{\gamma_2+1-\beta_2}} - \frac{\mu_1(1-\theta_1) + \mu_2(1-\theta_2)}{v_2} - \delta.$$

The price in each good changes according to

$$\frac{\dot{q}_i}{q_i} = \rho = r_i = \rho - a_i N_i^{\beta_i}, \quad i = 1, 2.$$

By the definition of v_i ($= q_i k_i$), we thus obtain

$$\frac{\dot{v}_1}{v_1} = (1-a_1)\,\eta_1 v_1^{\frac{\beta_1}{\gamma_1+1-\beta_1}} + \rho - \frac{\mu_1\theta_1 + \mu_2\theta_2}{v_1} - \delta, \tag{6.85a}$$

$$\frac{\dot{v}_2}{v_2} = (1-a_2)\,\eta_2 v_2^{\frac{\beta_2}{\gamma_2+1-\beta_2}} + \rho - \frac{[\mu_1(1-\theta_1) + \mu_2(1-\theta_2)]}{v_2} - \delta. \tag{6.85b}$$

Differential equations (6.85a) and (6.85b) constitute a complete set of dynamic system.

The balanced growth of the world economy is attained when $\dot{v}_1 = \dot{v}_2 = 0$. Note that in the balanced-growth equilibrium, the real income of both countries need not grow at a common rate. If each country grows at a different rate, the relative price between goods x and y continue to change at a constant rate to keep the uncovered interest parity condition, $r_1 = \dot{p}/p + r_2$. Hence, letting g_i be the steady growth rate of country i, in the balanced-growth equilibrium, we obtain

$$g_i = a_i N_i^{\beta_i} - \rho - \delta_i = -\dot{q}_i/q_i, \quad i = 1, 2, \tag{6.86}$$

which means that change in the relative price on the balanced-growth path is

$$\frac{\dot{p}}{p} = \frac{\dot{q}_1}{q^1} - \frac{\dot{q}_2}{q_2} = a_2 N_2^{\beta_2} - a_1 N_1^{\beta_1}. \tag{6.87}$$

The rate of change in asset holding in country 1 is given by

$$\frac{\dot{B}_1}{B_1} = g_1 + \rho + \frac{\mu_1\theta_1}{q_1 b_1} - \frac{p\mu_2(1-\theta_2)}{q_2 b_1}.$$

In the balanced-growth equilibrium, b_1 changes at the rate of g_1, and thus it holds that

$$\frac{p\mu_2(1-\theta_2)}{q_2 b_1} - \frac{\mu_1\theta_1}{q_1 b_1} = \frac{py_1 - x_1}{b_1} = \rho.$$

Similarly, the balanced-growth condition in country 2 involves $x_2/p - y_1 = \rho b_2$.

Due to the assumption of log-additive utility functions, there is no interaction between the dynamic behaviors of v_1 and v_2. It is easy to confirm that the steady-state value of v_i is uniquely given if $\gamma_i + 1 > \beta_i$. We also find that if $\gamma_i + 1 < \beta_i$, then either there is no steady state or there are dual steady states. Here, we assume that both countries have dual balanced-growth paths when $\gamma_i + 1 < \beta_i$. Additionally, we can confirm that when there are two steady states, the one with a lower value of v_i is locally indeterminate and the other with a higher value of v_i is locally determinate.[13] Consequently, we obtain the following:

Proposition 6.8 *If $\gamma_i + 1 - \beta_i > 0$ for $i = 1, 2$, the world economy has a unique balanced-growth path that satisfies global determinacy. On the contrary, if $\gamma_i + 1 - \beta_i < 0$ for $i = 1, 2$, then there may exist four steady states: the one in which both countries grow at lower rates is locally determinate, while the other three are locally indeterminate.*

Figure 6.2a depicts the phase diagram of (6.85a) and (6.85b) for $\gamma_i + 1 > \beta_i$ $(i = 1, 2)$ (so that the world economy is globally determinate). If this is the case, the world economy stays on the balanced-growth path and has no transitional dynamics. In contrast, if $\gamma_i + 1 < \beta_i (i = 1, 2)$, then the world economy involves four steady states: the balanced-growth path on which both countries attain lower growth rates will not display indeterminacy, while other three are locally indeterminate. As Fig. 6.2b shows, the steady state where both countries attain higher growth rates is a sink. This suggests that the behaviors of the terms of trade and current accounts of both countries may be totally indeterminate around the high-growth steady state of the world economy.

It is worth emphasizing that in our setting each country may attain a different rate of balanced growth. In particular, in the case of Fig. 6.2b, the balanced-growth rate of each country may differ from each other even though both countries have identical production and preference structures. As shown above, in this case, the terms of trade changes in such a way that

$$\frac{\dot{p}}{p} = r_2 - r_1 = g_2 - g_1,$$

where g_i denotes the balanced-growth rate of country i. As a result, the growth rate of real income evaluated by a particular good (good x or good y) is the same for both countries.

---

[13] Denote the steady state values of v_i as v_i^* and v_i^{**} $(v_i^* < v_i^{**})$. It is seen that $d\dot{v}_i/dv_i < 0$ for $v_i = v_i^*$ and $d\dot{v}_i/dv_i > 0$ for $v_i = v_i^{**}$. Since v_i is not a predetermined variable, indeterminacy emerges around $v_i = v_i^*$.

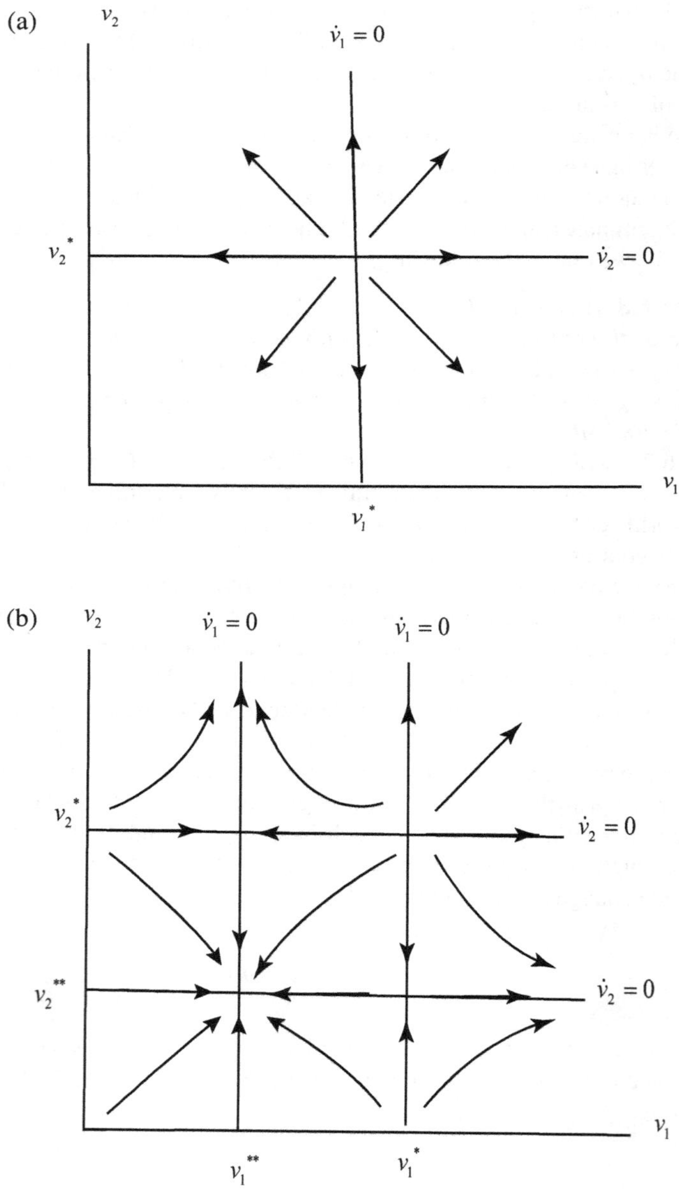

Fig. 6.2 (**a**) The case of $1 + \gamma_i > \beta_i (i = 1, 2)$ (**b**) The case of $\beta_i > 1 + \gamma_i (i = 1, 2)$

6.6 References and Related Studies

Earlier studies on indeterminacy in small open economies include Lahiri (2001), Weder (2001), and Meng and Velasco (2003, 2004). The two-secor model with nontraded invesment goods used by Meng and Velasco (2003) follows the dependent economy model discussed by Turnovsky and Sen (1995). As is well known, in the standard small open macroeconomic model in which the time discount rate of the households equals a fixed world interest rate, the steady state level of asset holding constitutes a continuum. If the equilibrium is determinate, the steady state asset position depends on the initial holding of the asset. As pointed out by Schmitt-Grohé and Uribe (2003), there are several alternative ways to pin down the steady state of a small open economy. Among others, endogenization of the time discount rate has been frequently employed in the literature. Bian and Meng (2004) explore the indeterminacy conditions in such an environment. All of studies mentioned above are based on the conventional open macroeconomic approach in which international lending and borrowing allowed. In contrast, Nishimura and Shimomura (2002a) reveal indeterminacy in a small open Hecsher-Ohlin model in which both invesment and consumption goods are traded but international financial transactions are not allowed.

Some authors examine indeterminacy in small open economies that allow endogenous growth. In addition to Chin et al. (2012), cited in Sect. 6.1.2, we refer to Meng (2003). Moreover, Chen et al. (2016), Meng (2015), and Huang and Meng (Balanced-budget income taxes and aggregate stability in a small open economy. Unpublished manuscript, 2016) analyze small open economy models with endogenous growth in which balanced budget rule gives rise to equilibrium indeterminacy. Similarly, Chen et al. (2016) examine the stabilization effect of nonlinear taxation in a small open economy model with endogenous growth.

The dynamic two-country Heckcsher-Ohlin model is studied in detail by several authors such as Chen (1992) and Caliendo (2010). As mentioned in Sect. 6.3, indeterminacy in the two-country Heckscher-Ohlin model is studied by Nishimura and Shimomura (2002b) for the first time. Subsequent studies such as Naito (2006), Sim and Ho (2007), Hu and Shimomura (2011), Iwasa and Nishimura (2014), and Nishimura et al. (2014) discuss the same issue in more general settings than Nishimura and Shimomura (2002b) do. The two-country model with financial transactions examined in Sect. 6.4 follows Hu and Mino (2013).

While many authors have studied two-country endogenous growth models, the issue of indeterminacy in these models has not been fully explored. In addition to the second part of Sect. 6.5, which is based on Mino (2008) and Farmer and Lahiri (2005, 2006) examine equilibrium indeterminacy in the context of two-country endogenous growth models. They employ a two-country version of Lucas's (1988) model of human capital accumulation in which human capital is associated with external effects.

Appendices

Appendix 1: Proof of Proposition 6.1

When $\dot{q} = \dot{q}^* = 0$ in (6.48a) and (6.48b), it holds that

$$a_1 A_1 k_1 (p)^{\alpha_1 - 1} = a_1 A_1 k_1 \left(p^*\right)^{\alpha_1 - 1} = \rho + \delta.$$

Hence, by use of (6.15a), we find

$$p = p^* = \left(\frac{A_2}{A_1}\right)\left(\frac{a_2}{a_1}\right)^{\alpha_2}\left(\frac{b_2}{b_1}\right)^{1-\alpha_2}\left(\frac{\rho+\delta}{a_1 A_1}\right)^{\frac{\alpha_2-\alpha_1}{\alpha_1-1}}.$$

These conditions show that the steady state levels of p and p^* are uniquely given and it holds that $p = p^*$ in the steady state. The steady state levels of capital stocks satisfying $\dot{K} = \dot{K}^* = 0$ in (6.47a) and (6.47b) are determined by the following conditions:

$$\frac{K - k_2(p)}{k_1(p) - k_2(p)} A_1 k_1 (p)^{\alpha_1} = \delta K,$$

$$\frac{K^* - k_2(p^*)}{k_1(p^*) - k_2(p^*)} A_1 k_1 \left(p^*\right)^{\alpha_1} = \delta K^*.$$

Using the conditions for $\dot{p} = \dot{p}^* = 0$ and the fact that $p = p^*$ holds in the steady state, we confirm that the steady state level of capital stock in each county has the same value given by

$$K = K^* = \frac{(aA_1)^{\frac{1}{1-\alpha_1}}(\rho+\delta)^{\frac{\alpha_1}{\alpha_1-1}}}{\rho + \delta\left(1 - \delta + \frac{a_2 b_1}{b_2}\right)}\left(\frac{a_2 b_1}{a_1 b_2}\right),$$

which has a positive value. We also find that the steady state values of labor allocation to the investment good sector are

$$L_1 = L_1^* = \frac{a_1 \delta \left(\frac{a_2 b_1}{a_1 b_2}\right)}{\rho + (1 - a_1)\delta + a_1 \delta \left(\frac{a_2 b_1}{a_1 b_2}\right)} \in (0, 1).$$

Hence, (6.20) is fulfilled so that both countries specialize imperfectly.

Appendix 2: Proof of Proposition 6.2

Since the functional form of $R(K, K^*, p, p^*)$ in (6.55) is complicated, it is simpler to treat a dynamic system with respect to K, K^*, q, and q^*. We thus focus on the dynamic system consisting of (6.47a), (6.47b), (6.48a), and (6.48b) with $p = \pi(K, K^*, q, q^*; \bar{m})$ and $p^* = \pi^*(K, K^*, q, q^*; \bar{m})$, where $\bar{m}$ is fixed.[14]

To prove Proposition 6.2, the following facts are useful:

Lemma A.1 *In the symmetric steady state in which $K = K^*$ and $q = q^*$, the following relations are satisfied:*

$$y^i_K(K, p) = y^i_{K^*}(K^*, p^*), \quad i = 1, 2,$$
$$y^i_p(K, p) = y^i_{p^*}(K^*, p^*), \quad i = 1, 2,$$
$$\pi_K(K, K^*, q, q^*) = \pi^*_K(K, K^*, q, q^*) = \pi_{K^*}(K, K^*, q, q^*) = \pi^*_{K^*}(K, K^*, q, q^*),$$
$$\pi_q(K, K^*, q, q^*) = \pi^*_{q^*}(K, K^*, q, q^*),$$
$$\pi_{q^*}(K, K^*, q, q^*) = \pi^*_q(K, K^*, q, q^*).$$

Proof By the functional forms of $y^i_j(\cdot)$ $(i = 1, 2, j = K, K^*, p, p^*)$, it is easy to see that $y^i_K(K, p) = y^i_{K^*}(K^*, p^*)$ and $y^i_p(K, p) = y^i_{p^*}(K^*, p^*)$ are established when $p = p^*$ and $K = K^*$.As for the rest of the results, we use $p\lambda(\cdot) = q$ and $p^*\lambda(\cdot)\bar{m}^{-\sigma} = q^*$. the total differentiation of $p\lambda(\cdot) = q$ and $p^*\lambda(\cdot)\bar{m}^{-\sigma} = q^*$ yields the following:

$$\frac{\partial p}{\partial K} = \pi_K = -\frac{p\lambda_K}{\lambda + p\lambda_P + p^*\lambda_{p^*}}, \quad \frac{\partial p}{\partial K^*} = \pi_{K^*} = -\frac{p\lambda_{K^*}}{\lambda + p\lambda_P + p^*\lambda_{p^*}},$$

$$\frac{\partial p^*}{\partial K} = \pi^*_K = -\frac{p^*\lambda_K}{\lambda + p\lambda_P + p^*\lambda_{p^*}}, \quad \frac{\partial p^*}{\partial K^*} = \pi^*_{K^*} = -\frac{p^*\lambda_{K^*}}{\lambda + p\lambda_P + p^*\lambda_{p^*}},$$

$$\frac{\partial p}{\partial q} = \pi_q = \frac{\lambda + p^*\lambda_{p^*}}{\lambda(\lambda + p\lambda_P + p^*\lambda_{p^*})}, \quad \frac{\partial p}{\partial q^*} = \pi_{q^*} = -\frac{p\lambda_p}{\lambda(\lambda + p\lambda_P + p^*\lambda_{p^*})},$$

$$\frac{\partial p^*}{\partial q} = \pi^*_q = -\frac{p^*\lambda_{p^*}}{\lambda + p\lambda_P + p^*\lambda_{p^*}}, \quad \frac{\partial p^*}{\partial q^*} = \pi^*_{q^*} = \frac{\lambda + p\lambda_p}{\lambda + p\lambda_P + p^*\lambda_{p^*}}.$$

[14] When the dynamic system of (K, K^*, q, q^*) satisfies equilibrium determinacy under a given level of $\bar{m}$, then the equilibrium paths of K and K^* are uniquely determined under given levels of K_0 and K^*_0. Therefore, the equilibrium path of (6.55) is also uniquely determined. Conversely, if the dynamic system of (K, K^*, q, q^*) exhibits local indeterminacy, the equilibrium paths of K and K^* cannot be uniquely determined by selecting K_0 and K^*_0. This means that (6.55) also holds equilibrium indeterminacy.

Since $\lambda_K(\cdot) = \lambda_{K^*}(\cdot)$ and $\lambda_p(\cdot) = \lambda_{p^*}(\cdot)$ in the steady state where $K = K^*$ and $p = p^*$, we obtain $\pi_K = \pi_K^* = \pi_{K^*} = \pi^*$, $\pi_q = \pi_{q^*}^*$ and $\pi_{q^*} = \pi_q^*$. ■

Under a given level of $\bar{m}$, let us linearize the dynamic system of (6.47a), (6.47b), (6.48a), and (6.48b) at the steady state. The coefficient matrix of the linearized system is given by

$$J = \begin{bmatrix} y_K^1 - \delta + y_p^1 \pi_K & y_p^1 \pi_{K^*} & y_p^1 \pi_q & y_p^1 \pi_{q^*} \\ y_{p^*}^1 \pi_K^* & y_{K^*}^1 - \delta + y_{p^*}^1 \pi_{K^*}^* & y_{p^*}^1 \pi_q^* & y_{p^*}^1 \pi_{q^*}^* \\ -q\hat{r}' \pi_K & -q\hat{r}' \pi_{K^*} & -q\hat{r}' \pi_q & -q\hat{r}' \pi_{q^*} \\ -q\hat{r}' \pi_K^* & -q\hat{r}' \pi_{K^*}^* & -q\hat{r}' \pi_q^* & -q\hat{r}' \pi_{q^*}^* \end{bmatrix}.$$

By use of Lemma A.1, we see that the characteristic equation of J is written as

$$\begin{aligned} \Gamma(\eta) &= \det[\eta I - J] \\ &= \det \begin{bmatrix} \eta - (y_K^1 - \delta + y_p^1 \pi_K) & -y_p^1 \pi_K & -y_p^1 \pi_q & -y_p^1 \pi_{q^*} \\ -y_p^1 \pi_K & \eta - (y_K^1 - \delta + y_p^1 \pi_K) & -y_p^1 \pi_{q^*} & -y_p^1 \pi_q \\ q\hat{r}' \pi_K & q\hat{r}' \pi_K & \eta + q\hat{r}' \pi_q & q\hat{r}' \pi_{q^*} \\ q\hat{r}' \pi_K & q\hat{r}' \pi_K & q\hat{r}' \pi_q & \eta + q\hat{r}' \pi_q \end{bmatrix} \\ &= \det \begin{bmatrix} \eta - (y_K^1 - \delta) & 0 & \eta & 0 \\ 0 & \eta - (y_K^1 - \delta) & 0 & \eta \\ q\hat{r}' \pi_K & q\hat{r}' \pi_K & \eta + q\hat{r}' \pi_q & q\hat{r}' \pi_{q^*} \\ q\hat{r}' \pi_K & q\hat{r}' \pi_K & q\hat{r}' \pi_q & \eta + q\hat{r}' \pi_q \end{bmatrix} \\ &= \left[\eta - (y_K^1 - \delta)\right]\left[\eta + q\hat{r}'(\pi_q - \pi_{q^*})\right]\xi(\eta), \end{aligned}$$

where η denotes the characteristic root of J and

$$\xi(\eta) \equiv \eta^2 + \left[q\hat{r}'\left(\pi_q + \pi_{q^*}\right) - \left(y_K^1 - \delta\right) - 2y_p^1 \pi_K\right]\eta - q\hat{r}'\left(y_K^1 - \delta\right)\left(\pi_q + \pi_{q^*}\right).$$

Our assumptions mean that $\frac{a_1}{b_1} - \frac{a_2}{b_2} < 0$ and $\alpha_1 - \alpha_2 > 0$. Thus from (6.21a) we see that $y_K^1 - \delta < 0$. In addition, as to the partial derivatives of $\pi(.)$ function displayed above, we see that $\pi_q - \pi_{q^*} = 1/\lambda\,(> 0)$. Hence, using $\hat{r}(p) \equiv a_1 A_1 k_1(p)^{\alpha_1 - 1}$, we obtain

$$\hat{r}'\left(\pi_q - \pi_{q^*}\right) = a_1(a_1 - 1)A_1(k_1(p))^{a_1 - 2}\frac{k_1'(p)}{\lambda} > 0.$$

As a consequence, at least two roots of $\Gamma(\eta) = 0$ have negative real parts. Similarly, we find that

$$\pi_q + \pi_{q^*} = \frac{1}{\lambda + 2p\lambda_p},$$

where

$$\lambda_p = \frac{\partial}{\partial p}(1+\bar{m})^{\frac{1}{\sigma}}\left[y^2(K,p)+y^2(K^*,p^*)\right]^{-\frac{1}{\sigma}}$$
$$= -\frac{y_p^2}{\sigma}(1+\bar{m})^{\frac{1}{\sigma}}\left[y^2(K,p)+y^2(K^*,p^*)\right]^{-\frac{1}{\sigma}-1} < 0.$$

Therefore, in the steady state equilibrium. the following holds:

$$\lambda + 2p\lambda_p = \frac{1}{\sigma}\left[\sigma - \frac{py_p^2(K,p)}{y^2(K,p)}\right].$$

Note that under our assumptions, it holds that $y_p^2(K,p) > 0$. Suppose that σ is small enough to satisfy $\sigma < py_p^2/y^2$. Then, $\lambda_p + 2p\lambda_p > 0$ so that $\pi_q + \pi_{q^*} < 0$, which leads to

$$-q\hat{r}'\left(y_K^1 - \delta\right)\left(\pi_q + \pi_{q^*}\right) < 0.$$

This means that $\xi(\eta) = 0$ has one positive and one negative root. As a result, $\Gamma(\eta) = 0$ has three stable roots. Hence, if σ is smaller than the price elasticity of supply function of consumption goods, then there locally exists a continuum of equilibrium paths converging to the steady state.

Now suppose that σ is larger than py_p^2/y^2. Then, we obtain $\pi_q + \pi_{q^*} > 0$. Furthermore, it holds that

$$-2y_p^1\pi_K = -2y_p^1\left(-\frac{p\lambda_K}{\lambda + 2p\lambda_p}\right)$$
$$= -\frac{2py_p^1}{\lambda + 2p\lambda_p}y_K^2\left[\frac{(1+\bar{m})^{\sigma-1}}{\sigma}\right]\left(2y^2\right)^{-\sigma^{-1}-1} > 0,$$

because $y_p^1 < 0$ and $y_K^2 > 0$ under our assumptions. Consequently, the following inequalities are established:

$$-q\hat{r}'\left(y_K^1 - \delta\right)\left(\pi_q + \pi_{q^*}\right) > 0,$$
$$q\hat{r}'\left(\pi_q + \pi_{q^*}\right) - \left(y_K^1 - \delta\right) - 2y_K^1\pi_K > 0.$$

These conditions mean that $\xi(\eta) = 0$ has two roots with negative real parts and, hence, all the roots of $\Gamma(\eta) = 0$ are stable ones. In sum, if $\frac{a_1}{b_1} - \frac{a_2}{b_2} < 0$ and $\alpha_1 - \alpha_2 > 0$, then the characteristic equation of the linearized system involves at least three stable roots, meaning that the converging path towards the steady state is locally indeterminate.

Chapter 7
New Directions

In this short chapter, we refer to the recent development of macroeconomic models with equilibrium indeterminacy. The global financial crisis of 2007–2008 forced macroeconomists to rethink about their analytical frameworks. The mainstream dynamic stochastic general equilibrium (DSGE) approach was severely criticized by practitioners and policy makers because it failed to offer useful policy recommendations for the financial crisis as well as for the prolonged slumps in many countries after the crisis. In the search for new directions in macroeconomic analysis, there is renewed interest in macroeconomic models with equilibrium indeterminacy. In what follows, we pick out a notable sample of the recent studies in the field.

7.1 Microfoundations of Keynesian Economics

In a series of studies, Roger Farmer claims that the New Keynesian models, that is, DSGE models with sticky prices, fail to capture the core idea of Keynes (1936); see Farmer (2008a, 2008b, 2010, 2012, 2013). In order to provide a microfoundation to Keynes's theory of unemployment equilibrium, he adds labor market frictions to an otherwise standard general equilibrium model of macroeconomy. Unlike the conventional macroeconomic models with search frictions in labor markets, in Farmer's model, the wage is not settled by a Nash bargaining. Instead, the wage is determined competitively in the process of random matching between workers and firms. However, in the presence of labor market frictions, the competitive wage cannot be determined by the usual labor market equilibrium condition, that is, the equality between the marginal rate of substitution of consumption for labor and the marginal productivity of labor. As a consequence, the economy involves a continuum of steady state equilibria, so that the steady state levels of real wage and unemployment of labor become indeterminate as well.

K. Mino, *Growth and Business Cycles with Equilibrium Indeterminacy*, Advances in Japanese Business and Economics 13,
DOI 10.1007/978-4-431-55609-1_7

To close the model, Farmer introduces the "belief function" that relates households' expected wealth to a specific steady state equilibrium. (Since the steady state constitutes a continuum, every belief can be self-fulfilled, and, hence, rationality of expectations still holds.) In this model, the households' consumption demand depends on their beliefs (animal spirits), which determine the steady state levels of real wage and unemployment. Therefore, the main outcome of the model analysis is close to Keynes's business cycle theory in which animal spirits of entrepreneurs play a key role in determining the level of effective demand (Keynes 1936, Chapter 22).

In a different context, Benhabib et al. (2015) also examine the demand constrained equilibria of a macroeconomy. In their model, each firm produces a different consumption good in monopolistically competitive markets. Firms should produce before the demand for their products materializes. The firms determine their production plans based on the information about demand conditions, but the signal they receive contains aggregate as well as idiosyncratic noises. On the other hand, households should decide their consumption demand before their income materializes. They expect their income based on their sentiments and their decisions are sent to the firms as noisy signals.

In the foregoing studies on equilibrium indeterminacy, including Farmer's theory just mentioned above, it is demonstrated that there may exist (infinitely) many fundamental equilibria and the selection of a specific equilibrium is affected by extrinsic uncertainty. In contrast, the model of Benhabib et al. (2015) involves a unique fundamental equilibrium. However, in the presence of imperfect information, there may also exist "sentiments-driven" equilibria in addition to the fundamental equilibrium, and the selection of a particular equilibrium depends on the households' sentiments (animal spirits). The modelling strategy of Benhabib et al. (2015) is closely related to a contribution of Angeletos and La'O (2013). These authors empathize that agents hold heterogeneous expectations under imperfect information. They show that in the presence of expectations heterogeneity, correlated shocks to the agents' higher-order beliefs may yield sentiment-driven business fluctuations.

7.2 Financial Frictions and Bubbles

The general equilibrium models with financial constraints initiated by Kiyotaki and Moore (1997) and others have regained research interest after the financial crisis of 2007–2008. Some authors examine the role of financial frictions for generating equilibrium indeterminacy. Harrison and Weder (2013) introduce financial constraints into a real business cycle model with external increasing returns. In their model, the production function includes land as well as labor and capital. Firms should pay for wages before production takes place, and they borrow their payments from household by using the value of land they hold as collateral. Harrison and Weder

(2013) show that if the borrowing constraint is effective, equilibrium indeterminacy may arise under an empirically plausible degree of increasing returns.

In a similar vein, Benhabib and Wang (2013) examine a model in which intermediate goods are produced in monopolistically competitive markets. The final good firms must pay for intermediate goods in advance, and they borrow the payments from the households. It is also assumed that each financial transaction is associated with a fixed borrowing cost. In this situation, markups determined by the intermediate good firms are affected by the final good firms' borrowing constraints. Since the presence of the fixed borrowing cost generates nonconvexity, it plays the same role as external increasing returns in the model of Benhabib and Farmer (1994). The authors confirm that equilibrium indeterminacy may emerge even though the final good production technology satisfies constant returns to scale.

Liu and Wang (2014) also explore the relation between financial constraints and equilibrium indeterminacy in a different setting. In their model, there is a continuum of firms, each of whom has a different productivity. Each firm borrows its advance payments for production factors under a financial constraint in which the value of the firm (the value of stocks) acts as collateral. Given this setting, the presence of borrowing constraints determines the cutoff level of firm productivity, and firms that have productivity higher than the cutoff level participate in production activities. As a consequence, the financial constraints affect the total productivity of final goods. Liu and Wang (2014) reveal that equilibrium indeterminacy arises even though the production technology is not associated with external increasing returns.

Miao and Wang (2012), on the other hand, focus on bubbles in the presence of financial constraints. Like Liu and Wang (2014), in their model, firms face financial constraints for their investment and the firm value acts as a collateral. The authors first confirm that the bubble-less equilibrium is uniquely determined. However, there may also exist a continuum of bubbly equilibria. If the economy stays on a bubbly equilibrium path, the burst of bubbles caused by changes in agents' expectations yields an abrupt downturn of economic activities. This model, therefore, provides us with a possible theoretical exposition about the huge negative impact on the real side of the US economy caused by the collapse of the housing bubbles in 2007.

7.3 Search Frictions

If market transactions are decentralized, the matching technology of search activities of agents is relevant in characterizing the equilibrium conditions. Early studies on labor market dynamics such as Diamond (1982), Diamond and Fudenberg (1989), and Howitt and McAfee (1992) reveal that external effects associated with matching technology easily bring about equilibrium indeterminacy. In addition, Mortensen (1999) shows that a search-matching model of labor market yields global indeterminacy if the production technology exhibits increasing returns. The source of indeterminacy in these search-matching models is similar to the nonconvexity of social production technology emphasized by Benhabib and Farmer (1994).

The Diamond-Mortensen-Pssarides modelling of labor market frictions has been incorporated into the DSGE models. While the majority of the these studies focus on the case of equilibrium determinacy, some authors explore the possibility of sunspot-driven business cycles generated by labor market frictions. For example, Hashimzade and Ortigueira (2005) confirm that the presence of external effects in search activities generates sunspot-driven business cycles even in the absence of external increasing returns of production technology. Furthermore, using a model without capital and investment, Krause and Lubik (2010) demonstrate that indeterminacy may hold even though both production and matching technologies exhibit constant returns to scale.

More recently, Kaplan and Menzio (2016) and Dong et al. (2015) present new insights on business fluctuation caused by search frictions. Kaplan and Menzio (2016) consider search frictions in commodity markets and find that equilibrium indeterminacy is generated by "shopping externalities.", In their model. there are two kinds of consumption goods: one is traded in a competitive, centralized market, while the other is traded in decentralized markets. Therefore, transactions are decentralized not only in the labor markets but also in a part of final goods markets. The key idea of Kaplan and Menzio (2016) is that employed workers have higher income and spend less time to search commodities with lower prices than unemployed workers. In this situation, if a positive sunspot shock make firms increase employment of labor, then the number of workers with higher income increases, which brings about larger aggregate demand and higher commodity prices. As a result, the optimistic anticipation of firms are self-fulfilled, which yields multiple equilibria even in the absence of increasing returns in production and matching technologies. Kaplan and Menzio (2016) give a detailed discussion of the global dynamics of the model economy. They find that the dynamic system involves multiple steady states and that there is a continuum of equilibrium paths converging to each steady state. Consequently, the analytical properties of their model resembles these of the growth models with multiple steady states discussed in Sects. 4.2 and 4.3 in Chap. 4. The authors claim that their model is consistent with the empirical findings about the difference in shopping behaviors between employed and unemployed workers.

Dong et al. (2015) introduce search frictions into credit markets. These authors assume that there are search frictions in transactions between depositors (households) and banks as well as in transactions between borrowers (firms) and banks. Given this setting, business booms enhance search activities, which raises the matching probabilities of financial transactions. This mechanism generates increasing returns of the aggregate production technology. As a result, although production technology of individual firm and matching technologies in credit markets satisfy constant returns, the equilibrium path of the economy becomes indeterminate.

7.4 Agent Heterogeneity

In recent times, introducing heterogeneous agents into the business cycle models is an active research topic in macroeconomics. In an economy with heterogeneous households and firms, the distribution of income and wealth among households as well as firm size distribution may affect the behavior of the aggregate economy. Hence, the determinacy/indeterminacy conditions would be affected by the pattern of distribution of these variables. Based on this idea, some authors explore the relation between agents' heterogeneity and equilibrium indeterminacy.

For example, Ghiglino and Sorger (2002) introduce two types of households into Benhabib and Farmer's (1994) model of real business cycles with external increasing returns. Both types of households are assumed to have identical preference and labor efficiency but different initial wealth holdings. Since the separable utility function used in the Benhabib and Farmer model does not hold homotheticity, the behavior of the aggregate economy is not independent of wealth distribution among the households. The authors confirm that the conditions under which indeterminacy emerges is affected by the initial distribution of wealth, so that heterogeneity matters for the equilibrium determinacy/indeterminacy conditions. In a similar vein, Ghiglino and Olszak-Duquenne (2005) and Ghiglino and Venditti (2007) treat a two-sector Ramsey model with production externalities. Again, there are two types of households. In addition to their initial wealth holdings, the households' labor efficiencies are different from each other. The authors inspect the relation between equilibrium indeterminacy and the degree of heterogeneity of households. They show that depending on parameter magnitudes concerning preference structures, a higher heterogeneity may or may not enhance the possibility of emergence of indeterminacy.

Mino and Nakamoto (2012), on the other hand, explore the effects of consumption externalities in the presence of heterogenous households. In their model, there are two groups of household, and. each household's felicity is affected by the intragroup consumption externalities as well as by the intergroup consumption externalities. Mino and Nakamoto (2012) demonstrate that if the degree of intergroup externalities are sufficiently high, that is, each household's consumption behavior is strongly affected by the consumption of households in other group, then the presence of consumption externalities yield equilibrium indeterminacy.[1]

Finally. it is worth emphasizing that heterogeneity of agents also plays a key role in models with financial and search frictions as well as in sentiment-driven business cycles models explored by Angeletos and La'O (2013) and Benhabib et al. (2015). Therefore, the recent development in macroeconomic models with equilibrium indeterminacy has shifted its main concern from the representative agent settings to the heterogeneous agent settings.

---

[1]Mino and Nakamoto (2016) examine a more general model in which there is a continuum of households, each of whom has different degree of conformism. They, however, do not consider the indeterminacy issue.

It still remains to be seen whether the recent development cited above can present effective policy recommendations for long-stagnated economies such as Japan. However, it is fair to say that the research on growth and business cycle models with equilibrium indeterminacy continues serving as an attractive alternative when the standard macroeconomic models with equilibrium determinacy fail to provide us convincing explanations for relevant macroeconomic phenomena.

Bibliography

Abel, A. (1990). Asset prices under habit formation and catching up with the Joneses. *American Economic Review, 80*, 38–42.
Aghion, P., & Howitt, P. (1992). A model of growth through creative destruction. *Econometrica, 60*, 323–351.
Aiyagari, R. (1995). The econometrics of iindeterminacy: An applied study: A comment. *Carnegie-Rochester Conference Series on Public Policy, 43*, 273–284.
Akao, K., Kamihigashi, T. & Nihimura, K. (2011). Monotonicity and continuity of the critical capital stock in the Dechert–Nishimura model. *Journal of Mathematical Economics, 47*, 677–682.
Alonso-Carrera, J., Caballe, J., & Raurich, X. (2008). Can consumption spillovers be a source of equilibrium indeterminacy? *Journal of Economic Dynamics and Control, 32*, 2883–2902.
Altug, S. (2009). *Business cycles: Facts, fallacy and fantasy*. Singapore: World Scientific.
Amano, D., & Itaya, J. (2013). Taxation in the two-sector neoclassical growth model with sector-specific externalities and endogenous labor supply. *Japanese Economic Review, 64*, 248–275.
Amano, D., Itaya, J., & Mino, K. (2008). Tax incidence in dynamic economies with externalities and endogenous labor supply. In T. Kamihigashi & L. Zhao (Eds.), *International trade and economic growth: Essays in memory of Koji Shimomura* (pp. 361–382). Springer.
Anagnostopoulos, A., & Giannitsarou, C. (2013). Indeterminacy and period length under balanced budget rules. *Macroeconomic Dynamics, 19*, 898–919.
Angeletos, G.-M., & La'O, J. (2013). Sentiments. *Econometrica, 81*, 739–779.
Antoci, A., Galeotti, M., & Russu, P. (2014). Global analysis and indeterminacy in a two-sector growth model with human capital. *International Journal of Economic Theory, 10*, 313–338.
Antras, P., & Caballero, R. (2009). Trade and capital flows: A financial frictions perspective. *Journal of Political Economy, 117*, 701–744.
Atkeson, A., & Kehoe, P. (2000). *Paths of development for early- and late-bloomers in a dynamic Heckscher-Ohlin model* (Staff Report 256). Federal Reserve Bank of Minneapolis.
Azariadis, C. (1981). Self-fulfilling prophecies. *Journal of Economic Theory, 25*, 380–396.
Azariadis, C., & Drazen, A. (1990). Threshold externalities in economic development. *Quarterly Journal of Economics, 105*, 501–526.
Azariadis, C., & Guesnerie, R. (1986). Sunspots and cycles. *Review of Economic Studies, 53*, 725–736.
Bajona, C., & Kehoe, T. (2010) Trade, growth, and convergence in a dynamic Heckscher-Ohlin model. *Review of Economic Dynamics, 13*, 487–513.

K. Mino, *Growth and Business Cycles with Equilibrium Indeterminacy*,
Advances in Japanese Business and Economics 13,
DOI 10.1007/978-4-431-55609-1

Bambi, M., & Venditti, A. (2016). *Time-varying consumption tax, productive government spending, and aggregate instability* (Discussion Papers 16/01). Department of Economics, University of York.

Basu, S., & Fernald, J. (1997). Returns to scale in U.S. production: Estimates and implications. *Journal of Political Economy, 105*, 249–283.

Baxter, M., & Crucini, M. (1995). Business cycles and the asset structure of foreign trade. *International Economic Review, 36*, 821–854.

Beaudry, P., & Portier, F. (2004). An exploration into Pigou's theory of cycles. *Journal of Monetary Economics, 51*, 183–1216.

Beaudry, P., & Portier, F. (2014). News-driven business cycles: Insights and challenges. *Journal of Economic Literature, 52*, 993–1074.

Becker, G. S. (1975). *Human capital*. Chicago: The University of Chicago Press.

Bella, G., & Mattana, P. (2014). Global indeterminacy of the equilibrium in the Chamley model of endogenous growth in the vicinity of a Bogdanov–Takens bifurcation. *Mathematical Social Sciences, 71*, 69–79.

Ben-Gad, M. (2003). Fiscal policy and indeterminacy in models of endogenous growth. *Journal of Economic Theory, 108*, 322–344.

Benhabib, J. (2014). Multiple equilibria in the Aghion-Howitt model. *Ricerche Economiche, 68*, 112–116.

Benhabib, J., & Eusepi, S. (2005). The design of monetary and fiscal policy: A global perspective. *Journal of Economic Theory, 123*, 40–73.

Benhabib, J., & Farmer, R. (1994). Indeterminacy and increasing returns. *Journal of Economic Theory, 63*, 19–41.

Benhabib, J., & Farmer, R. E. (1996). Indeterminacy and sector specific externalities. *Journal of Monetary Economics, 37*, 397–419.

Benhabib, J., & Farmer, R. (1999). Indeterminacy and sunspots in macroeconomics. In J. B. Taylor Michael Woodford (Ed.), *Handbook of macroeconomics* (Vol. 1, Part A, pp. 387–448). Amsterdam: Elsevier.

Benhabib, J., & Gali, J. (1995). On growth and indeterminacy: Some theory and evidence. *Carnegie-Rochester Conference Series on Public Policy, 43*(1), 163–211.

Benhabib, J., & Nishimura, K. (1998). Indeterminacy and sunspots with constant returns. *Journal of Economic Theory, 81*, 58–96.

Benhabib, J., & Perli, R. (1994). Uniqueness and indeterminacy: Transitional dynamics. *Journal of Economic Theory, 63*, 113–142.

Benhabib, J., & Wang, P. (2013). Financial constraints, endogenous markups, and self-fulfilling equilibria. *Journal of Monetary Economics, 60*, 789–805.

Benhabib, J., Perli, R., & Xie, D. (1994). Monopolistic competition, increasing returns and growth. *Ricerche Economiche, 48*, 279–298.

Benhabib, J., Meng. Q., & Nishimura, K. (2000). Indeterminacy under constant returns to scale in multisector economies. *Econometrica, 68*, 1541–1548.

Benhabib, J., Schmitt-Grohé, S., & Uribe, M. (2001a). Monetary policy and multiple equilibria. *American Economic Review, 91*, 167–186.

Benhabib, J., Schmitt-Grohe, S., & Uribe, M. (2001b). The perils of Taylor rules. *Journal of Economic Theory, 96*, 40–69.

Benhabib, J., Wang, P., & Wen, Y. (2015). Sentiments and aggregate demand fluctuations. *Econometrica, 83*, 549–585, 03.

Bennett, R., & Farmer, R. (2000). Indeterminacy with nonseparable utility. *Journal of Economic Theory, 93*, 118–143.

Bian, Y., & Meng, Q. (2004). Preferences, endogenous discount rate, and indeterminacy in a small open economy model. *Economics Letters, 84*, 315–322.

Black, F. (1974). Uniqueness of the price level in monetary growth models with rational expectations. *Journal of Economic Theory, 7*, 53–65.

Blanchard, O., & Kahn, C. (1980). The solution of linear diserence models under rational expectations. *Econometrica, 48*, 1305–1310.

Boldrin, M. (1992). Dynamic externalities, multiple equilibria, and growth. *Journal of Economic Theory, 58*, 198–218.

Boldrin, M., & Rustichini, A. (1994). Growth and indeterminacy in dynamic models with externalities. *Econometrica, 62*, 23–342.

Boldrin, M., & Woodford, M. (1990). Equilibrium models displaying endogenous fluctuations and chaos: A survey. *Journal of Monetary Economics, 25*, 189–222.

Bond, E., Wang, P., & Yip, C.-K. (1996). A general two-sector model of endogenous growth with physical and human capital. *Journal of Economic Theory, 68*, 149–173.

Brock, W. (1974). Money and growth: The case of long run perfect foresight. *International Economic Review, 15*, 750–777.

Caballe, J., & Santos, M. (1993). On endogenous growth with physical and human capital. *Journal of Political Economy, 101*, 1042–1067.

Caliendo, L. (2010). *On the dynamics of the Hecksher-Ohlin theory* (Working Papers 2010–011). Becker Friedman Institute for Research in Economics.

Calvo, G. (1979). On models of money and perfect foresight. *International Economic Review, 20*, 83–103.

Carlstrom, C., & Fuerst, T. (2005). Investment and interest rate policy: A discrete-time analysis. *Journal of Economic Theory, 123*, 4–20.

Cass, D., & Shell, K. (1983). Do sunspots matter? *Journal of Political Economy 90*, 193–227.

Chamley, C. (1993). Externalities and dynamics in models of learning or doing. *International Economic Review, 34*, 583–609.

Chen, Z. (1992). Long-run equilibria in a dynamic Heckscher-Ohlin model. *Canadian Journal of Economics, 25*, 923–943.

Chen, B.-L. (2006). Public capital, endogenous growth, and endogenous fluctuations. *Journal of Macroeconomics, 28*, 768–774.

Chen, B.-L., & Chu, A. (2010). On R&D spillovers, multiple equilibria and indeterminacy. *Journal of Economics, 100*, 247–263.

Chen, B.-L., & Hsu, M. (2007). Admiration is a source of indeterminacy. *Economics Letters, 95*, 96–103.

Chen, B.-L., Hus, Y.-S., & Mino, K. (2013). Can Consumption habit spillovers be a source of equilibrium indeterminacy? *Journal of Economics, 109*, 245–269.

Chen, B.-L., Hsu, Y.-S., & Mino, K. (2015). Welfare implications and equilibrium indeterminacy in a two-sector growth model with consumption externalities. *Macroeconomic Dynamics, 19*, 535–577.

Chen, B.-L., Hu, Y., & Mino, K. (2016). *Stabilization effects of taxation rules in small-open economies with endogenous growth* (KIER Working Papers 946). Institute of Economic Research, Kyoto University.

Chen, S.-H., & Guo, J.-T. (2013). Progressive taxation and macroeconomic (In) stability with productive government spending. *Journal of Economic Dynamics and Control, 37*, 951–963.

Chen, S.-H., & Guo, J.-T. (2014). Progressive taxation and macroeconomic (In)stability with utility-generating government spending. *Journal of Macroeconomics, 42*, 174–183.

Chen, S.-H., & Guo, J.-T. (2015). Progressive taxation, endogenous growth, and macroeconomic (In)stability. (Working Paper) Department of Economics, University of Calfornia, Riverside.

Chen, S.-H., & Guo, J.-T. (2016). *Progressive taxation as an automatic destabilizer under endogenous growth* (Working Paper). Department of Economics, University of California, Riverside.

Chin, C.-T., Guo, J.-T., & Lai, C.-C. (2012). A note on indeterminacy and investment adjustment costs in an endogenously growing small open economy. *Macroeconomic Dynamics, 16*, 438–450.

Christiano, L., & Harrison, S. (1999). Chaos, sunspots and automatic stabilizers. *Journal of Monetary Economics, 44*; Cooper, R., & John, A. (1988). Coordinating coordination failures in Keynesian models. *Quarterly Journal of Economics, 103*, 441–463.

Cooper, R. (1999). *Macroeconomic complementarities*. Cambridge: Cambridge University Press.

Cooper, R., & John, A. (1988). Coordinating coordination failures in Keynesian models. *Quarterly Journal of Economics, 103*, 441–463.

Coury, T., & Wen, Y. (2009). Global indeterminacy in locally determinate real business cycle models. *International Journal of Economic Theory, 5*, 49–60.

Daito, I. (2009). Productive consumption and population dynamics in an endogen growth model: Demographic trends and human development aid in developing economies. *Journal of Economic Dynamics and Control, 34*, 696–709.

Dechert, W., & Nishimura, K. (1983). A complete characterization of optimal growth paths in an aggregated model with a non-concave production function. *Journal of Economic Theory, 31*, 332–354.

Diamond, P. (1982). Aggregate demand management in search equilibrium. *Journal of Political Economy, 90*, 881–894.

Diamond, P., Fudenberg, D. (1989). Rational expectations business cycles in search equilibrium. *Journal of Political Economy, 97*, 606–619.

Dong, F., Wen, Y., & Wang, P. (2015). Credit search and credit cycles. *Economic Theory, 61*(2), 215–239.

Drugeon, J.-P., & Venditti, A. (2001). Intersectoral external effects, multiplicities and indeterminacies. *Journal of Economic Dynamics and Control, 25*, 765–787.

Dufourt, F., Nishimura, K., & Venditti, A. (2015). Indeterminacy and sunspots in two-sector rbc models with generalized no-income-effect preferences. *Journal of Economic Theory, 157*, 1056–1080.

Dupor, W. (2001). Investment and interest rate policy. *Journal of Economic Theory, 98*, 85–113.

Edge, R. M., & Rudd, J. B. (2007). Taxation and the Taylor principle. *Journal of Monetary Economics, 54*, 2554–2567.

Eicher, T., & Turnovsky, S. (1999). Convergence in a two-sector nonscale growth model. *Journal of Economic Growth, 4*, 413–428.

Eusepi, S. (2009). On expectations-driven business cycles in economies with production externalities. *International Journal of Economic Theory, 5*, 9–23.

Farmer, R. (2004). *Macroeconomics of self-fulfilling prophecies* (2nd ed.). Cambridge: MIT Press.

Farmer, R. (2008a). Aggregate demand and supply. *International Journal of Economic Theory, 4*, 77–93.

Farmer, R. (2008b). Animal spirits. In L. Blume & S. Durlauf (Eds.), *The new Palgrave dictionary of economics* (2nd ed.). Basingstoke/Hampshire: Palgrave MacMillan.

Farmer, R. (2010). *Expectations, employment and prices*. Oxford/New York: Oxford University Press.

Farmer, R. (2012). Confidence, crashes and animal spirits. *Economic Journal, 122*, 155–172.

Farmer, R. (2013). Animal spirits, financial crises and persistent unemployment. *Economic Journal, 123*, 317–340.

Farmer, R. (2016). The evolution of endogenous business cycles. *Macroeconomic Dynamics, 20*, 544–557.

Farmer, R., & Guo, J.-T. (1994). Real business cycles and animal spirit hypothesis. *Journal of Economic Theory, 63*, 42–72.

Farmer, R., & Guo, J.-T.(1995). The econometrics of indeterminacy: An applied study. *Carnegie-Rochester Conference Series on Public Policy, 43*, 225–271.

Farmer, R., & Lahiri, A. (2005). A two-country model of endogenous growth. *Review of Economic Dynamics, 8*, 68–88.

Farmer, R., & Lahiri, A. (2006). Economic growth in an interdependent world economy. *Economic Journal, 116*, 969–990.

Frankel, D., & Pauzner, A. (2000). Resolving indeterminacy in dynamic setting: The role of shocks. *Quarterly Journal of Economics, 105*, 285–304.

Fujisaki, S., & Mino, K. (2007). Generalized Taylor rule and determinacy of growth equilibrium. *Economics Bulletin, 5*(11), 1–7.

Fujisaki, S., & Mino, K. (2008). *Income taxation, interest-rate control and macroeconomic stability with balanced-budget* (Discussion papers in Economics and Business 08–20). Graduate School of Economics and Osaka School of International Public Policy (OSIPP), Osaka University.

Fukao, K., & Benabou, R. (1993). History versus expectations: A comment. *Quarterly Journal of Economics, 108*, 535–542.

Fukuda, S. (1993). The emergence of equilibrium cycles in a monetary economy with a separable utility function. *Journal of Monetary Economics, 32*, 321–334.

Futagami, K., & Mino, K. (1993). Threshold externalities and cyclical growth in a stylized model of capital accumulation. *Economics Letters, 41*, 99–105.

Futagami, K., & Mino, K. (1995). Public capital and patterns of growth in the presence of threshold externalities. *Journal of Economics, 61*, 123–146.

Futagami, K., Iwaisako, T., & Ohdoi, R. (2008). Debt policy rule, productive government spending, and multiple growth paths. *Macroeconomic Dynamics, 12*, 445–462.

Futagami, K., Hori, T., Maebayashi, N., & Morimoto, K. (2017). Debt policy rules in an open economy. *Journal of Public Economic Theory, 19*, 158–187.

Gali, J. (1994). Keeping up with the Joneses: Consumption externalities, portfolio choice, and aasset prices. *Journal of Money, Credit and Banking, 26*, 1–8.

Gali, J. (1995). Product diversity,eendogenous markups, and development traps. *Journal of Monetary Economics, 36*, 39–63.

Ghiglino, C., & Sorger, G. (2002). Poverty traps, indeterminacy, and the wealth distribution. *Journal of Economic Theory, 105*, 120–139.

Ghiglino, C., & Olszak-Duquenne, M. (2005). On the impact of heterogeneity on indeterminacy. *International Economic Review, 46*, 171–188.

Ghiglino, C., & Venditti, A. (2007). Wealth inequality, preference heterogeneity and macroeconomic volatility in two-sector economies. *Journal of Economic Theory, 135*, 414–441.

Ghilardi, M., & Rossi, R. (2014). Aggregate stability and balanced-budget rules. *Journal of Money, Credit and Banking, 46*, 1787–1809.

Giannitsarou, C. (2007). Balanced budget rules and aggregate instability: The role of consumption taxes. *Economic Journal, 117*, 1423–1435.

Greenwood, G., Hercowitz, Z., & Huffman, G. (1988). Investment, capacity utilization, and the real business cycle. *American Economic Review, 78*, 402–417.

Greiner, A., & Semmler, W. (1995). Multiple steady states, indeterminacy and cycles in a basic model of endogenous growth. *Journal of Economics, 63*, 79–99.

Greiner, A., & Semmler, W. (1996). Saddle path stability, fluctuations, and indeterminacy in economic growth. *Studies in Nonlinear Dynamics and Econometrics, 1*, 1–16.

Guo, J.-T., & Harrison, S. (2001a). Indeterminacy with capital utilization and sector-specific externalities. *Economics Lettes, 72*, 355–360.

Guo, J.-T., & Harrison, S. (2001b). Tax policy and stability in a model with sector-specific externalities. *Review of Economic Dynamics, 4*, 75–89.

Guo, J.-T., & Harrison, S. (2004). Balanced-budget rules and macroeconomic (In)stability. *Journal of Economic Theory, 119*, 357–363.

Guo, J.-T., & Harrison, S. (2008). Useful government spending and macroeconomic (In)stability under balanced-budget rules. *Journal of Public Economic Theory, 10*, 383–397.

Guo, J.-T., & Harrison, S. (2010). Indeterminacy with no-income-effect preferences and sector-specific externalities. *Journal of Economic Theory, 145*, 287–300.

Guo, J.-T., & Lansing, K. (1998). Indeterminacy and stabilization policy. *Journal of Economic Theory, 82*, 481–490.

Guo, J.-T., & Lansing, K. (2002). Fiscal policy, increasing returns, and endogenous fluctuations. *Macroeconomic Dynamics, 6*, 633–664.

Guo, J.-T., Sirbu, A.-L., & Suen, R. (2012). On expectations-driven business cycles in economies with production externalities: A comment. *International Journal of Economic Theory, 8*, 313–319.

Hansen, G. (1985). Indivisible labor and the business cycle. *Journal of Monetary Economics, 16*, 309–327.

Harrison, S. (2001). Indeterminacy in a model with sector-specific externalities. *Journal of Economic Dynamics and Control, 25*, 747–764.
Harrison, S. (2003). Returns to scale and externalities in the consumption and investment sectors. *Review of Economic Dynamics, 6*, 963–976.
Harrison, S., & Weder, M. (2013). Sunspots and credit frictions. *Macroeconomic Dynamics, 17*, 1055–1069.
Hashimzade, N., & Ortigueira, S. (2005). Endogenous business cycles with frictional labor markets. *Economic Journal, 115*, 161–175.
Herrendorf, V. & Walldman, R. (2000). Ruling out multiplicity and indeterminacy: the role of heterogeneity. *Review of Economic Studies, 67*, 295–307.
Hintermaier, T. (2003). On the minimum degree of returns to scale in sunspot models of the business cycle. *Journal of Economic Theory, 110*, 400–409.
Hori, T, Maebayashi, N. (2016). Debt policy rule, utility-generating government spending, and indeterminacy of the transition path in an AK model. Forthcoming in *Macroeconomic Dynamics*.
Howitt, P., & McAfee, P. (1992). Animal spirits. *American Economic Review, 82*, 493–507.
Hu, Y., & Mino, K. (2013). Trade structure and belief-driven fluctuations in a global economy. *Journal of International Economics, 90*, 414–424.
Hu, Y., & Shimomura, K. (2011). Multiple equilibria and welfare effects of transfers in a two-country dynamic general equilibrium model. *International Journal of Development and Conflict, Gokhale Institute of Politics and Economics, 1*, 379–397.
Huang, K., & Meng, Q. (2007) Capital and macroeconomic instability in a discrete-time model with forward-looking interest rate rules. *Journal of Economic Dynamics and Control, 31*, 2802–2826.
Huang, K., & Meng, Q. (2009). On interest rate policy and equilibrium stability under increasing returns: A note. *Macroeconomic Dynamics, 13*, 535–552.
Itaya, J., & Mino, K. (2003). Inflation, transaction costs and indeterminacy in monetary economies with endogenous growth. *Economica, 70*, 1–20.
Itaya, J., & Mino, K. (2004). Interest-rate rule and multiple equilibria with endogenous growth. *Economics Bulletin, 5*(6), 1–8.
Itaya, J., & Mino, K. (2007). Technology, preference structure and the growth effect of momey supply. *Macroeconomic Dynamics, 11*, 589–612.
Iwasa, K., & Nishimura, K. (2014). Dynamic two-country Heckscher–Ohlin model with externality. *International Journal of Economic Theory, 10*, 53–74.
Jaimovich, N. (2007). Firm dynamics and markup variations: Implications for sunspot equilibria and endogenous economic fluctuations. *Journal of Economic Theory, 137*, 300–325.
Jaimovich, N. (2008). Income effects and indeterminacy in a calibrated one-sector growth model. *Journal of Economic Theory, 143*, 610–623.
Jevons, W. (1884). The solar period and the price of corn. In W. Stanley Jevons (Ed.), *Investigations in currency and finance* (pp. 194–205). London: Macmillan.
Jin, K. (2012). Industrial structure and capital flows. *American Economic Review, 102*, 2111–2146.
Jones, L., & Manuelli, R. (1990). A convex model of equilibrium growth: Theory and policy implications. *Journal of Political Economy, 98*, 1008–1038.
Kamihigashi, T. (1996). Real business cycles and sunspot fluctuations are observationally equivalent. *Journal of Monetary Economics, 37*, 105–117.
Kaplan, G., & Menzio, G. (2016). Shopping externalities and self-fulfilling unemployment fluctuations. *Journal of Political Economy, 124*, 771–825.
Kaplan, G., Moll, B., & Violante, G. (2016). *Monetary policy according to HANK* (NBER Working Papers No. 21897). National Bureau of Economic Research, Inc.
Keynes, J. M. (1936). *The general theory of employment, interest and money*. London: Macmillan/Cambridge University Press.
Kim, J. (2003). Indeterminacy and investment adjustment costs: An analytical result. *Macroeconomic Dynamics, 7*, 394–406.

King, R., Plosser, C., & Rebelo, S. (1988a). Production, growth and business cycles: I. The basic neoclassical model. *Journal of Monetary Economics, 21*, 195–232.
King, R., Plosser, C., & Rebelo, S. (1988b). Production, growth and business cycles: II. New directions. *Journal of Monetary Economics, 21*, 309–341.
Kiyotaki, N., & Moore, J. (1997). Credit cycles. *Journal of Political Economy, 105*, 211–248.
Krause, M., & Lubik, T. (2010). Instability and indeterminacy in a simple search and matching model. Economic Quarterly, Federal Reserve Bank of Richmond, Issue 3Q, 259–272.
Krugman, P. (1991). History versus expectations. *Quarterly Journal of Economics, 106*, 651–667.
Kurozumi, T. (2006). Determinacy and expectational sability of equilibrium in a monetary sticky-price model with Taylor rules. *Journal of Monetary Economics, 53*, 827–846.
Kurozumi, T., & Van Zandweghe, W. (2008). Investment, interest rrate policy, and equilibrium stability. *Journal of Economic Dynamics and Control, 35*, 1489–1516.
Kurozumi, T., & Zandweghe, W. (2011). Determinacy under inflation targeting interest rate policy in a sticky price model with investment (and labor bargaining). *Journal of Money, Credit and Banking, 43*, 1019–1033.
Kydland, F., & Prescott, E. (1982). Time to build and aggregate fluctuations. *Econometrica, 50*, 1345–1370.
Ladrón-de-Guevara, A., Ortigueira, S., & Santos, M. S. (1997). Equilibrium dynamics in two sector models of endogenous growth. *Journal of Economic Dynamics and Control, 21*, 115–143.
Lahiri, A. (2001). Growth and equilibrium indeterminacy: The role of capital mobility. *Economic Theory, 17*, 197–208.
Leeper, E. (1991). Equilibria under 'Active' and 'Passive' monetary and fiscal policies. *Journal of Monetary Economics, 27*, 129–147.
Linnemann, L. (2006). Interest rate policy, debt, and indeterminacy with distortionary taxation. *Journal of Economic Dynamics and Control, 30*, 487–510.
Linnemann, L. (2007). Balanced budget rules and macroeconomic stability with non-separable utility. *Journal of Macroeconomics, 30*, 199–215.
Liu, Z., & Wang, P. (2014). Credit constraints and self-fulfilling business cycles. *American Economic Journal: Macroeconomics, 6*, 32–69.
Long, J., & Plosser, C. (1983). Real business cycles. *Journal of Political Economy, 91*, 39–69.
Lubik, T. (2003). *Investment spending, equilibrium determinacy, and the interactions of monetary and fiscal policy* (Economics Working Paper Archive 490). Department of Economics, The Johns Hopkins University.
Lucas, R. E. (1988). On the mechanics of development. *Journal of Monetary Economics, 22*, 3–42.
Lucas, R. E. (1993). Making a miracle. *Econometrica, 42*, 293–316.
Matsuyama, K. (1990). Sunspot Equilibria (rational bubbles) in a model of money-in-the-utility-function. *Journal of Monetary Economics, 25*, 137–144.
Matsuyama, K. (1991). Increasing returns, industrialization, and indeterminacy of equilibrium. *Quarterly Journal of Economics, 106*, 617–650.
Mattana, P., Nishimura, K., & Shigoka, T. (2009). Homoclinic ifurcation and global indeterminacy of equilibrium in a two-sector endogenous growth model. *International Journal of Economic Theory, 5*, 25–47.
McCallum, B. (1983). On non-uniqueness in rational expectations models: An attempt at perspective. *Journal of Monetary Economics, 11*, 139–168.
Meng, Q. (2003). Multiple transitional growth paths in endogenously growing open economies. *Journal of Economic Theory, 108*, 365–376.
Meng, Q. (2015). Balanced-budget consumption taxes and aggregate stability in a small open economy. *Economics Letters, 137*, 214–217.
Meng, Q., & Velasco, A. (2003). Indeterminacy in a small open economy with endogenous labor supply. *Economic Theory, 22*, 661–670.
Meng, Q., & Velasco, A. (2004). Market imperfections and the instability of open economies. *Journal of International Economics, 64*, 503–519.
Meng, Q., & Yip, C.-K. (2004). Investment, interest rate rules, and equilibrium determinacy. *Economic Theory, 23*, 863–878.

Miao, J., & Wang, P. (2012). Bubbles and total factor productivity. *American Economic Review, 102*, 82–87.

Milesi-Ferretti, G., & Roubini, N. (1998). On taxation of human capital in models of endogenous growth. *Journal of Public Economics, 70*, 237–254.

Mino, K. (1996). Analysis of a two-sector model of endogenous growth with capital income taxation. *International Economic Review, 37*, 227–251.

Mino, K. (1998). *Equilibrium determinacy of a two-sector AK model* (MPRA Paper No. 17323). University Library of Munich.

Mino, K. (1999). Non-separable utility function and indeterminacy of equilibrium in a model with human capital. *Economics Letters, 62*, 311–317.

Mino, K. (2001). Indeterminacy and endogenous growth with social constant returns. *Journal of Economic Theory, 97*, 203–222.

Mino, K. (2002). *Indeterminacy in two-sector models of endogenous growth with leisure* (MPRA Paper 16994). University Library of Munich, Germany.

Mino, K. (2008). Preference structure and volatility in a financially integrated world. In T. Kamihigashi & L. Zhao (Eds.), *International trade and economic dynamics: Essays in memory of Koji Shimomura* (323–). Berlin/Hiderberg: Springer.

Mino, K., & Nakamoto, Y. (2012). Consumption externalities and equilibrium dynamics with heterogeneous agents. *Mathematical Social Sciences, 64*, 225–233.

Mino, K., & Nakamoto, Y. (2016). Heterogeneous conformism and wealth distribution in a neoclassical growth model. *Economic Theory, 62*, 689–717.

Mino, K., & Shibata, A. (1995). Monetary policy, overlapping generations, and patterns of growth. *Economica, 62*, 179–194.

Mino, K., Nishimura, K., Shimomura, K., & Wang, P. (2008). Equilibrium dynamics in discrete-time endogenous growth models with social constant returns. *Economic Theory, 34*, 1–23.

Mitra, T. (1998). On equilibrium dynamics under externalities in a model of economic development. *Japanese Economic Review, 49*, 85–107.

Mortensen, D. (1999). Equilibrium unemployment dynamics. *International Economic Review, 40*, 889–914.

Mulligan, C., & Sala-i-Martin, X. (1993). Transitional dynamics in two-sector models of endogenous growth. *Quarterly Journal of Economics, 103*, 739–773.

Naito, T. (2006). Pattern of trade and indeterminacy. *Journal of Macroeconomics, 28*, 409–427.

Naito, T., & Ohdoi, R. (2008). Dynamics of a two-sector endogenous growth model with intersectoral knowledge spillovers. *Economic Theory, 35*, 599–605.

Naito, T., & Ohdoi, R. (2011). A two-country model of trade and growth with intersectoral knowledge spillovers. *Journal of Economics, 103*, 39–58.

Nishimura, K., & Shimomura, K. (2002a). Indeterminacy in a dynamic small open economy. *Journal of Economic Dynamics and Control, 27*, 271–281.

Nishimura, K., & Shimomura, K. (2002b). Trade and indeterminacy in a dynamic general equilibrium model. *Journal of Economic Theory, 105*, 249–259.

Nishimura, K., Venditti, A., & Yano, M. (2014). Destabilization effect of international trade in a perfect foresight dynamic general equilibrium model. *Economic Theory, 52*, 357–392.

Nishimura, K., Seegmuller, T., & Venditti, A. (2015). Fiscal policy, debt constraint and expectations-driven volatility. *Journal of Mathematical Economics, 61*, 305–316.

Obstfeld, M., & Rogoff, K. (1983). Speculative hyperinflations in maximizing models: Can we rule them out? *Journal of Political Economy, 91*, 675–687.

Ono, Y., & Shibata, A. (2010). Time patience and specialization patterns in the presence of asset trade. *Journal of Money, Credit and Banking, 42*, 93–112.

Palivos, T., Yip, C.-K., & Zhang, J. (2003). Transitional dynamics and indeterminacy of equilibria in an endogenous growth model with a public input. *Review of Development Economics, 7*, 86–98.

Park, H., & Philippoulos, A. (2004). Indeterminacy and fiscal policy in a growing economy. *Journal of Economic Dynamics and Control, 28*, 645–660.

Pavlov, O., & Weder, M. (2012). Variety matters. *Journal of Economic Dynamics and Control, 36*, 629–641.
Pelloni, A., & Waldmann, R. (1998). Stability properties of a growth model. *Economics Letters, 61*, 55–60.
Pelloni, A., & Waldmann, R. (2000). Can west improve welfare? *Journal of Public Economics, 77*, 45–79.
Rebelo, S. (1991). Long-run policy analysis and long-run growth. *Journal of Political Economy, 99*, 500–521.
Rogerson, R. (1988). Indivisible labor, lotteries and equilibrium. *Journal of Monetary Economics, 21*, 3–16.
Romer, P. (1986). Increasing returns and long-run growth. *Journal of Political Economy, 94*, 1002–1037.
Romer, P. (1990). Endogenous technological change. *Journal of Political Economy, 98*, S71–102.
Schmitt-Grohé, S. (1997). Comparing four models of aggregate fluctuations due to self-fulfilling expectations. *Journal of Economic Theory, 72*, 96–147.
Schmitt-Grohé, S. (2000). Endogenous business cycles and the dynamics of output, hours, and consumption. *American Economic Review, 90*, 1136–1159.
Schmitt-Grohé, S., & Uribe, M. (1997). Balanced-budget rules, distortionary taxes, and aggregate instability. *Journal of Political Economy, 105*, 976–1000.
Schmitt-Grohé, S., & Uribe, M. (2003). Closing small open economy models. *Journal of International Economics, 61*, 163–185.
Sim, H., & Ho, K.-W. (2007). Autarkic indeterminacy and trade determinacy. *International Journal of Economic Theory, 4*, 315–328.
Skiba, A. (1978). Optimal growth with a convex-concave production function. *Econometrica, 46*, 527–539.
Steger, T. (2002). Productive consumption, the intertemporal consumption trade-off and growth. *Journal of Economic Dynamics & Control, 26*, 1053–1068.
Suen, M.-H., & Yip, C.-K. (2005). Superneutrality, indeterminacy and endogenous growth. *Journal of Macroeconomics, 27*, 579–595.
Taylor, J. (1993). Discretion versus policy rules in practice. *Carnegie-Rochester Conference Series on Public Policy, 39*, 195–214.
Turnovsky, S. (1997). *International macroeconomics*. MIT Press., Cambridge MA
Turnovsky, S. (1999). Fiscal policy and growth in a small open economy with elastic labor supply. *Canadian Journal of Economics, 32*, 1191–1214.
Turnovsky, S. (2000). Fiscal policy, elastic labor supply, and endogenous growth. *Journal of Monetary Economics, 45*, 185–210.
Turnovsky, S., & Monteiro, G. (2007). Consumption externalities, production externalities, and efficient capital aaccumulation under time non-separable preferences. *European Economic Review, 51*, 479–504.
Turnovsky, S., & Sen, P. (1995). Investment in a two-sector dependent economy. *Journal of the Japanese and International Economies, 9*, 29–55.
Uzawa, H. (1963). On a two-sector model of economic growth II. *Review of Economic Studies, 30*, 105–118.
Weder, M. (2000). Consumption externalities, production externalities and indeterminacy. *Metroeconomica, 51*, 435–453.
Weder, M. (2001). Indeterminacy in a small open economy Ramsey growth model. *Journal of Economic Theory, 98*, 339–356.
Weder, M. (2006a) Interest rate rules and macroeconomic stabilization. *Recherches Economique de Louvain, 72*, 195–204.
Weder, M. (2006b). Taylor rules and macroeconomic instability or how the central bank can preempt sunspot expectations. *Journal of Money, Credit and Banking, 38*, 655–678.
Weder, M. (2008). Sticky prices and indeterminacy. *Journal of Money, Credit and Banking, 40*, 1073–1082.
Weil, D. (1989). Animal spirits and increasing returns. *American Economic Review, 79*, 889–894.

Wen, Y. (1998). Capacity utilization under increasing returns to scale. *Journal of Economic Theory, 81*, 7–36.

Wen, Y. (2001). Understanding self-fulfilling rational expectations equilibria in real business cycle models. *Journal of Economic Dynamics and Control, 25*, 1221–1240.

Wong, T.-N., & Yip, C.-K. (2010). Indeterminacy and the elasticity of substitution in one-sector models. *Journal of Economic Dynamics and Control, 34*, 623–635.

Xie, D. (1994). Divergence in economic performance: Transitional dynamics with multiple equilibria. *Journal of Economic Theory, 63*, 97–112.

Yip, C. K., & Li, K. F. (2004). Monetary policy and equilibrium indeterminacy in a cash-in-advance economy with investment. *Economic Bulletin, 5*(2), 1–7.

Yong, B., & Meng, Q. (2004). Preferences, endogenous discount rate, and indeterminacy in a small open economy model. *Economics Letters, 84*, 315–322.

Zhang, Y. (2008). Does the utility function form matter for indeterminacy in a two sector small open economy. *Annals of Economics and Finance, 9–1*, 61–71.

Author Index

K. Mino, *Growth and Business Cycles with Equilibrium Indeterminacy*, Advances in Japanese Business and Economics 13, DOI 10.1007/978-4-431-55609-1

Subject Index

K. Mino, *Growth and Business Cycles with Equilibrium Indeterminacy*,
Advances in Japanese Business and Economics 13,
DOI 10.1007/978-4-431-55609-1

FSC
www.fsc.org
MIX
Papier | Fördert gute Waldnutzung
FSC® C083411

Kolibri 360 GmbH
Ferdinand-Jühlke-Straße 7
99095 Erfurt, Deutschland
produktsicherheit@kolibri360.de